James Martin

The Collection

with 300 classic recipes

James Martin

The Collection

with 300 classic recipes

Photographs by
Jean Cazals and
Simon Wheeler

MITCHELL BEAZLEY

THE COLLECTION
by James Martin

First published in Great Britain in 2008 by Mitchell Beazley,
an imprint of Octopus Publishing Group Ltd,
2–4 Heron Quays, London E14 4JP
An Hachette Livre UK Company
www.octopusbooks.co.uk

Copyright © Octopus Publishing Group Ltd 2008
Text copyright © James Martin 2008
Photographs copyright © Jean Cazals / Simon Wheeler 2008

The recipes in this book are taken from the following James
Martin titles: *Eating In with James Martin*, *James Martin's
Great British Dinners*, *James Martin's Easy British Food*,
James Martin's Great British Winter Cookbook and
Delicious! The Deli Cookbook.

ISBN: 978 1 84533 350 8

A CIP record for this book is available from the British Library.

Set in Helvetica Neue LT and LubalinGraph LT.

Colour reproduction in China by Sang Choy.
Printed and bound in China by Toppan Printing Company Ltd.

Commissioning Editor Rebecca Spry
Art Director Tim Foster
Project Editor Leanne Bryan
Editor Susan Fleming
Indexer Diana Lecore
Executive Art Editor Yasia Williams-Leedham
Designer Nicky Collings
Prop Stylists Isabel De Cordova, Sue Rowlands
Food Stylists Lisa Harrison, Bethany Heald,
  Katherine Ibbs, Chris Start, Karen Taylor, Linda Tubby
Photography Jean Cazals and Simon Wheeler
Production Manager Peter Hunt

contents

introduction

I'm probably best known for cooking British food, which isn't all that surprising, as it's been a major part of my life since I was a kid. My love of British foods developed as I watched my mum, gran and auntie cooking. Many of their dishes are included in this book, and you can't get more traditional than that.

If I grew up enjoying my gran's sponge cakes, my mum's roast beef and my grandad's poached haddock, I also grew up with dishes that we have adopted from abroad. Many of them are definitely 'British' now: I'm talking about things like kedgeree, moussaka, burgers and chicken tikka masala. They all taste fantastic, and so I've included them too.

I've also added to my collection of British dishes over the years, due to my work as a chef: through cooking at the Hotel du Vin and on the *Ocean Village* cruise ships; through speedy invention on *Ready Steady Cook* and presenting *Saturday Kitchen*; through researching British desserts for *Sweet Baby James*; and through travelling around the country meeting new people and tasting dishes for *The Great British Village Show*.

None of these recipes is difficult; in fact I've simplified the original in many cases. Although I trained as a chef, I'm not against shortcuts in cooking, and I will happily use bought stocks, ice creams and pastries. (But I've given recipes for many of these, so you can choose.)

Purist foodies may turn their noses up at some of the dishes here, but I don't care. I've been eating quiche and pizza, for instance, since my teens, and to me they're as much part of my experience of British food as apple pie and bacon butties. This book is my all-singing, all-dancing (well, I did reach the semi-finals of *Strictly Come Dancing* in 2005!) collection of foods that we celebrate in Britain, and I hope you enjoy them as much as I do.

breakfasts

I once presented a show for UK Food on asparagus and was lucky enough to visit a farm in Sussex. The season for English asparagus normally runs from May to June, for about six weeks. The most amazing thing I found at the farm was that it seemed like you could see the asparagus stalks growing; the farmer told me it was common to finish picking the field one day and then to go back to start picking the same field again almost immediately as the asparagus grows so quickly.

Asparagus Spears with Poached Egg and Tarragon Butter

SERVES 4

20–30 asparagus spears, trimmed

salt, to taste

1 tbsp white wine vinegar

4 free-range eggs

100g (3¹/₂ oz) butter

juice of 2 lemons

2 tbsp chopped fresh tarragon

4 slices brioche, toasted

Steam the asparagus over plenty of boiling water for 3–5 minutes, depending on the thickness of the spears.

Bring a pan of salted water to the boil and add the vinegar. Whisk to make a whirlpool. Once it's settled crack an egg in the middle. Simmer for 2–3 minutes, remove and keep warm. Repeat with the other eggs.

Melt the butter in a pan and stir in the lemon juice and tarragon. Pile the spears of asparagus on to each toasted brioche. Top with a poached egg and spoon on the butter sauce.

My Dad's Cheese on Toast

My father taught me this recipe – it's proper cheese on toast. This has to be one of the first culinary skills people master when they leave home!

SERVES 4

4 slices brown bread, toasted

25g (1oz) butter, softened

225g (8oz) Cheddar, grated

3 tbsp double cream

a dash of Worcestershire sauce

a dash of Tabasco sauce (optional)

salt and pepper, to taste

Preheat the grill to its highest setting.

Spread the toasts with the butter.

Put the cheese in a bowl and add the cream, Worcestershire sauce, Tabasco (if using) and seasoning. Mix well. Spoon the mixture on to the buttered toasts.

Place the toasts under the grill, and then grill until the cheese starts to bubble on the top and turn golden brown. Remove and eat immediately.

Oatcakes

I suppose the main reason why oats are thought to be Scottish is that they are the country's most successful cereal crop. There's a saying that Scottish housewives are born with a rolling pin under their arms; it's not to whack men with, but because of their love for baking. You can use finer flour for a lighter biscuit, if you like.

MAKES 16 BISCUITS

100g (3 1/2 oz) medium fine oatmeal

a pinch of salt

25g (1oz) butter, melted

3 tbsp water

plain flour, for dusting

Preheat the oven to 180°C/350°F/gas mark 4. Place the oatmeal and salt in a bowl and stir in the melted butter. Mix in enough water to create a firm, pliable dough.

Sprinkle the worktop with flour and knead the dough for a few minutes. Roll out the dough until it is about 3mm (1/8 in) thick and cut out large round cakes. On each one, mark out six to eight segments on the surface, but not right the way through. Bake in the oven for 8–10 minutes, until golden brown. Serve with any cheese you like – as long as it's British!

I'm lucky enough to have a local farmer deliver fresh eggs to me each day. But when doing my research for this book, I learned a simple thing that we take for granted – that the standard British egg has not always been British. In 1900, we imported two billion fresh eggs from as far away as Eastern Europe, so they can't have been that fresh, after all, can they?

Plain and Sweet Omelettes

SERVES 1–2

PLAIN OMELETTE

3 free-range eggs

salt and pepper, to taste

25g (1oz) unsalted butter

SWEET OMELETTE

3 free-range eggs

25g (1oz) unsalted butter

100g (3¹/₂ oz) fresh raspberries

3 tbsp fresh raspberry coulis

icing sugar

Have ready a 20cm (8in) omelette pan. Beat the eggs lightly with some salt and pepper (leave out the seasoning if you're making a sweet omelette).

Heat the pan, then add the butter. When it melts, swirl it around the pan to coat the bottom. Add the eggs and shake the pan to spread them out evenly. Use a fork to draw the edges of the egg towards the centre, allowing unset egg to run to the sides. Continue until the egg is neatly set but still soft, with a little liquid on top. Take off the heat.

If you're making a sweet omelette, now add the raspberries to one half of the omelette, then flip the opposite side over it. Turn the omelette out of the pan on to a plate. Serve with the coulis and a sprinkling of icing sugar.

Yes, I know people are going to say it's an omelette Arnold Bennett, but who cares? I made this while filming in Whitby. I got the haddock from a shop called Fortune's, which is famous for smoked kippers mainly, but the haddock was brilliant. I used fresh farm eggs and cream – English, of course – and it was one of the nicest dishes I've ever made.

Smoked Haddock Omelette

SERVES 2

300ml (10fl oz) milk

3 bay leaves

2 slices onion

6 black peppercorns

280g (10oz) undyed smoked haddock fillet

6 free-range eggs

salt and pepper, to taste

20g ($^3/_4$ oz) unsalted butter

50ml (2fl oz) double cream

2 tbsp freshly grated Parmesan

Mix the milk with 300ml (10fl oz) of water, pour it into a large shallow pan and bring to the boil. Add the bay leaves, onion and peppercorns, and bring back to the boil. Add the smoked haddock, bring back to a simmer and poach for about 3–4 minutes, until the fish is cooked. Lift the fish out on to a plate and leave until cool, then break into flakes, discarding any skin and bones. Preheat the grill to high.

Whisk the eggs and season. Heat a 23–25cm (9–10in) nonstick frying pan over a medium heat, then add the butter and swirl it around to coat the base and sides of the pan. Pour in the eggs and, as they start to set, drag the back of a fork over the base of the pan, lifting up little folds of egg to allow the uncooked egg to run underneath.

When the omelette is set underneath but still moist on top, sprinkle over the flaked smoked haddock. Pour the cream over, add the Parmesan, and grill the omelette until lightly golden. Slide on to a warmed plate, and serve with a crisp green salad.

Kedgeree

My father used to cook the best kedgeree, always for breakfast. The prawns are optional, but the curry powder is a must to kick-start the flavour. A little chopped green chilli will give it the same kick if you don't have any curry powder.

SERVES 4

750ml (1 pint 6fl oz) milk

500g (1lb 2oz) undyed smoked haddock

40g (1¹/₂ oz) butter

1 onion, finely chopped

175g (6oz) long-grain rice

1 tsp medium curry powder

1 handful frozen cooked prawns, defrosted

salt and pepper, to taste

3 soft-boiled free-range eggs, shelled and quartered

2 tbsp chopped fresh flat-leaf parsley

Put the milk in a pan and bring to the boil. Add the haddock, making sure it is covered by milk, and simmer for 2 minutes. Take off the heat and allow to cool slightly. Flake the fish and pick off any bones and skin. Reserve the milk.

In a heavy-bottomed pan, melt 25g (1oz) of the butter and fry the onion for 2–3 minutes. Add the rice and curry powder, then the milk. Stir well. Bring to a gentle simmer and cook for 20–25 minutes, until the rice is cooked. Add a little more milk if it begins to dry out.

When the rice is cooked, add the haddock, then the prawns. Be careful when stirring not to break up the haddock too much. Season and put in a serving dish. Arrange the soft-boiled eggs around the edge, sprinkle with the parsley and top with the remaining butter.

Chive Blinis with Smoked Salmon and Crème Fraîche

Perhaps not so traditionally British, but this is the first dish I remember making at catering college. It is a must for any canapé tray. It's sometimes poshed up with a spoonful of caviar, but it's at its best when freshly made, and served with sliced Scottish smoked salmon and some thick, creamy crème fraîche.

SERVES 4

BLINIS
5 free-range egg whites

175g (6oz) plain flour

200ml (7fl oz) milk

1 free-range egg, beaten

1 free-range egg yolk

1 tsp bicarbonate of soda

salt and pepper, to taste

TO COOK AND SERVE
butter, for cooking

200g (7oz) smoked salmon

100g (3 1/2 oz) thick crème fraîche

2 tbsp finely chopped fresh chives

Whisk the egg whites until stiff.

Mix together the remaining blini ingredients, then carefully fold the egg whites into the mixture.

Put a teaspoonful of the mixture on to a very hot, lightly buttered, heavy-bottomed frying pan and cook in a little butter for approximately 2–3 minutes on each side, until golden brown. When bubbling, flip over with a palette knife. Repeat with the remainder of the mixture.

Cut the smoked salmon into small strips. Arrange a squiggly shape of salmon on each blini and add a teaspoon of crème fraiche and a sprinkling of finely chopped chives.

I remember cooking this at college and wondering why we spent a whole day learning how to poach an egg. Now I know, as I have asked everybody I have interviewed since then to do it, and probably 50 per cent of them make a mess of it. Why? Because most of them are too busy thinking about the next fancy garnish to go on their plate, and not about what is really important. Good cooking is all about getting the basics right, and doing them well, before progressing. Delia, you are correct about that, and I thank you.

Eggs Benedict with Smoked Haddock

SERVES 4

4 x 100g (3 1/2 oz) pieces thick undyed smoked haddock fillet, cooked (*see* page 15)

1 tbsp white wine vinegar

4 free-range eggs

TO SERVE AND GARNISH

1 quantity Hollandaise Sauce (*see* page 238)

2 English muffins

a few coarsely crushed black peppercorns

a few chopped fresh chives

Make the Hollandaise sauce and keep it warm, off the heat, over a pan of warm water.

Cook the smoked haddock as described on page 15. Lift the haddock out on to a plate, peel off the skin, discard any bones and keep warm.

Bring about 5cm (2in) water to the boil in a medium-sized pan, add the vinegar and reduce it to a gentle simmer. Break the eggs into the pan one at a time, and poach for 3 minutes each.

Meanwhile, slice the muffins in half and toast them until lightly browned. Lift the poached eggs out of the water with a slotted spoon and drain briefly on kitchen paper.

To serve, place the muffin halves on to four warmed plates and top with the haddock and poached eggs. Spoon over the hollandaise sauce and garnish with a sprinkling of black pepper and chives.

Scrambled Eggs with Chilli and Crisp Streaky Bacon on Toast

Scrambled egg is so simple to make, but still people overcook it and end up with rubbery, gelatinized stuff on toast. To prevent this, add double cream halfway through the cooking while you whisk everything together in the pan.

SERVES 4

12 streaky bacon rashers

55g (2oz) unsalted butter

6 free-range medium eggs, beaten

salt and pepper, to taste

100ml (3 1/2 fl oz) double cream

TO SERVE

4 pieces sliced bread, toasted and buttered

1 green chilli, deseeded and finely diced

Heat a sauté pan on a medium heat. Add the bacon with half the butter, and cook until crisp and golden brown, a few minutes only. Remove from the pan and keep warm.

Wipe the pan and return to the heat with the remaining butter. Season the eggs well with salt and pepper, then pour into the pan. Quickly mix the eggs with a whisk and, when half-cooked, add the cream, whisking all the time.

Just as the eggs are beginning to set, remove from the heat, and season again. Spoon on to the toast, with a scattering of chopped chilli on top and bacon on the side. Serve immediately.

Gammon with Pineapple Salsa

This is an up-to-date gammon and pineapple, but do you know where I think the best gammon and pineapple can be tasted in the UK? In truckers' roadside cafés. Gammon with a grilled tinned pineapple ring, HP Sauce and chips may not be the lowest cholesterol dish in the world, but it tastes fantastic!

SERVES 4

4 slices gammon

6 pineapple rings, fresh or tinned with natural juice, chopped

juice of 2 limes

1 red chilli, deseeded and chopped

1 tbsp roughly chopped fresh mint

2 tbsp olive oil

salt and pepper, to taste

Grill or fry the slices of gammon until cooked.

Mix the remaining ingredients together for the salsa. Serve the gammon with chips, potato wedges or vegetables and a generous of serving of salsa on the side.

Smoked Bacon Welsh Rarebit

You can make loads of this cheese mixture in one go, and it can sit in the fridge for a week. Then, any time of day or night you fancy a quick snack, it's so easy to use. But serve your rarebit with the Tomato and Apple Chutney on page 370, and it becomes a very serious dish indeed.

SERVES 4–6

12 slices good streaky bacon

4–6 thin slices white bread

RAREBIT

375g (13oz) strong Cheddar

75ml (2 1/2 fl oz) milk

100ml (3 1/2 fl oz) double cream

1 free-range egg plus 1 free-range egg yolk

1/2 tbsp mustard powder

25g (1oz) plain flour

25g (1oz) fresh white breadcrumbs

a dash of Worcestershire sauce

a dash of Tabasco sauce

salt and pepper, to taste

To make the rarebit, grate the cheese into a pan with the milk and cream, and gently warm until the cheese has melted. Do not boil. Leave to cool slightly. Preheat the grill.

Add the egg and egg yolk, mustard, flour, breadcrumbs and a dash of both Worcestershire and Tabasco sauces to the cheese mixture. Season, mix well and allow to cool.

Grill the bacon until cooked, then grill the bread on one side only. Place the bread, ungrilled-side up, into an ovenproof dish, and top with the bacon. Pour the rarebit mixture over the bacon and bread, return to the grill and allow to colour.

Remove from the grill and cool a bit before serving with the Tomato and Apple Chutney on page 370.

Hot Stilton Rarebit

Rarebits or rabbits are centuries old, and were traditionally served as a savoury before or instead of a sweet. You can use leftovers from cans of beer, but don't replace the beer with milk as some recipes suggest; this ruins the taste.

SERVES 4

25g (1oz) butter

3 free-range egg yolks

1 tsp English mustard

90ml (3fl oz) ale or lager

a dash of Tabasco sauce

a dash of Worcestershire sauce

salt and pepper, to taste

225g (8oz) Stilton cheese, grated

4 slices toast

Preheat the grill to its highest setting.

Melt the butter over a low heat, then remove from the heat and cool slightly. Mix in the egg yolks, mustard, ale or lager, and the Tabasco and Worcestershire sauces. Season well with salt and pepper, and fold in the cheese.

Place on the toast (either on its own or with sliced tomatoes or flat-leaf parsley leaves underneath), and grill until brown on the top.

Sausage and Ketchup Sarnie

Shop around for good-quality sausages for this recipe; if you use cheap, poor-quality sausages your sarnie will suffer!

SERVES 2

450g (1lb) sausages

4 slices bread

TO SERVE

Ketchup (bought or homemade, *see* page 241)

Grill or fry the sausages until cooked.

Spread the ketchup on 2 slices of bread, then top each of these slices with sausages and another slice of bread.

If there were one meal I could request before I died, it would be my gran's bacon buttie. She's no longer with us, but if I could make a buttie as well as she could, I would be a very rich man.

Bacon Buttie

SERVES 2

30g (approx. 1oz) dripping

8 slices streaky smoked bacon

4 slices bread (bloomer or pain de campagne)

40g (1¹/₂ oz) butter

2 ripe tomatoes, sliced

black pepper, to taste

Warm a large pan on the stove and add the dripping. Separate the bacon and add to the pan – watch out for the fat spitting out of the pan.

While the bacon is cooking, toast the bread, either on a griddle or under the grill. When the bacon is nice and crispy, remove from the pan. Add the butter to the pan and melt.

Dip the bread into the pan and then place on to the plates and build up the sandwich with the bacon and sliced fresh tomatoes. Pour over the rest of the juices from the pan, grind over some pepper, top with the other slice of bread and serve.

I remember hating bees from the moment, when I was a kid, that my father decided it was a good idea to visit a local honey farm in the North Yorkshire moors. The heather-flavoured honey was great, but what of those mad people who, daily, had to face what seemed like certain death to collect it? Since then, I have tried to avoid going anywhere near bees again. This recipe is a tribute to all you beekeepers. Oh, and by the way, I think you're all bloody mad!

Pancakes with Honeycomb

SERVES 2–3

PANCAKES

1 large free-range egg

a pinch of salt

100g (3 1/2 oz) plain flour

300ml (10fl oz) cold milk

2 tbsp melted butter, plus extra for cooking

HONEYCOMB BUTTER

100g (3 1/2 oz) unsalted butter, softened

85g (3oz) honeycomb

2 tbsp runny honey

Make the pancakes by mixing together the egg, salt and flour and then slowly whisking in the milk. Just before cooking, mix in the melted butter.

Heat a heavy-bottomed saucepan on the stove. Add a small knob of butter and place a spoonful of the batter in the centre of the pan. Swirl the pan to coat the base with the pancake.

Place the pan back on the heat to cook the base of the pancake. Once the base is cooked, either flip the pancake over or use a palette knife to turn it, then cook the other side. Continue making pancakes until all the batter is used up. Keep the pancakes warm.

To make the honeycomb butter, place all the ingredients in a food processor and blend until smooth. This will keep in a covered container in the fridge.

Serve two to three pancakes per portion topped with a spoonful or so of the fragrant butter.

Hot cross buns are traditionally baked for Good Friday and are thought to originate from pagan times, but they are far too good to eat only at Easter. Here is a great way to use them as a nice breakfast or dessert (not forgetting, of course, the 'true' way to eat them – toasted with butter – but I don't need to tell you that!).

Blueberry Sauce for Hot Cross Buns

SERVES 2

250ml (9fl oz) milk

15g (1/2 oz) caster sugar

2 free-range eggs

a knob of butter

2 hot cross buns (bought or homemade, *see* page 363)

BLUEBERRY SAUCE

300g (10 1/2 oz) blueberries (or strawberries)

45g (a good 1 1/2 oz) caster sugar

a splash of port or orange juice

TO SERVE

honeyed cream, crème fraîche, clotted cream or ice cream

Put the milk and sugar into a bowl and, using a whisk, beat in the eggs. Leave to one side.

Prepare the blueberry sauce by mixing together all the ingredients, crushing the berries lightly to allow the juices to run.

Heat the butter in a pan. Slice the hot cross buns in half, dip into the eggy mixture, and cook in the butter for about 2 minutes on each side.

Remove the buns from the pan and place on a serving plate. Pile the blueberry sauce on top of the bottom half of each bun, top with 2 spoonfuls of cream or ice cream, then add the lid of the bun. Serve immediately.

soups

Watercress is near to my heart. I am lucky enough to live in a part of England where watercress is famous. Hampshire, in particular Alresford, is the home of the famous 'watercress line' that used to deliver freshly cut watercress from the beds up to London. Sadly, this doesn't happen any more – instead, the cress travels by road. But the line does still exist and, for a small fee, you can travel a stretch of it in the original steam train and carriage. Watercress is grown in beds fed by spring water from underground. It needs a constant flow of this water to grow, and is available most of the year.

Watercress Soup

SERVES 4–6

1 onion, sliced

2 cloves garlic, chopped

25g (1oz) butter

1.2 litres (2 pints) chicken stock

450g (1lb) Estima potatoes, peeled and diced

2 bunches watercress

freshly grated nutmeg (optional)

200ml (7fl oz) double cream

salt and pepper, to taste

bread croûtons, to garnish (optional)

In a heavy-bottomed saucepan, fry the onion and garlic in the butter until softened but not coloured.

Add the stock and potatoes and bring to the boil. Simmer for 15–20 minutes, until the potatoes are cooked.

Chop up the watercress (leaves and stalks) and add to the soup with the freshly grated nutmeg, if using.

Simmer for 2–3 minutes before blending in a food processor in batches, adding the cream as you go.

Return to the pan to heat through gently and season with salt and pepper. Garnish with bread croûtons – baked or fried – if you like.

Rich Onion Soup with Cheese Toasts

French in inspiration, but a real favourite in Britain now. The start of this recipe is most important. The knack of making a good onion soup is colouring the onions well first, as this will give flavour and a deep colour to the finished dish. No gravy browning – that's cheating!

SERVES 6

5 onions, thinly sliced

3 cloves garlic, thinly sliced

20g ($^3/_4$ oz) duck fat

300ml (10fl oz) red wine

150ml (5fl oz) fresh beef stock

50ml (2fl oz) brandy

100ml ($3^1/_2$ fl oz) good balsamic vinegar

salt and pepper, to taste

10g ($^1/_4$ oz) fresh flat-leaf parsley

55g (2oz) unsalted butter

CHEESE TOASTS

8 thick slices white bread

280g (10oz) Gruyère cheese, grated

Sauté the onion and garlic in a large pan in the duck fat for about 20–30 minutes, colouring very well.

Stir before adding the red wine and stock. Bring to the boil and simmer for about 10 minutes. Add the brandy and balsamic vinegar and simmer for another 20 minutes.

Preheat the grill. Toast the bread on both sides, top with the grated cheese and place under the grill to melt.

Season the soup well with salt and pepper and add the chopped parsley. Pour into soup bowls. Top with the grilled cheese toasts and a knob of butter.

Leek, Potato and Stilton Soup

A classic soup with that most classic of all British ingredients: Stilton, the king of cheeses. Stilton has conquered the world, but is still exclusively made in seven dairies in Leicestershire, Nottinghamshire and Derbyshire. The best Stilton is made in the summer, with summer milk, which gives it a creamy yellow colour. It is usually sold at Christmas time. When buying Stilton, look for evenly distributed veins and a good contrast between the blue veins and the creamy cheese.

SERVES 4

1 chicken stock cube

600ml (1 pint) hot water

100ml (3 1/2 fl oz) white wine

1 medium leek, split, washed and thinly sliced

1 shallot, finely chopped

2 cloves garlic, finely chopped

1 large baking potato, peeled and finely chopped

125g (4 1/2 oz) strong Stilton cheese

125ml (4fl oz) double cream

salt and pepper, to taste

1 packet shop-bought croûtons

1 tbsp chopped fresh parsley

Place the stock cube, water and wine in a pan and bring to the boil. Add the leek to the pan with the shallot, garlic and potato. Cover and cook for 10 minutes.

Add the Stilton and cook for 4–5 minutes to melt the cheese. Add the cream, salt and pepper and blend.

Warm the croûtons. Serve the soup hot, sprinkled with the parsley, and offer the warmed croûtons separately.

I made this soup while filming in York. It's a nice twist to an old English favourite, almond soup. The vegetables came from a man called John Mannion, who is an old friend of the family. I remember going to his stall in York Market (and his shop nearby) as a kid with my gran and watching her squeeze all the fruit first before buying them. What's great now is that most of the market stalls are selling a mixture of new and traditional fruit and veg. I wonder what my gran would have thought of garlic and ginger grown in Yorkshire! Probably nothing, as they were never her thing, but she could make a great broccoli soup, and this is as near as I can get to it.

Broccoli and Almond Soup

SERVES 4

25g (1oz) butter

2 cloves garlic, crushed

1 large white onion, diced

225g (8oz) potato, peeled and diced

75ml (2 1/2 fl oz) white wine

700ml (1 1/4 pints) vegetable stock

2 heads broccoli, cut into small florets

150ml (5fl oz) double cream

85g (3oz) flaked almonds, toasted

2–3 sprigs fresh parsley, finely chopped

salt and pepper, to taste

Heat a large saucepan and add the butter. Once foaming, add the garlic and onion, and sweat without colouring for a few minutes. Next add the potato, white wine and stock. Bring to the boil and simmer for 5 minutes to get the potato cooking.

Add the broccoli to the pan and continue to cook for a further 6–8 minutes. Add the cream, half the almonds and all the parsley. Bring to the boil, remove from the heat and allow to cool slightly.

Blend in a food processor, then return the liquid to the pan. Bring to the boil and season with salt and pepper.

To serve, spoon the soup into bowls or mugs and top with the remaining toasted almonds. You could also add a little partly whipped double cream.

A twist on our traditional tomato soup. Roasting vegetables for soups, as I've done here and in the Butternut Squash and Lime Soup with Pine Nuts and Herb Oil on page 38, makes the soup taste even better. Serve with thick slices of crusty bread.

Roast Tomato and Cumin Soup

SERVES 6–8

1.25kg (2 3/4 lb) ripe tomatoes

6 tbsp olive oil

2 medium onions, roughly chopped

3 cloves garlic, roughly chopped

1 large fresh red chilli pepper, deseeded and chopped

2 tbsp cumin seeds, roasted and ground

500ml (18fl oz) tomato passata

salt and pepper, to taste

Preheat the oven to 170°C/325°F/gas mark 3.

Slice the tomatoes in half and place them on a large, heavy baking sheet. Sprinkle over 2 tbsp of the olive oil and roast for about 1 hour, or until the tomatoes are dehydrated and have caramelized. Remove the tomatoes from the baking sheet and set aside.

Place the onion, garlic and chilli in a large saucepan with the remaining olive oil. Cook over a low heat, stirring occasionally, until the onion is soft and translucent, about 10 minutes. Add the cumin and fry for another 5 minutes. Add the roasted tomatoes and the tomato passata and cook for 10 minutes.

Purée the mixture in a food processor or blender.

To serve, transfer the mixture back into a saucepan and reheat gently until warm. Taste and add salt and pepper as desired. Ladle into warm bowls. Serve with some charred ciabatta.

One-minute Chilled Tomato Soup
This soup takes only a minute as the ice cubes chill it instantly. I use plum tomatoes only if they are good ones. But if you are unsure about the tomatoes' quality, use a 400g tin of plum tomatoes.

SERVES 4

6 plum tomatoes, quartered

2 cloves garlic, roughly chopped

1 small red onion, roughly chopped

50ml (2fl oz) white wine

50ml (2fl oz) water

1 tsp tomato purée

5 ice cubes

1 x 15g packet fresh basil leaves

salt and pepper, to taste

olive oil

Put the tomatoes, garlic and onion in a food processor or blender. Then add the wine, water, tomato purée, ice cubes, fresh basil, lots of black pepper and a pinch of salt.

Place the lid on securely and blitz for about 30 seconds until all the ingredients are mixed together well. There may be some funny noises from the machine, but that's only the ice being ground up.

Remove and serve in chilled bowls, drizzled with a little olive oil, with some hot French bread and butter. You can garnish it further with some ripped-up fresh basil leaves, if you like.

Sweetcorn and Crab Soup
This may be taking its place in a British cookbook, but the idea came from one of the Indian chefs in my restaurant.

SERVES 6

1 large white onion

250g (9oz) potatoes, peeled

curry powder, to taste

30g (1¼ oz) unsalted butter

1.2 litres (2 pints) chicken stock

a handful of fresh basil leaves

300ml (10fl oz) double cream

salt and pepper, to taste

450g (1lb) frozen sweetcorn kernels

meat from 2 freshly cooked crabs

olive oil

Dice the onion and potatoes. In a large, heavy pan, sweat them with curry powder to taste in the butter until soft. Pour in the stock, stir, and bring to the boil, then simmer until the potato is tender, about 15 minutes.

Meanwhile, whizz most of the basil in a blender until finely chopped. Add 250ml (9fl oz) of the double cream and mix. Season and chill.

Add the sweetcorn to the soup, simmer for 3 minutes, then add the crabmeat and remove from the heat. Purée while still hot, then return to the pan, add the remaining cream, and simmer for 3 minutes. Season again. Spoon into bowls. Garnish with a little basil cream and olive oil and a basil leaf.

Not long ago I tried to grow squash in the garden and was amazed by all the different kinds available. The one we are most familiar with must be the common butternut, and since growing these I've become an even bigger fan. This soup is different to the norm; I roast the squash first as I think it tastes much better.

Butternut Squash and Lime Soup with Pine Nuts and Herb Oil

SERVES 6–8

1 butternut squash, about 1kg (2¼lb)

2 tbsp clear honey

extra virgin olive oil

1 white onion, chopped

2 cloves garlic, chopped

150ml (5fl oz) white wine

500ml (18fl oz) chicken stock

25g (1oz) pine nuts

150ml (5fl oz) double cream

finely grated zest and juice of 3 limes

salt and pepper, to taste

50ml (2fl oz) crème fraîche

10g (¼ oz) fresh basil, torn

HERB OIL

10g (¼ oz) fresh basil

20g (¾ oz) fresh chervil

75ml (2 ½ fl oz) olive oil

Preheat the oven to 200°C/400°F/gas mark 6.

Cut the squash in half, scoop out the seeds, then peel it and dice the flesh into 2.5cm (1in) chunks. Place in a large oven tray with the honey and a little olive oil. Roast for 30–40 minutes.

Meanwhile, fry the onion and garlic in a little olive oil to soften, then add the wine and stock. Bring to the boil and simmer for 3–4 minutes.

Sauté the pine nuts in a little olive oil until golden brown. Remove and leave to one side.

To make the herb oil, chop the basil and chervil and place in a blender with the olive oil. Blend to a fine purée. Season and leave to one side.

Remove the squash from the oven and place it in a blender with the stock mixture, cream, lime juice and lime zest, and blend. Season well. Return to the pan to the heat and check the seasoning.

Pour into individual bowls, and top with a dollop of crème fraîche. Drizzle with the puréed herb oil, pine nuts and the basil. Serve.

I thought this dish up in Prince Charles's Duchy Estate in Cornwall, where I stumbled across a farm shop while filming for the BBC. It had over 30 different types of squashes! I bought a pumpkin, which I roasted when I got home and made into a great, inexpensive, vegetable soup.

Puff Pastry Crusted Pumpkin and Rosemary Soup

SERVES 6

1 small pumpkin, about 1kg (2¹/4 lb), peeled, deseeded and diced into 2.5cm (1in) chunks

1 white onion, chopped

2 cloves garlic, chopped

2 tbsp clear honey

3 fresh rosemary sprigs

extra virgin olive oil

500ml (18fl oz) chicken stock

100ml (3¹/2 fl oz) white wine

150ml (5fl oz) double cream

juice of 1 lemon

salt and pepper, to taste

TOPPING

200g (7oz) ready-rolled puff pastry

1 free-range egg yolk, beaten

Preheat the oven to 200°C/400°F/gas mark 6.

Place the pumpkin, onion and garlic in a large oven tray with the honey, rosemary sprigs and a little olive oil. Roast for 25–30 minutes, until the pumpkin is cooked and golden brown. Keep basting the pumpkin as the honey may catch on the bottom of the tray. Remove from the oven.

Heat the stock and wine on the stove. Place into a blender with the pumpkin mixture, cream and lemon juice, and blend until smooth. Check the seasoning, and keep to one side.

On a slightly floured worktop, open out the ready-rolled pastry and, either using four large ovenproof soup dishes or four smaller deep dishes, cut the pastry out into four circles, 2cm (³/4in) bigger than the rim of each dish.

Fill the dishes no more than three-quarters full with soup and brush the edges of the dishes with the beaten egg yolk. Place the pastry on top and crimp it down on to the egg to seal. Use any of the leftovers to make a small pumpkin-shaped piece on the top.

Brush the pastry with the egg and bake for 15 minutes, until golden brown on the top. Serve piping hot.

This cheap soup has great strong flavours, but go carefully; a common mistake is to use too much saffron, as it takes a while to get the right colour and flavour. The soup goes well with the caramelized onions, which I like to make loads of at a time – I also use them in sandwiches and with cheese, especially Cheddar.

Mussel and Saffron Soup with Caramelized Onions

SERVES 6

50 mussels, scrubbed and bearded (discard any that do not close when tapped)

75ml (2 1/2 fl oz) dry white wine

1 tbsp olive oil

2 tsp minced garlic

a pinch of crushed red pepper flakes

1/2 small onion, chopped

1 tsp tomato purée

200ml (7fl oz) double cream, whipped

500ml (18fl oz) fresh chicken stock

1 tsp saffron strands

1 tbsp chopped fresh chives

salt and pepper, to taste

CARAMELIZED ONIONS

2 tbsp unsalted butter

2 onions, halved and thinly sliced

Caramelize the onions first. Melt the butter in a medium sauté pan over a low heat. Add the onions and sauté until caramel brown, about 30 minutes, stirring occasionally.

To make the soup, combine the mussels and wine in a large, heavy pot over a high heat. Cover and cook, shaking the pot occasionally, until the mussels open, about 4–5 minutes. Discard any mussels that do not open. Drain, reserving the mussel liquor. Shell 40 of the mussels. Strain the reserved mussel liquor through a fine sieve.

In a large saucepan over a medium heat, heat the olive oil, and sauté the garlic and pepper flakes until the garlic is light brown. Add the chopped onion and sauté until tender, about 5 minutes. Add the reserved mussel liquor, the tomato purée, cream and stock. Bring to a boil and skim off any foam that develops.

Lower the heat, add the saffron and simmer for 5 minutes. Add the shelled mussels and the chives, and season with salt and pepper. Liquidize.

To serve, place a spoonful of caramelized onions in the centre of each bowl and scatter a few mussels around in their shells. Then pour the soup over the lot.

Pea Soup

I was brought up on this, and I love it! My gran used to put chunks of leftover ham with the bone in this soup, which adds extra flavour. I like it with fresh mint leaves thrown in at the end. But soups can be easily overcooked and none more so than this: the last thing you want is a wrinkly bullet in the bottom of your soup bowl.

SERVES 6–8

1 bunch spring or young green-stemmed onions, chopped

2 cloves garlic, chopped

25g (1oz) unsalted butter

600g (1lb 5oz) podded young peas

675g (1½ lb) leftover cooked/boiled ham, roughly chopped

600ml (1 pint) fresh chicken stock

250ml (9fl oz) double cream (optional)

salt and pepper, to taste

1 fresh mint sprig (8–12 leaves), chopped

Sweat the onion and garlic in the butter in a covered pan for 5 minutes, without colouring.

Add the peas, ham and stock, and bring to the boil. If using the cream, add now and simmer until the peas are tender, about 10 minutes.

Season to taste, and liquidize if you like, adding another 25g (1oz) butter. But why bother blending? I think it looks and tastes so much better when you can see the bits of food you're eating (and without the extra cream). Serve sprinkled with the mint.

salads, terrines & pâtés

Salad of Chargrilled Leeks and Red Onions with Mozzarella

The thing I love most about this dish is the dressing; I sometimes serve it with plain little gem lettuce and some croûtons or, even better, warm French beans and seared tuna or salmon. You can change this salad totally by adding smoked chicken or plainly cooked chicken. You could also use a mild British cheese instead of the mozzarella.

SERVES 4

a pinch of caster sugar

salt and pepper, to taste

24 young leeks, trimmed

2 red onions, cut into wedges

2 x 200g mozzarella balls, cut into 4 slices each

DRESSING

4 tbsp tarragon vinegar

1 tsp Dijon mustard

1 tbsp chopped fresh tarragon

50ml (2 fl oz) extra virgin olive oil

1 tomato, deseeded and finely diced

1 tbsp fine capers, rinsed and drained

1 tbsp stoned green olives, finely chopped

1 hard-boiled free-range egg, shelled and finely chopped

Make the dressing first. Combine all the ingredients and leave for an hour or so for the flavours to come together.

Bring a large pan of water to the boil with the sugar and a little salt. Throw in the leeks, return to the boil and cook gently for 2–3 minutes. Drain them well and dry on a cloth.

Grill the leeks and onions on a hot, ridged cast-iron griddle pan. When they are tender and slightly blackened, remove from the heat and season with salt and pepper.

Toss the leeks and onions in most of the dressing, then divide between four plates. Arrange two slices of mozzarella over each portion, sprinkle with the remaining dressing, and serve.

Stilton and Red Onion Salad

This is another one of those dishes I did in my first year at college, and I remember it because it's so simple. So once more, it's very 1970s, I suppose, but then again I did eat it a lot in Berni Inns …. Stilton, to my mind, needs a strong robust flavour to accompany it, and red onion fits the bill for this salad.

**SERVES 4 AS
A STARTER**

4 red onions

2 tbsp olive oil

2 tbsp groundnut oil

2 tbsp balsamic vinegar

a squeeze of lemon juice

salt and pepper, to taste

10 very thin slices baguette

**225–350g (8–12oz) mixed
green leaves**

**115g (4oz) Stilton cheese,
broken into pieces**

DRESSING

3 tbsp port

2 tbsp Dijon mustard

2 tbsp red wine vinegar

4 tbsp walnut oil

4 tbsp groundnut oil

Cut each onion into six wedges, keeping the root of the onion in place to prevent it falling apart. Bring a pan of water to the simmer, add the cut onions and cook for 2 minutes.

Warm together the oils, balsamic vinegar and lemon juice. Drain the onions and add them to the oil/vinegar mix. Remove from the heat, season with some salt and pepper, and leave the onions to marinate at room temperature, turning every so often to ensure an even flavour. The onions will be at their best after an hour or so.

Preheat the oven to 200°C/400°F/gas mark 6. To make the dressing, boil and reduce the port by half and allow to cool. Mix the mustard with the red wine vinegar. Whisk together the oils and pour slowly on to the mustard and vinegar mixture, while continuing to whisk vigorously. Once all has been added, whisk in the reduced port and season with salt and pepper.

Crisp up the sliced bread by drizzling with a little extra oil and baking for 5–10 minutes.

To serve, separate the red onion wedges, and remove from the marinade. Mix with the green leaves and Stilton. Add some of the red wine/port dressing to bind. Place on a plate, trickle over some more of the dressing and sit the crispy toasts on top.

Seared Salmon with Sesame Watercress Salad
This is a modern twist to a recipe that uses two great British ingredients: salmon and watercress.

SERVES 2

2 x 200g (7oz) salmon fillets (no skin or bone), cut on a slant

olive oil

salt and pepper, to taste

50g (1 3/4 oz) watercress

2 tbsp sesame seeds, toasted

WATERCRESS DRESSING

50g (1 3/4 oz) watercress, blanched

25ml (1fl oz) rice wine vinegar

125ml (4fl oz) grapeseed oil

Make the dressing first. Blend together all the ingredients in a food processor and leave to one side for the flavours to infuse.

Heat a cast-iron griddle or frying pan on the stove until very hot and brush the salmon on both sides with a little oil. Season and then fry on both sides for 3–4 minutes.

While the fish is cooking, place the watercress on the plate and then put the cooked salmon in the middle.

Sprinkle the toasted sesame seeds over the top, drizzle with the watercress dressing and serve immediately.

This salad is great: charred aubergine (which we Brits have come to love) served warm with roast loin of lamb. I put watercress and coriander in the salad with red onions, but spring onions will work well, too. The lamb comes from the best end, which has been removed from the bone and trimmed down.

Lamb, Aubergine and Watercress Salad

SERVES 6

1 x 600g (1lb 5oz) lamb loin, trimmed of fat and silver skin

olive oil

salt and pepper, to taste

2 small aubergines, cut into 1.5cm (5/8 in) slices

BALSAMIC VINAIGRETTE

4 tbsp balsamic vinegar

1 clove garlic, finely chopped

a pinch of caster sugar

125ml (4fl oz) olive oil

leaves from 2 fresh thyme sprigs

WATERCRESS SALAD

100g (3 1/2 oz) watercress, stems removed

25g (1oz) fresh coriander, leaves picked

1 red chilli, deseeded and cut into strips

1 red onion, halved and sliced

rind of 1/2 salted lemon or preserved lemon, cut into strips

Preheat the oven to 220°C/425°F/gas mark 7.

Brush the lamb with olive oil and season with salt and pepper. Heat a frying pan over a high heat and seal the lamb on all sides until browned. Transfer the lamb to a baking tray and roast for 6–8 minutes for medium. Set aside to rest for 5 minutes before slicing.

Preheat an overhead grill or ridged cast-iron grill to a high heat. Lightly brush the aubergine with olive oil and cook for 5–8 minutes, or until tender and browned. Keep warm.

Meanwhile, to make the balsamic vinaigrette, whisk all the ingredients together until combined. Season to taste with salt and pepper.

To make the salad, combine the watercress, coriander, chilli, onion and lemon rind. Add enough balsamic vinaigrette to moisten it.

To serve, place two to three slices of aubergine on each serving plate. Slice the lamb loin into discs, about 5mm (1/4 in) thick. Arrange the salad over the aubergine, and the lamb on top. Finish with a further light drizzle of balsamic vinaigrette.

Egg and Bacon Salad

Here is an easy salad that can be served on its own or as a starter. You can, of course, poach the eggs as a change, or use pancetta instead of streaky bacon. When doing the latter, though, crisp up the pancetta on an oven tray. This will stop the pancetta sticking to the grill tray while cooking.

SERVES 4

4 slices thick-sliced white bread, crusts removed

4 soft-boiled free-range eggs (boiled from room temperature for 5 minutes in simmering water)

6 rashers thick-sliced back or streaky bacon

4 little gem lettuces, leaves separated, rinsed and drained

salt and pepper, to taste

4 spring onions, washed and finely shredded

3 tbsp red wine vinegar

2 tbsp each of olive and groundnut oil, mixed

Cut the slices of bread into 1cm (1/2 in) dice. Shell the boiled eggs, and cut into quarters.

The bacon can now be pan-fried until crispy in a nonstick pan with no oil. Any fat content will be released into the pan from the bacon. This will also happen if grilling. Whichever method you choose, keep the bacon fat for frying the bread. Once cooked, remove the bacon from the pan and keep warm.

Add the bread dice to the bacon fat, and fry until golden and crispy. You might need a little extra oil to achieve a golden colour.

Season the salad leaves with salt and pepper. It's best, whenever making salads, to sprinkle salt around the bowl and not directly on to the leaves. This prevents the salt from falling on to wet leaves and sticking in lumps.

Chop the bacon into chunky strips, and mix into the leaves with the spring onions and fried bread. Mix together the red wine vinegar and the oils. This can be spooned over the leaves, adding just enough to coat.

Arrange in a large bowl as one large salad. The soft-boiled egg quarters can now also be seasoned with salt and pepper and placed among the leaves. Serve immediately.

Bacon and Bean Salad

The dressing is the key to this delicious salad. Its texture is a bit like that of a Caesar salad, but less creamy and heavy. It's a pain to remove the shells of broad beans, but it will be worth it. You'll need about 200g (7oz) fresh or frozen large beans to end up with 100g (3 1/2 oz) here.

SERVES 4

8 slices dry-cured streaky bacon or 10 slices Parma ham

50g (1 3/4 oz) fresh white bread, crusts removed, cubed

a knob of unsalted butter

150g (5 1/2 oz) mixed red and white chicory and rocket

100g (3 1/2 oz) cooked French beans

100g (3 1/2 oz) podded, blanched and peeled broad beans

5g (1/8 oz) fresh flat-leaf parsley, picked and washed

extra virgin olive oil

Parmesan shavings (optional)

DRESSING

2 slices white bread, crusts removed

4 tbsp milk

juice and finely grated zest of 1 lemon

2 cloves garlic

140g (5oz) fresh shelled walnuts

150ml (5fl oz) extra virgin olive oil

salt and pepper, to taste

To make the dressing, tear the bread into the blender and moisten with the milk. Add the lemon zest and juice, garlic and walnuts and blend to a paste. Add, and blend in, the olive oil and some salt and pepper to taste.

Grill the bacon or Parma ham until crisp. Fry the cubed bread in a little butter until golden brown.

Place the salad leaves and the beans into a bowl. Add the dressing and some salt and pepper and mix.

Place a portion of the salad on each plate and top with the crisp bacon, the parsley and croûtons. Drizzle with the olive oil and top with the Parmesan shavings (if using).

Good sausages are used as the base of this simple terrine. Play around with the flavours by using beef or game sausages instead of pork. I've used plum sauce, as this combines with the orange segments to give a sweet-and-sour flavour. When making terrines, don't overcook them or they will break up while being sliced.

Pork Terrine with Apricots and Pistachios

SERVES 8–12

olive oil

250g (9 oz) streaky bacon rashers

900g (2lb) or 14–15 large sausages (Lincolnshire are best)

10 fresh sage leaves, chopped

5g (1/8 oz) fresh flat-leaf parsley, chopped

100g (3 1/2 oz) dried apricots, chopped

75g (2 3/4 oz) shelled pistachio nuts, roughly chopped

salt and pepper, to taste

SALAD

2 oranges, peeled and segmented

55g (2oz) wild rocket leaves

1 large potato, peeled, cooked and diced

8 tbsp plum sauce (make your own, or buy the Chinese stuff from the supermarket)

3 tbsp olive oil

Preheat the oven to 180°C/350°F/gas mark 4. Take a terrine dish, 30–35cm (12–14in) long, 10cm (4in) wide, and 9–10cm (3 1/2 –4in) deep, and brush it with olive oil. Line the dish with streaky bacon, leaving 5–6cm (2–2 1/2 in) overlapping the edge of the terrine.

Make the filling by removing all the meat from the sausage skins (discard these). Add the sage, parsley, chopped apricots and pistachio nuts and mix well with plenty of seasoning.

Pile the meat mixture into the terrine mould and press down well. Fold over the bacon and either cover with the lid or with foil, and place in a bain-marie half-filled with hot water. Cook in the oven for 60 minutes. Remove from the oven, cover with foil, and press down with a weight. Cool, then place in the fridge.

When ready to serve, make the salad by mixing the orange segments, rocket and potato together in a bowl. Mix the plum sauce with the olive oil and season to taste.

Cut the terrine into slices and serve in the centre of the plates with the salad to one side and the dressing spooned over the top.

Yorkshire Ham Terrine with Spiced Pickle

Scott's Butchers in York is still the best place to buy Yorkshire pork products, but if you visit you have to queue. Last time I was there it was obviously pension day, as the place was like a bingo hall on a jackpot night!

SERVES 10

3 ham knuckles

4 bay leaves

6 black peppercorns

1 large onion, halved

1 medium leek, halved

1 medium carrot, halved

extra virgin olive oil

6–8 thin slices York ham, or other cooked sliced ham

2 shallots, finely chopped

1 clove garlic, chopped

salt and pepper, to taste

20g (^{3}/$_4$oz) fresh parsley leaves, finely chopped

a pinch of ground mixed spice

2 gelatine leaves, soaked in cold water for 5 minutes

55g (2oz) mixed salad leaves and herbs, such as chervil and wild rocket

PINEAPPLE PICKLE

1 clove garlic, crushed

1 tsp grain mustard

5 tbsp white wine vinegar

a good pinch of turmeric powder

150g (5^1/$_2$ oz) demerara sugar

1 medium pineapple, skinned, cored and finely chopped

DRESSING

4 tbsp each of grain mustard, extra virgin olive oil and cider vinegar

Put the ham knuckles, bay leaves, peppercorns, onion, leek and carrot in a large saucepan. Cover with cold water, bring to the boil and simmer, covered, for 3 hours, until the meat is tender.

Meanwhile, grease a 20 x 8cm (8 x 3 ^{1}/$_4$ in) terrine mould with olive oil. Line with clingfilm, then with the sliced York ham.

When the ham knuckles are nearly cooked, heat a little olive oil in a small pan and gently sweat the shallots and garlic.

Remove the cooked ham knuckles from the pan, reserving the stock, and leave to cool slightly. While warm, remove the meat in pieces from the bone. Place in a small bowl with the shallot and garlic, some salt and pepper and the parsley. Mix well, then pack into the terrine mould.

Strain the ham stock. Taste and, if it is too salty, dilute with water. Pour 500ml (18fl oz) into a pan and add the mixed spice. Warm gently and add the soaked gelatine; leave for 2–3 minutes for the gelatine to dissolve before stirring. Pour into the terrine and overlap the edges of the ham. Cover with clingfilm; the terrine needs to be quite solid and 'packed'. Put a uniform weight on the terrine to press it down (I use a brick) and leave overnight in the fridge.

To make the pickle, put all the ingredients together in a pan except for the pineapple. Simmer for 3 minutes, then add the pineapple and cook for a further 3 minutes. Put into sterilized jars (*see* page 368 for sterilizing instructions) and cool.

To make the mustard seed dressing, whisk all the ingredients together, then use some of it to dress the salad leaves at the last minute.

To serve, turn out the terrine and remove the clingfilm. Using a sharp knife, cut into 2cm (^{3}/$_4$ in) slices and place a slice in the centre of each plate. On each plate, spoon a pile of pineapple pickle, placing a few dressed leaves on, too. Grind over a little black pepper, and serve.

Chicken and Ham Terrine

This is one of the dishes I put on the menu at The Bistro on board *Ocean Village*, and I love it. But as with most terrines and pâtés, I think it should be served with fruit chutney or caramelized onions, or something else to break up the taste.

SERVES 10–12

16–20 slices streaky bacon (depending on the size of the terrine)

300g (10 1/2 oz) chicken meat, minced

300g (10 1/2 oz) shoulder of pork, minced

600ml (1 pint) double cream

1 free-range egg, beaten

100ml (3 1/2 fl oz) Armagnac

3 tbsp each of chopped fresh parsley and chives

2 tbsp chopped fresh tarragon

salt and pepper, to taste

25g (1oz) butter

2 shallots, finely chopped

300g (10 1/2 oz) chicken breast meat, cut into 5mm (1/4 in) strips

225g (8oz) sliced cooked ham

140g (5oz) chicken livers, cleaned

TO GARNISH
Pear Chutney (*see* page 370)

mixed dressed salad leaves

First, line a terrine dish measuring 28 x 16 x 6cm (11 x 6 1/2 x 2 1/2 in) with streaky bacon, allowing the slices to overlap the mould at the sides by a few centimetres.

Put the chicken and pork into a bowl, and work the mixture with a wooden spatula. Stir in the cream, egg, Armagnac and chopped herbs. Season with salt and pepper, to taste.

Heat the butter in a small saucepan and sweat the shallots for 2–3 minutes. Cool and add to the meat mixture.

Spread half the mixture over the bottom of the terrine, then make a layer with some of the sliced chicken breast, then some of the sliced ham, and fill with some of the remaining mince mixture. Continue with two or three layers of the ham, mince mixture and chicken breast, with a layer of the chicken livers running though the middle of the terrine. Finally, fold the bacon over the terrine from the sides and either cover with a lid or cover with foil.

Preheat the oven to 200°C/400°F/gas mark 6.

Place the terrine in a roasting tray, and half-fill the tray with warm water. Cook in the oven for 1 hour. Remove from the oven and place a weighted board (maximum weight 500g/1lb 2oz) on the terrine to compress it gently until it has cooled completely.

Serve in thick slices with pear chutney and dressed salad leaves.

Duck Liver Pâté

I hated liver as a kid, as most kids do. The only two dishes my grandad would cook were calf's liver and poached haddock. I used to watch him with his Brylcreemed stick-back hair as he pan-fried his slice of liver with precision. He never failed to try to get me to eat some as I ran out of the door in horror. I now know I was missing out on something great.

SERVES 14–16

1kg (2 1/4 lb) organic duck livers, left whole, but all green and thready bits removed

Cognac

2 cloves garlic, finely chopped

a handful of fresh basil leaves

salt and pepper, to taste

350g (12oz) unsalted butter

GARNISH

brown bread, sliced and toasted, or Melba toast

Pear Chutney (*see* page 370)

mixed salad leaves, dressed

Place the livers in a single layer in a heatproof dish, and scatter over some Cognac. It should not cover them, but they need to wallow in it for several hours. Turn them over so both sides absorb the alcohol. Throw the garlic, all but 2 of the basil leaves (torn and minus the stalks) and some salt and pepper into the brew just before poaching.

Gently poach the livers, turning them over after a couple of minutes, and continue to stew until they are cooked on the outside but pink within, about 3–4 minutes. Do not overcook them or you will end up with a drab, brown, crumbly result.

Tip the contents of the dish straight into your blender with 225g (8oz) of the softened butter, and whizz until smooth. Check the seasoning, then scrape into a large terrine dish and leave to cool.

Meanwhile, clarify the remaining butter. Gently melt it, and pour into another container, leaving behind all the curd-like sediment. Cool a little.

Pour the buttercup-coloured clear liquid butter over the surface of the pâté, place the reserved basil leaves in the centre, and put it into the fridge until it is set.

Using a hot knife, slice the terrine. Serve with a slice of toast, a spoonful of chutney and some dressed mixed salad leaves.

grills
& fry-ups

Rib-eye Steak with Caesar Salad

Rib-eye steak has only really become popular in Britain over the past ten years, but it is such a great piece of meat. It comes from the end of the sirloin part of the beef that the rib joint is attached to (where you get the rib joint for roasting from). I love steak and salad, and Caesar salad works particularly well in this case. The recipe for the dressing was invented by a chef I used to work with – cheers, Adam!

SERVES 4

4 rib-eye steaks, about 225g (8oz) each

salt and pepper, to taste

olive oil

CAESAR SALAD

2 cos lettuces

2 thick slices white bloomer bread, cubed

about 25g (1oz) butter

4 cloves garlic

150ml (5fl oz) white wine

4 free-range egg yolks

2 anchovy fillets

140g (5oz) Parmesan, freshly grated

300ml (10fl oz) vegetable oil

1 tbsp Dijon mustard

To start the salad, separate the lettuce leaves, and wash and dry well, then tear into chunky pieces. Place in a serving bowl. Gently cook the bread cubes in the butter in a frying pan until golden brown.

To start the Caesar dressing, peel the garlic and place in a pan with the wine. Bring to the boil and cook for about 5 minutes, until the cloves are soft. Using a hand blender, blend the wine and garlic together with the egg yolks, anchovy fillets and cheese, adding the oil slowly to stop the mix from splitting. (This shouldn't happen, as the cheese should make the mix blend together more easily.) Add the mustard and seasoning to taste.

Preheat a frying pan on the stove. Season the steaks with salt and pepper, and cook in a little olive oil. If you want medium, this should take about 3–4 minutes on both sides. Once cooked, remove the steaks from the pan and place them on the plate while you sort out the salad.

To serve, throw the bread cubes into the bowl with the lettuce, add the dressing, and mix together well. Season, place on plates alongside the steaks and munch away.

Rib-eye Steak with Herbs and Mustard served with Honeyed Oven Chips

Nothing beats sirloin steak, deep-fried onion rings, peas and jacket potatoes or chips. This is just a more up-to-date version of our classic steak and chips. It uses rib-eye steak that is now, thankfully, found in most stores and butchers.

SERVES 4

4 rib-eye steaks, about 225g (8oz) each

olive oil

salt and pepper, to taste

8 tbsp Dijon mustard

125g (4¹/₂ oz) chopped herbs, such as parsley, coriander, basil, thyme and chervil

1 lemon, quartered

HONEYED OVEN CHIPS

500g (1lb 2oz) Estima potatoes, peeled

4 tbsp runny honey

1 tsp fresh thyme, chopped

1 clove garlic, chopped

4 tbsp olive oil

Preheat the oven to 200°C/400°F/gas mark 6.

For the chips, cut the potatoes into large, chip-sized pieces. Mix together the honey, thyme and garlic in a bowl. Whisk in the olive oil and use the mixture to coat the potatoes well.

Season the chips and place on a baking tray in the oven for 35–45 minutes.

Meanwhile, heat a ridged, cast-iron griddle pan until it is very hot. Brush the steaks with a little olive oil and season with salt and pepper. Seal on the griddle and cook to taste, probably about 3–4 minutes on both sides.

Once cooked, brush the steaks with mustard and dip into the herbs. Slice each steak into four to six slices, arrange on a plate and serve with chips and a lemon quarter.

Fillet Steak with Stilton Rarebit

Rarebits are usually associated with toast – and, in one celebrated chef's recipe, with smoked fish – but the combination here of Stilton cheese, beer and beef is great. It's a dish I created at the Hotel du Vin and Bistro; there I served the steak on toast with a liver pâté. This is a simpler version.

SERVES 4

4 x 200g (7oz) fillet steaks

salt and pepper, to taste

3 tbsp olive oil

400ml (14fl oz) red wine

600ml (1 pint) fresh beef stock

approx. 20g (3/4 oz) cold butter, diced

2 tbsp pesto

RAREBIT

2 free-range egg yolks

1 tsp mustard

2 tbsp fresh breadcrumbs

a dash of Worcestershire sauce

a dash of Tabasco sauce

100ml (31/2 fl oz) milk

100ml (31/2 fl oz) beer

115g (4oz) Stilton cheese

Season the fillet steaks well and place in a hot frying pan with the olive oil. Cook on both sides for a total of about 5–6 minutes, then remove from the pan and keep warm. (This gives you a medium steak; if you prefer it cooked more or less than this, cook to the degree you prefer as no further cooking is necessary.)

Keep the pan on full heat and add the wine. Boil to reduce by half, then add the beef stock and continue to reduce.

For the rarebit, place the egg yolks, mustard and breadcrumbs in a bowl along with the Worcestershire and Tabasco sauce. Then stir in the milk and beer, and season well with salt and pepper. Grate the Stilton cheese, and fold in as well. Mix everything together until it has formed a very thick paste.

Preheat the grill to a high heat. Top the steaks with the rarebit and place under the grill until golden brown on the top. Remove from the grill and place on the four plates.

Season the reduced sauce and add the butter to give it a nice glaze. To finish, add the pesto to the sauce, then pour it around the steaks and serve.

Classic Beef Burgers with Soft Onions

Make these burgers with quality mince so you can serve them pink. Prepare them in advance so they can firm up in the fridge before frying. If you plan to barbecue them, seal them in a pan first.

SERVES 4

900g (2lb) best minced beef

salt and pepper, to taste

3 white onions, thinly sliced

30g (1¼oz) unsalted butter

olive oil

TO SERVE

4 burger buns

1 head little gem lettuce, leaves separated

2 medium tomatoes, sliced

Place the meat in a bowl and season. Weigh the meat into 225g (8oz) portions and mould them with your hands into burger shapes. Place the burgers on a tray or plate, cover with clingfilm and leave in the fridge.

When you want to eat the burgers, sauté the onions in a pan in the butter until golden brown, about 10–15 minutes.

Heat a little olive oil in a ridged cast-iron griddle or sauté pan and fry the burgers, depending how you like them. You need 3 minutes each side for medium. Serve the burgers in the buns with a couple of lettuce leaves, some sliced tomato and some soft onion.

Beef Burgers with Bacon

Although beef burgers are usually thought to be American, so many of us have grown up eating them, either from frozen, bought from one of the burger chains or – best of all – homemade, that they have attained British status.

SERVES 4

675g (1½ lb) minced beef

1 tsp French mustard

salt and pepper, to taste

1 shallot, finely diced

1 clove garlic, finely diced

1 tbsp chopped fresh flat-leaf parsley

1 free-range egg

TO COOK AND SERVE

1 tbsp olive oil

25g (1oz) butter

4 rashers bacon

lettuce leaves, shredded

4 burger buns

Combine all of the burger ingredients in a large bowl. Form into four oval-shaped patties.

Sauté the patties in a hot pan in the olive oil and butter for 3–4 minutes on each side. While sautéing, grill the bacon until cooked through.

Place the salad leaves in your bun and put the burger and then bacon on top of the leaves.

Everybody loves burgers, from burnt to a cinder by the old man who once a year takes over the cooking on the barbecue, to the 'drive-thru' eaten from in-between your legs as you drive off to the next meeting. But there's one thing that gets me going, and it's those pretentious chefs who slag off burgers in favour of fillet steak.

The Best Cheeseburger

SERVES 4

2 shallots, chopped

a splash of olive oil

675g (1½ lb) tail of beef fillet

4 tbsp chopped gherkins

2 tbsp double cream

½ tsp Dijon mustard

a splash of Worcestershire sauce

salt and pepper, to taste

1 ball mozzarella cheese, drained and cut into 4 slices

Sauté the chopped shallots quickly in the oil to take off the rawness, then allow to cool.

Mince the fillet of beef into a bowl through the fine plate of a mincer. Add the shallots, gherkins, cream, mustard and Worcestershire sauce. Beat well together and season to taste with salt and pepper.

Using a little oil on your hands, shape the mixture into four even-sized burger shapes. Then, using the palm of your other hand, mould the burger into a bowl shape and place a slice of the mozzarella in the middle. Fold over the meat to enclose it, then reshape into a burger. Leave in the fridge to firm up for at least 30 minutes.

Preheat the grill, then cook the burgers medium-rare, about 4 minutes on each side. Season well.

Kids love to make this recipe as it's great fun to do. It's even better if you can buy a sausage-making machine (they're not too expensive – sometimes under £50). If you can't find one, you can use a piping bag, although it's harder work. Get sausage skins – at least 60cm (2ft) in length – from your local butcher; you can find synthetic ones now as well.

Cumberland Sausage

SERVES 4–6

450g (1lb) boned, skinned shoulder of pork

175g (6oz) hard back pork fat

4 rashers smoked bacon

1 tsp each of grated nutmeg and mace

25g (1oz) white breadcrumbs, soaked in 8 tbsp hot water

salt and pepper, to taste

Cut the pork, fat and bacon into strips, and put first through the coarse blade of a mincing machine, then through the medium blade. Add the spices, then the soaked, squeezed breadcrumbs. Mix well together with your hands, then add salt and plenty of pepper.

Rinse the salt from the sausage skins. Ease one end of a piece of skin on to the cold tap. Run cold water gently through the skin, to make sure there are no splits or large holes. Turn off the tap, remove the skin and ease it on to the long spout of the sausage-making attachment. Screw the whole thing on to the mincing machine with a coarse blade in position.

Feed the pork sausage meat through the mincer again and, as it comes through, slide the skin gently off the attachment and coil it on to a large plate. Leave in the fridge until next day.

When ready to cook, preheat the oven to 180°C/350°F/gas mark 4. Prick the sausage, place on a greased ovenproof tray then bake for 30–45 minutes. Alternatively, fry the coil in a pan on top of the stove, in a little oil – but the oven is easier. The sausage coil is enough for four on its own, or six as part of a meal.

The fact that black pudding is made from pig's blood mixed with oatmeal, suet and onion may not appeal to you, but I consider it one of the best of British tastes (which is good for breakfast as well). Try to buy from good butchers' shops, as black pudding is usually made fresh on the premises. These have much more flavour and taste than the commercial, branded black puddings. I believe black puddings should be sliced and pan-fried. The cooking time is important as well as the heat of the pan, and you don't need much fat. A cooked slice of black pudding should be slightly crisp on the edges but moist in the centre.

Black Pudding with Caramelized Apple and Cider

SERVES 2

1 Golden Delicious apple

55g (2oz) butter

1 tbsp caster sugar

175g (6oz) black pudding, cut into 1cm (1/2 in) slices

50ml (2fl oz) cider

salt and pepper, to taste

Place two frying pans on the stove and heat up to a high heat while you prepare the apple. Core the apple whole, then cut it in half and slice each half into five slices.

Divide the butter between the two pans, and put the sugar in one of them. Place the black pudding into the non-sugared pan, reduce the heat and cook for 2–3 minutes, turning occasionally.

When the sugar and butter in the other pan have started to turn golden brown, add the apple slices. Turn up the heat and quickly caramelize the apple: about 3 minutes. Pour in the cider to deglaze the pan, stirring well, and season quickly with salt and pepper.

To serve, either put the apple mixture and the black pudding into separate bowls or plates for the two of you to help yourselves from, or arrange the black pudding on the two plates with the apple on top.

Corned beef and Spam were the basis of so much food we ate as kids, but they're not deemed trendy any more. Or are they? I cook corned beef hash to remind me of what my auntie used to cook for me. Served with a little salad, it is a satisfying snack that can be eaten at any time of the day. It's good for breakfast, perhaps topped with a fried egg. It can also be made into little patties – when the mix might need to be bound with an egg. In America, corned beef hash is served with Ketchup (*see* page 241) or chilli sauce.

Corned Beef Hash

SERVES 4

2 onions, chopped

1 tbsp fresh thyme leaves

25g (1oz) butter

1 tsp yeast extract

350ml (12 fl oz) beef stock

150ml (5 fl oz) red wine

375g (13 oz) corned beef

2 tbsp chopped fresh flat-leaf parsley

salt and pepper, to taste

FILLING

250g (9oz) potatoes, peeled

milk, for mashing potatoes

25g (1 oz) butter

50g (1 3/4 oz) Cheddar, grated

25g (1oz) fresh breadcrumbs

Preheat the oven to 200°C/400°F/gas mark 6.

For the filling, boil the potatoes in plenty of simmering, salted water. When they are just cooked, remove from the heat and cool in cold water. Drain, dice and leave to one side.

In a large frying pan, fry the onions and thyme in the butter for about 3 minutes. Add the yeast extract, stock and red wine and reduce by half. Add the corned beef, parsley and and some salt and pepper and cook for 5–10 minutes, breaking the beef up with a fork.

Season the cooled potatoes and mash them thoroughly with some milk and the butter.

Place the corned beef mixture into an ovenproof dish and top with the mashed potatoes. Mix the grated cheese together with the breadcrumbs. Sprinkle the mixture over the mashed potatoes and bake for 20 minutes to cook through and brown the top.

Serve with a dressed green salad.

I like calf's liver with onions, but what I really remember is the tripe and onions I had when I was a kid. It's hard to find now. There is one place that still does good tripe and onions, and that's a café in Leeds city centre vegetable market. It tastes great, but what's even better is that the café is full of old blokes telling stories of the old days. A fab place.

Pan-fried Calf's Liver with Bacon and Onions

SERVES 4

8 medium onions, sliced

85g (3oz) butter

8 rashers smoked streaky bacon

100ml (3 1/2 fl oz) Madeira, plus extra for deglazing

900ml (1 1/2 pints) beef or chicken stock

salt and pepper, to taste

675g (1 1/2 lb) calf's liver, thinly sliced

TO SERVE
Mashed Potatoes (*see* page 222)

Preheat the grill to high. Sauté the onions in 25g (1oz) of the butter until well caramelized. This will take about 15 minutes. While the onions are cooking, crisp the bacon under the grill.

Once the onion is ready, add the Madeira and stock and reduce by half, until you have a rich sauce. Check the seasoning and leave to one side.

Heat a frying pan on a high heat and add a knob of the remaining butter. Cook the liver in batches to keep the pan really hot. Season while in the pan. The liver will only take about 1–2 minutes to cook on each side, and should be nice and pink in the middle.

Remove the liver from the pan and deglaze the pan with a little more Madeira, then add the reduced onion sauce as well, and season.

To serve, place the mashed potatoes on the plate, top with the liver and spoon over the sauce. Top with the crispy bacon.

Meatballs with Tomato Sauce

A grown-up version of a kid's delight. I remember hating meatballs as a child, as my nana used to cook them all the time, but they were truly awful, always from a tin and never heated through, and served with a mound of overcooked rice. My sister and I used to be made to sit through this ordeal, and we weren't allowed to leave the table until we had finished. I used to hide mine, anywhere and everywhere I could….But these are infinitely more delicious!

SERVES 4

2 shallots, chopped

1 clove garlic, chopped

olive oil

450g (1lb) tail of beef fillet

2 tsp Dijon mustard

a dash of Worcestershire sauce

50ml (2 fl oz) double cream

salt and pepper, to taste

BASIC TOMATO SAUCE

1.5kg (3lb 5oz) ripe and meaty tomatoes

4 tbsp olive oil

1 medium onion, very finely sliced

1 clove garlic, coarsely chopped

1 tbsp chopped fresh oregano

10 small fresh basil leaves, shredded

For the tomato sauce, plunge the tomatoes into boiling water for 1 minute to loosen the skin. Remove the skin, and cut the tomatoes in half. Discard the inner liquid and seeds. Coarsely chop the remaining flesh.

Heat the oil in a pan and fry the onion for 5 minutes. Add the garlic and fry for a further minute. Add the tomatoes and bring to the boil, then add the oregano, reduce the heat and simmer for 30–40 minutes. Halfway through, add the basil leaves.

When the sauce has finished cooking, add some salt to taste, and liquidize. Keep warm. (The sauce keeps for a few days in the fridge, but is best if eaten when freshly made.)

Meanwhile, to make the meatballs, sauté the shallots and garlic quickly in a little oil to take off the rawness, then allow to cool. Mince the beef through the fine plate of a mincer into a bowl. Add the shallots, garlic, mustard, Worcestershire sauce and cream. Beat well together, then season to taste with salt and pepper.

Using a little oil on your hands, shape the mixture into eight to ten even-sized shapes about the size of a golf ball. Leave for 10 minutes, covered, in the fridge to firm up.

Preheat a pan on the stove and add a little olive oil. Fry the meatballs until golden brown all over, and serve with the warm tomato sauce.

pies
& tarts

Masham, which is just off the A1 near Thirsk, has two breweries: Theakstons and the Black Sheep Brewery. It was once also home to one of the largest sheep markets in the country, which was held in the town's market square. That trade has now gone, but the breweries are still going strong. Run by Paul Theakston, the Black Sheep Brewery is open·to the public and is well worth a visit. Their strongest beer is Riggwelter; the words 'rigged' and 'welted' in old Yorkshire slang would suggest to a farmer that one of his sheep is upside down. Trust me, a few pints of this stuff, and you'd be rigged too!

Beef and Black Sheep Ale Pie

SERVES 4

900g (2lb) stewing beef, diced

25g (1oz) plain flour

salt and pepper, to taste

butter

2 white onions, sliced

2 cloves garlic, sliced

2 medium carrots, sliced

140g (5oz) button mushrooms, wiped

2 sprigs fresh thyme

1 bay leaf

400ml (14fl oz) Black Sheep Ale

500ml (18fl oz) fresh beef stock

1 free-range egg, beaten, for egg wash

300g (10 1/2 oz) ready-rolled puff pastry

Preheat the oven to 180°C/350°F/gas mark 4, and place a large casserole dish over a medium heat on the stove.

While the dish is heating, place the meat in a bowl, and add the flour and seasoning, turning to coat. When the pan is hot, melt about 15g (1/2 oz) of the butter. Add the meat in batches, adding more butter if necessary, and seal until golden brown all over.

Once browned, add the vegetables, herbs and liquids to the meat and bring to a simmer on the stove. Cover with a lid or some foil, and either gently simmer on top of the stove for 1½ hours or (what I would do) cook it in the oven for 1¼ hours. Once the meat is tender, season and tip into an ovenproof oven-to-table pie dish. Increase the oven temperature to 200°C/400°F/gas mark 6.

Brush the beaten egg along the edges of the dish and top with the puff pastry. Pinch the edges of the dish so that the pastry will stick to it, and trim off any remaining pieces of pastry from around the edge. Use the pastry trimmings to make leaves, berries and a decorative rope to go along the outside. Make holes in the top for steam to escape. Brush the pastry all over with the remaining egg wash, and place the pie dish on a baking tray.

Bake for 30–40 minutes, until the pastry is golden brown on the top. (Use a baking tray, as the mixture inside the pie dish can sometimes bubble out and make one hell of a mess on the bottom of your cooker.)

Steak and Kidney Pie

Great pub food is one of the joys of where I live, and steak and kidney pie is one of my faves. There are so many variations of this classic. Some say it should have oysters, beer or stout in the mix, but I think this one is the nicest I've cooked. Besides, would you want me to give you a recipe with beef, kidneys and oysters topped with pastry? I don't think so. Although purists say this pie should be made with shortcrust pastry, I feel puff pastry makes a much better topping.

SERVES 4

1 x 300g pack puff pastry

1 free-range egg and 1 extra free-range egg yolk, beaten together

FILLING

25g (1oz) beef dripping or 2 tbsp vegetable oil

700g (1lb 9oz) stewing beef, diced

200g (7oz) lamb's kidney, diced

2 medium onions, diced

8 button mushrooms, halved

25g (1oz) plain flour

1/2 tbsp tomato purée

700ml (1 1/4 pints) beef stock

150ml (5fl oz) red wine

salt and pepper, to taste

2 tbsp chopped fresh parsley

a dash of Worcestershire sauce

Heat the dripping or vegetable oil in a large frying pan, and use to seal the beef in batches until well coloured. Browning the meat is important, as it gives the pie a really deep golden colour.

Brown the kidney in the same pan, then add the onions and mushrooms and cook for 3–4 minutes.

Return all the meat to the pan, then sprinkle the flour over to coat the meat and vegetables. Add the tomato purée, stock and red wine to the pan, stir well and bring to the boil. Turn the heat down and simmer for 1 1/2 hours without a lid on. If the liquid is evaporating too much, add a little more stock.

Shortly before the end of the cooking time, preheat the oven to 220°C/425°F/gas mark 7.

Add some salt and pepper, the parsley and Worcestershire sauce to the filling. Leave to cool slightly.

Place the cooked meat mixture into a pie dish. Roll out the pastry to 5mm (1/4in) thick, and 5cm (2in) larger than the dish you are using. Cut a strip of pastry to fit around the edge of the pie dish, and stick it down using a little water. Brush the top with beaten egg.

Use the rolling pin, lift the pastry and place it over the top of the pie dish. Trim and crimp the edges with your fingers and thumb. Brush all over the surface with the beaten egg and decorate with any pastry trimmings. Brush any decorations with beaten egg. Bake for 30–40 minutes. I love this with either mash, peas or carrots or – to hell with it – have all three!

Cornish Pasty

You can find all sorts of fancy recipes for Cornish pasties, but the simple ones are the best. This dish was never invented to achieve stars in restaurants. It is what it is: a good gut filler (and even better warm, of course). I have kept this recipe very simple and made it here with ready-made pastry, but you can make your own pastry if you wish.

SERVES 2

500g (1lb 2oz) ready-made shortcrust pastry

1 free-range egg, beaten, to glaze

FILLING

250g (9oz) rump steak

115–140g (4–5oz) onions, chopped

85g (3oz) turnip, chopped

225g (8oz) potato, peeled and thinly sliced

salt and pepper, to taste

a pinch of dried thyme

To make the filling, remove the fat from the lean meat, and cut the meat into rough cubes. Mix together with the vegetables, salt, pepper and thyme.

Preheat the oven to 180°C/350°F/gas mark 4.

Roll out the pastry and cut it into two large dinner-plate circles. Divide the steak mixture between the two, putting it down the middle. Brush the rim of the pastry with beaten egg. Fold over the pastry, to make a half circle, or bring up the two sides to meet over the top of the filling, and pinch them together into a scalloped crest going right over the top of the pasty. Make two holes on top, so that the steam can escape.

Place the pasties on a baking sheet and brush them with beaten egg. Bake for 40 minutes. Serve hot or cold.

Why is cottage pie always mixed up with shepherd's pie? Think about it: how many shepherds do you see looking after beef cattle?

Cottage Pie

SERVES 4–6

675g (1½ lb) minced beef

salt and pepper, to taste

25ml (1fl oz) olive oil

butter

3 onions, finely chopped

3 carrots, cut into 1cm (½ in) dice

4 celery sticks, cut into 1cm (½ in) dice

½ tsp ground cinnamon

½ tsp chopped fresh rosemary

1 tbsp tomato purée

1 tbsp tomato ketchup

2 tsp Worcestershire sauce

150ml (5fl oz) red wine

25g (1oz) plain flour

200ml (7fl oz) beef stock

900g (2lb) Mashed Potatoes (*see* page 222)

Season the minced beef with salt and pepper, and pan-fry in the oil in a hot frying pan. For the best results, fry in batches. As one lot is fried and coloured, pour off from the pan and drain in a colander.

In another large saucepan, melt a knob of butter. Add the vegetables and season with salt, pepper and cinnamon, then add the rosemary. Cook for 5–6 minutes, until beginning to soften. Add the mince, tomato purée, ketchup and Worcestershire sauce, and stir into the mix. Add the red wine in three parts and turn the heat up, reducing each time. Sprinkle the flour into the pan and cook for 2–3 minutes.

Pour in the beef stock, bring to a soft simmer, cover and gently cook for about 1–1½ hours on top of the stove. During the cooking time, the sauce may become too thick; if so, add a little water to loosen. However, remember that the mash will spread on top, so don't allow the sauce to become too thin.

Make the mashed potatoes during the last 30 minutes of the cooking time. Reduce the quantities of the butter and cream given in the recipe on page 222, to give a slightly firmer topping.

Once the cottage pie mince is ready, spoon into a suitable ovenproof serving dish. The mashed potatoes can now be spooned or piped on top, brushed with a little butter and finished in a very hot oven or under the grill to become golden. Another method is to allow the mince to become cold in the dish before covering with the potato. This can now be refrigerated until needed, then reheated at 200°C/400°F/gas mark 6 for 35–40 minutes.

Shepherd's Pie
I think you might have got the idea by now. *This* is the pie that uses lamb….I've put cheese on the mashed potato topping for extra flavour.

SERVES 4

1 onion, cut into chunks

50g (1 3/4 oz) swede, cut into chunks

100g (3 1/2 oz) carrots, cut into chunks

1/2 tsp ground cinnamon

1 tsp chopped fresh thyme

1 tbsp chopped fresh flat-leaf parsley

10g (1/4 oz) plain flour

350g (12 oz) minced lamb

salt and pepper, to taste

1 tbsp tomato purée

425ml (15fl oz) vegetable stock

TOPPING

900g (2lb) Desirée or King Edward potatoes

75ml (2 1/2 fl oz) double cream

50ml (2fl oz) semi-skimmed milk

40g (1 1/2 oz) Cheddar, grated

25g (1oz) Parmesan, freshly grated

Preheat the oven to 140°C/275°F/gas mark 1.

Place the onion, swede and carrots into the bowl of a food processor. Add the cinnamon, herbs and flour and whizz everything until it is finely chopped, but not puréed. Place in a casserole dish, add the lamb and season well.

Heat the tomato purée and stock together to boiling point. Stir this into the casserole and mix together well. Place the casserole over a gentle heat and bring it up to simmering point. Cover with the lid and place it in the oven for 2 hours.

About 30 minutes before the end of the cooking time, peel the potatoes, cut them into chunks and put them into a pan of cold water. Bring to the boil and simmer for 20 minutes, or until tender.

Drain the potatoes thoroughly, then mash them well. Add the cream, milk and some salt and pepper. Continue to beat the potatoes until they are light and fluffy.

Take the casserole out of the oven and turn the temperature up to 200°C/400°F/gas mark 6.

Transfer the meat to a shallow dish and cover it evenly with the mashed potato. Cover the potatoes with grated Cheddar and sprinkle with the grated Parmesan.

Place the pie in the oven for 15 minutes, or until the top is golden and crusty.

Chicken and Leek Pie

This is a tasty pie, making good use of the underrated leek. Serve with a green vegetable such as broccoli.

SERVES 4

225g (8oz) ready-made shortcrust or puff pastry

1 free-range egg, beaten

FILLING

4 chicken breasts (without skin or wing bone)

olive oil

250g (9oz) shallots

2 leeks, washed

25g (1oz) unsalted butter

300ml (10fl oz) crème fraîche

150ml (5fl oz) chicken stock

salt and pepper, to taste

Preheat the oven to 200°C/400°F/gas mark 6.

Seal the chicken breasts in a hot pan in a little oil or chargrill on both sides. Set aside to rest.

Pan-fry the shallots in a little oil, then bake in the preheated oven for 10 minutes. Chop the leeks and pan-fry in the butter until soft.

Heat the crème fraîche and stock together and season with salt and pepper. Cut the chicken into fork-sized pieces and add to the stock mixture. Simmer for 5 minutes, then add the leeks and shallots. Put into a suitably sized pie dish.

Roll out the pastry and cut a strip to go around the rim of the pie dish. Top the pie with the piece of pastry and crimp the edges to seal. Decorate if you like, and brush with the beaten egg

Bake in the oven for 30 minutes.

This pie tastes fantastic, and while it is cooking your kitchen will be filled with the most mouthwatering aromas. It is my belief that, no matter where you are, you can judge how good a butcher is by his pork pie. Although the main spice in a pork pie is usually pepper, other spices such as mace, cinnamon, nutmeg, coriander and ginger can also be added. You can make this as one large pie or two smaller ones (as in the photograph).

Pork Pie

MAKES 1 x 15–20CM (6–8IN) PIE

PASTRY

250g (9oz) lard

300ml (10fl oz) water

900g (2lb) plain flour, plus extra for dusting

a good pinch of salt

butter, for greasing

1 free-range egg, lightly beaten

FILLING

900g (2lb) lean pork mince or diced pork shoulder

2 medium onions, diced

2 pinches freshly grated nutmeg

salt and pepper, to taste

100ml (3 1/2 fl oz) dry white wine

1 x 284 ml tub ready-prepared chicken stock

Make the pastry by bringing the lard and water to the boil in a pan. Sieve the flour into a food processor and add the salt. While the processor is on, pour the hot water and lard on to the flour and blend until you have a smooth dough. When finished, turn the dough out into a large bowl and allow to cool slightly.

Grease a 15–20cm (6–8 in) pie mould with butter. On a lightly floured surface, roll out two-thirds of the pastry and line the pie tin, leaving an overhang. Don't worry if it's a bit like working with clay; it will be worth it in the end. Place in the fridge to set. Keep the remaining pastry covered and warm.

Preheat the oven to 180°C/350°F/gas mark 4. To make the filling, mix the pork with the onions and season with nutmeg, salt and pepper. Add the wine and mix. Pile the filling into the pastry crust.

On a lightly floured surface, roll out the remaining pastry, using a little extra flour if it's sticky. Put it on top of the pie, then trim and crimp the edges with your thumbs. Brush the top with some of the beaten egg.

Bake in the oven for 40 minutes. Carefully remove from the tin and brush the edges with the lightly beaten egg again. Return to the oven for a further 20–30 minutes to set the sides and cook through.

Remove from the oven and allow to cool. Warm the chicken stock, then make a little hole in the top of the pie. Pour as much stock as the pie will take in through the hole. Chill to set.

Toad in the Hole

Well, if I can't make Yorkshire puddings I shouldn't be writing this book. I'm going to give you some top tips. Make the batter well in advance, so it can rest, and make sure the dish is hot before you add the batter to it. When in the oven, keep the door closed for at least 20 minutes. So there you go: good luck and happy rising of your Yorkshires! You can make large toads or individual ones (as in the photograph).

SERVES 6

6 sausages, such as Cumberland or Lancashire

olive oil

3 tbsp grain mustard

25g (1oz) beef dripping or vegetable oil

YORKSHIRE PUDDING

225g (8oz) plain flour

4–5 medium free-range eggs

salt and pepper, to taste

600ml (1 pint) milk

1 tbsp chopped fresh thyme leaves

First, make the Yorkshire pudding batter by placing the flour and all the eggs into a bowl with some salt and pepper. Whisk until smooth and stir in all the milk and the chopped thyme.

Cover and place in the fridge for at least 2 hours, or preferably overnight.

Preheat the oven to 220°C/425°F/gas mark 7, and place a large Yorkshire pudding tin in the oven to warm.

Sauté the sausages in a hot pan with a little oil to colour them. Remove them from the pan and coat in the mustard. Remove the hot tray from the oven, add the dripping and heat again until very hot.

Put the sausages in the centre of the tray and, while the tray is hot, pour in the batter.

Bake for 25–30 minutes, until risen and golden brown.

Sausage Rolls

Weddings and funerals are usually where we see the very worst of buffet food. It's a chef's pet hate: those rows on rows of cheap, shop-bought sausage rolls, undercooked vol-au-vents filled with cold prawns and mushrooms, Scotch eggs, pickled eggs, warm ham, undressed salad, overcooked dry chipolatas on sticks, and cheap smoked salmon. However, these delicious homemade sausage rolls might just surprise you!

MAKES 15–20

450g (1lb) sausagemeat (either from your butcher or use normal sausages and take the meat out of the skins)

1 onion, finely chopped or grated

finely grated zest of 1/2 lemon

1 heaped tsp each of chopped fresh thyme and sage

salt and pepper, to taste

freshly grated nutmeg

225g (8oz) ready-made puff pastry

plain flour, for dusting

1 free-range egg yolk, mixed with 2 tsp milk

Preheat the oven to 200°C/400°F/gas mark 6.

Mix together the sausagemeat, onion, lemon zest and chopped herbs. Season with the salt, pepper and nutmeg. This can now be refrigerated to firm while the pastry is being rolled.

Roll the pastry thinly (3mm/1/8 in) on a floured surface, then cut into three long strips approximately 10cm (4 in) wide.

The sausagemeat can now be moulded, using your hands, into three long sausages, preferably 2.5cm (1in) thick. If the meat is too moist, then dust with flour.

Sit each 'sausage' on a pastry strip, 2–3cm (3/4–1 1/4 in) from the edge of the pastry. Brush the pastry along the other side, close to the sausage, with the egg yolk and milk mixture. Fold the pastry over the meat, rolling it as you do so. When the pastry meets, leave a small overlap before cutting away any excess. Once rolled all along, lift them carefully, making sure that the seal is on the base when put down. Cut each strip into 5cm (2in) sausage rolls.

These can now be transferred to a greased baking sheet. The sausage rolls can be left as they are, or you can make three to four cuts with scissors along the top. Brush each with the remaining egg yolk before baking for 20–30 minutes.

Once baked golden and crispy, remove from the oven and serve warm.

This is one of the first dishes that I cooked as a young chef at Castle Howard, when I was about eight or nine. It reminds me of the garden fêtes and village shows where wars were waged between grannies, aunties and the WI: rolling pins at dawn over the best sponge cake and scone in the show!

Quiche Lorraine

SERVES 4

PASTRY

175g (6oz) plain flour, plus extra for dusting

salt, to taste

75g (2 3/4 oz) butter, plus extra for greasing

water

FILLING

250g (9oz) Cheddar, grated

4 tomatoes, sliced (optional)

200g (7oz) bacon, rinded and chopped

5 free-range eggs, beaten

100ml (3 1/2 fl oz) milk

200ml (7fl oz) double cream

salt and pepper, to taste

2 sprigs fresh thyme

Sift the flour together with a pinch of salt in a large bowl. Rub in the butter until you have a soft breadcrumb texture. Add enough water to make the crumb mixture come together to form a firm dough, and then rest it in the fridge for 30 minutes.

Roll out the pastry on a lightly floured surface and line a 22cm (8 1/2 in) well-buttered flan dish. Don't cut off the edges of the pastry yet. Chill again.

Preheat the oven to 190°C/375°F/gas mark 5.

Remove the pastry case from the fridge and line the base of the pastry with baking parchment and then fill it with baking beans. Place on a baking tray and bake blind for 20 minutes. Remove the beans and parchment and return to the oven for another 5 minutes to cook the base.

Reduce the temperature of the oven to 160°C/325°F/gas mark 3.

Sprinkle the cheese into the pastry base and add the sliced tomatoes if you are using them. Pan-fry the bacon pieces until crisp and sprinkle them over the top.

Combine the eggs with the milk and cream in a bowl and season well with salt and pepper. Pour over the bacon and cheese. Sprinkle the thyme over the top and trim the edges of the pastry. Bake for 30–40 minutes, or until set.

Remove from the oven and allow to set. Trim the pastry edges to get a perfect edge (top cheffy tip there), then serve in wedges.

I love to make classic dishes easy – and this one really is simple. Tarte tatin is originally French, but over the years we've nicked it, and now it's ours, too!

Shallot Tarte Tatin

SERVES 4

350g (12oz) shallots

olive oil

115g (4oz) caster sugar

25g (1oz) unsalted butter

salt and pepper, to taste

200g (7oz) ready-rolled puff pastry

TO SERVE

225g (8oz) goat's cheese

8 tbsp runny honey

truffle oil

30g (1 1/4 oz) wild rocket leaves

Preheat the oven to 200°C/400°F/gas mark 6.

Roast the shallots with a little olive oil for 20 minutes.

In a clean nonstick ovenproof pan, melt the sugar to a caramel. Add the butter and mix with the caramel. While hot, pour the mixture into four 7.5cm (3 in) nonstick Yorkshire pudding tins. Add the roasted shallots until each tin is full and a tight fit. Season with salt and pepper.

Cut the puff pastry into four circles about 1cm (½ in) bigger than the tins. Place the pastry on top of the shallots, and tuck in the edges down the side of the tins to seal in the shallots. Place the tins in the oven and bake for 15 minutes, until the pastry is cooked.

Meanwhile, preheat the grill to medium. With a sharp knife, cut the goat's cheese into 1cm (½in) slices.

Turn the tarts out, while piping hot, on to an oven tray, pastry down. Top with slices of goat's cheese and place under the grill for a few minutes to brown.

Meanwhile, mix the honey and a little truffle oil together. Place a tart on each plate and garnish with the rocket dressed with the honey and truffle oil.

Red Onion and Crème Fraîche Tarts

I use red onions for these instead of Spanish white onions because they require much less cooking and because they start off red, but instantly turn a dark, deep, rich caramel when you add balsamic. I serve this in my restaurant on the ship, and it always proves popular. I've planted red onions in my garden and always look forward to the new season.

SERVES 4

250g (9oz) ready-rolled puff pastry (defrosted if frozen)

1 small free-range egg, beaten

salt and pepper, to taste

2 tbsp balsamic vinegar

100ml (3½ fl oz) olive oil, plus extra for drizzling

100g (3½ oz) fresh rocket leaves

FILLING

3 large red onions, thinly sliced

6 cloves garlic, crushed

4 fresh thyme sprigs

25g (1oz) unsalted butter

125g (4½ oz) full-fat crème fraîche

Preheat the oven to 220°C/425°F/gas mark 7. Roll the puff pastry out until it is half as thick as it was when it was opened (about 3mm/⅛ in thick, or as thin as you dare) and cut into four round circles the size of a side plate. Using a sharp knife, cut a small, frame-like edge around the whole pastry and lay this, in pieces, around the outer edge of the tarts. Alternatively, make 1 large rectangular tart, as in the photograph.

Break the egg into a bowl and whisk with a fork. Brush the pastry circles or rectangle around the edges. Prick with a fork before baking for 15–20 minutes, until the pastry is cooked.

For the filling, in a large pan fry the onions, garlic and thyme in the butter for 15 minutes, until well caramelized. Season well. Remove the cooked base/s from the oven and spread with the crème fraiche, then top with the caramelized onions, drizzle with olive oil and return to the oven for a few minutes, until cooked.

In a bowl, mix the balsamic vinegar with the olive oil and some salt and pepper. Combine the rocket with the dressing.

Remove the tart/s from the oven and place on a serving plate. Drizzle with a little olive oil and serve with a small pile of the dressed rocket in the middle of the tart.

Asparagus has a very short season in the UK: only about six to eight weeks in May and June. It's best eaten with melted butter, using your fingers, but is also great in a tart, cooked with a Quiche Lorraine filling.

Asparagus Tart

SERVES 4

400g (14oz) shortcrust pastry, ready-made (or 1 1/2 times the quantity on page 94)

a little flour, for dusting

10g (1/4 oz) butter

FILLING

4 free-range eggs

1 free-range egg yolk

1 shallot, finely chopped

400ml (14fl oz) crème fraîche

salt and pepper, to taste

2 tbsp chopped fresh flat-leaf parsley

100g (3 1/2 oz) Gruyère cheese, grated

400g (14oz) asparagus, blanched and cold, halved lengthways

Roll out the pastry on a lightly floured surface and line a 25cm (10in) well-buttered flan ring. Leave the excess to hang over the edge. Chill for 30 minutes.

Preheat the oven to 190°C/375°F/gas mark 5.

Remove the pastry case from the fridge. Line the base of the pastry with baking parchment and fill with baking beans. Place on a baking tray and bake blind for 20 minutes.

Remove the beans and parchment from the pastry case and return to the oven for another 5 minutes to cook the base.

Reduce the temperature of the oven to 160°C/325°F/gas mark 3.

For the filling, beat the eggs, egg yolk and shallot together with the crème fraîche and season well. Fold in the parsley and half the cheese and spoon the mixture on to the base of the tart. Top with the asparagus and cover with the remaining cheese.

Trim the pastry around the edges. Bake for a further 30 minutes, until set, and serve warm.

roasts

What can I say about roast beef that hasn't been said already? The picture says it all. I was brought up on this every week, and it's one of the best things we produce in the UK. When I was about 14, I went to work in two two-star Michelin restaurants in France and got treated like a skivvy for 10 weeks, as both head chefs thought all we cooked in the UK was roast beef and Yorkshire pudding. Roast beef; they don't know what they're missing.

Peppered Roast Beef

SERVES 8

675–900g (1¹/₂ – 2lb) sirloin or rib of beef on the bone

2–3 tbsp black peppercorns, finely crushed

salt

cooking fat or oil

1 large sprig fresh rosemary

Preheat the oven to 220°C/425°F/gas mark 7. Roll the beef in the crushed peppercorns until completely covered. Season with salt.

Heat some oil in a hot roasting pan, then add the meat to seal. Remove from the heat and tuck the rosemary underneath the meat or place it on top. Roast in the oven – a joint of this size will take between 25 and 40 minutes to cook, but this very much depends on how you would like to eat it. Cooking for 20 minutes will keep it rare; 30 minutes, medium; and 40 minutes, medium-to-well done.

Once cooked, leave the meat to rest for 15–20 minutes before carving. This will relax the meat, and it will become even more tender.

Roast Sirloin of Beef

Roast beef with Yorkshire pudding is the best meal in the world, full stop. But then I am Yorkshire born and Yorkshire bred: strong in the arm and bloody good at making Yorkshire puddings!

SERVES 8

1 x 2.25–2.7kg (5–6lb / 3 ribs) sirloin of beef on the bone

1 onion, quartered

1 tbsp plain flour

salt and pepper, to taste

TO SERVE
Yorkshire Pudding (*see* page 132)

Preheat the oven to 240°C/475°F/gas mark 9.

Place the beef upright in a roasting tin, tucking in the onions by the side.

Dust the flour liberally over the surface of the beef. Season with some salt and pepper. This floury surface will help to make the fat very crusty, while the onion will caramelize to give the gravy a rich colour and flavour.

Place the joint in the oven. After 20 minutes, turn the temperature down to 190°C/375°F/gas mark 5, and continue to cook for 30 minutes for rare beef, plus 45 minutes for medium-rare or 60 minutes for well done.

While the meat is cooking, baste with the juices at least three times. To see if the beef is cooked to your liking, insert a thin skewer and press out some of the juices; the red, pink or clear colour will indicate to what stage the beef is cooked.

Remove the cooked beef to a board for carving and leave it to rest for at least 30 minutes before serving. During this time you can make the Yorkshire pudding. Pour any juices that are released from the beef into the gravy.

Roast Loin of Pork with Five Vegetables

This is a must for a Sunday lunch: roast loin of pork with crackling, roast potatoes, a quartet of other vegetables, and gravy.

SERVES 4

1 x 1.8–2kg (4–4¹/2 lb) loin of pork with the skin on

2 tbsp white wine vinegar

1 tbsp sea salt

1 tbsp chopped fresh thyme

vegetable oil, lard or dripping

salt and pepper, to taste

300g (10¹/2 oz) cauliflower florets

200g (7oz) carrots, chopped

200g (7oz) green beans, trimmed

300g (10¹/2 oz) broccoli florets

2 tbsp yeast extract

150ml (5fl oz) red wine

600ml (1 pint) chicken stock

50g (1³/4 oz) butter

TO SERVE
Roast Potatoes (*see* page 221)

Preheat the oven to 180°C/350°F/gas mark 4.

Score the skin of the pork 12–15 times with a sharp knife. Rub the vinegar over the skin, then mix together the sea salt and thyme and rub into the skin.

Place in a roasting tray with some fat and roast in the oven for about 2 hours, basting every 15 minutes or so.

While the meat is in the oven, precook the vegetables separately in plenty of boiling salted water. Begin with the cauliflower, then remove and plunge into cold water. Do the same with the carrots, beans and broccoli – in this order. Once they are all cooked and cooled, set aside until needed. Blanch and roast the potatoes as described on page 221, but for an hour instead of 50 minutes.

Once the meat is cooked, remove from the tray and leave to rest. Pour off the excess fat.

To make the gravy, place the oven tray on the stove and add the yeast extract, red wine and stock. Boil to reduce by about half, stirring. Add half the butter and some seasoning before passing through a sieve. Keep warm until needed.

To serve, put the roast potatoes in a serving dish. Reheat the vegetables in boiling salted water, tip into a serving dish and dot with the remaining butter. Remove the crackling, break into pieces and carve the meat. Pour the gravy into a jug.

Roast Pork

Even cold roast pork with cold apple sauce is fantastic, let alone straight from the oven just roasted. How many of you are tempted to taste a thick slice while you're carving? All, if you're like me. And I can never walk past one of those hog roasts without grabbing a floury bun filled with sliced meat and stuffing. Delicious!

SERVES 6

1 x 1.8kg (4lb) boned and rolled shoulder or loin of pork

salt and pepper, to taste

bones from the joint (optional)

1–2 tsp yeast extract

100ml (3 1/2 fl oz) red wine

250ml (9fl oz) gravy, made from gravy granules

1 tsp cornflour mixed with a little cold water

TO SERVE

Roast Potatoes (*see* page 221)

Put your joint of pork on a rack set over a dish or small roasting tin, and leave it somewhere cool and airy for a few hours, so the skin can dry off. Preheat your oven to the highest possible setting.

Season the cut faces of the pork with salt and pepper, but leave the skin untouched. Place the pork skin-side up in a large roasting tin – on the bones, if you have them. Roast for 20 minutes, then lower the oven temperature to 180°C/350°F/gas mark 4, and continue to roast for 30 minutes per 450g (1lb) – so, for example, a 1.8kg (4lb) joint will take a further 2 hours – basting every 15 minutes or so.

Blanch and roast the potatoes as described on page 221, but for an hour instead of 50 minutes. Reserve the cooking water for the gravy.

Remove the pork from the oven, transfer to a tray and leave to rest.

For the gravy, pour off the excess fat from the roasting tin and put the tin over a medium heat. Add 600ml (1 pint) of the reserved potato cooking water and scrape the base of the tin with a wooden spoon to loosen all the caramelized juices. Add the yeast extract, red wine and liquid gravy. Bring to the boil, and boil for a few minutes. Thicken with the cornflour (you may not need it all – just enough to get a good consistency). Strain into a warmed sauceboat, and adjust the seasoning if necessary.

To carve, cut and remove the strings. Slide a knife under the crackling, lift it off and break it into pieces. Carve the pork across into thin slices, and arrange them on a warmed serving plate with the crackling and roast potatoes. Serve with the gravy and some vegetables.

Pot-roasted Shoulder of Pork with Chilli and Beer

Good pork is so hard to find nowadays. Supermarkets seem to sell pork that has been bred to run the 100 metres rather than for flavour. Why have our tastes changed? We seem to want pork with no fat on it. I visit the man I consider to be the best pork producer in the country, Martin Martindale, who is based in Hampshire and sells his pork at local farmers' markets. Get there early though – before me! No Linford Christie pigs here, this is the best-tasting pork I've ever had.

SERVES 8

1 x 2.7–3.25kg (6–7lb) small, whole boned shoulder of pork, with the skin on

10 cloves garlic, crushed

salt and pepper, to taste

juice of 3 lemons

4 tbsp dried red chillies

3 tbsp olive oil

1 x 300ml bottle bitter beer

SALSA VERDE

10g (1/4 oz) capers

10g (1/4 oz) gherkins

4 spring onions

30g (11/4 oz) mixed fresh herbs (chervil, basil, mint and parsley)

juice of 11/2 lemons

2 tbsp extra virgin olive oil

Preheat the oven to 230°C/450°F/gas mark 8.

Using a small sharp knife, score the whole skin of the shoulder of pork with deep cuts about 5mm (1/4 in) wide.

Mix the garlic with the salt, pepper, lemon juice, chillies and oil. Rub and push this mixture into and over the skin and on all the surfaces of the meat.

Place the shoulder on a rack in a roasting tin and pour the bottle of beer into the base. Roast for 45 minutes, or until the skin begins to crackle and turn brown. Baste the shoulder once or twice while cooking, turn the oven down to 180°C/350°F/gas mark 4 and leave the meat to pot-roast for 3–4 hours.

The shoulder is ready when it is completely soft under the crisp skin. You can tell by pushing with your finger: the meat will give way and might even split.

To make the salsa verde, chop the capers, gherkins, spring onions and herbs finely, then mix with the lemon juice and oil. Season well.

Serve each person with some of the crisp skin, meat cut from different parts of the shoulder and a spoonful of the salsa verde. I think this is best served cold with hot new potatoes.

Sugar and Mustard-glazed Gammon

I remember when I was a kid my gran used to take me to Scott's Butchers in York (which has some fantastic pork and great pork pies, by the way). They'd always give her a free ham bone for the dog: a six-inch high Yorkshire terrier. It's a wonder the bloody thing wasn't the size of a horse! Mind you, it did live to a ripe old age. I was always told that, originally, York hams took their flavour from smoke from the oak sawdust that was around when they were building York Minster. This recipe doesn't go to that extreme, but it's a must for any buffet party.

SERVES 20–26

1 x 5–6kg (11–13lb) whole gammon

3 tbsp English mustard

30 cloves

4 tbsp demerara sugar

6 tbsp runny honey

Soak the gammon in a sinkful of cold water overnight. (Ask your supplier how long you should soak it, as gammon pieces vary.)

Preheat the oven to 160°C/325°F/gas mark 3.

Remove the gammon from the water and pat dry. Put into a large oven tray and cover with foil. Put in the oven for about 3$1/2$ – 4$1/2$ hours, or about 20 minutes per 450g (1lb), depending on the size of your joint.

Half an hour before the end of the cooking time, remove the joint from the oven and turn the temperature up to 220°C/425°F/gas mark 7.

Remove the foil and peel off the skin, being careful not to burn yourself (rubber gloves can help here).

Using a sharp knife, score the fat in a criss-cross pattern all over the gammon. Rub the gammon with mustard and stud with the cloves, then sprinkle with the demerara sugar.

Drizzle with honey and return to the oven for about 20–30 minutes, until golden brown and well glazed. Keep basting with the juices in the pan and allow to cool before serving.

I remember queuing up at Scott's Butchers as a kid with my gran and auntie. Armed with their handbags and pensions every Thursday, they would wait for dry-cured smoked back bacon and York ham. Sadly they don't do York ham any more, but if you're in York it's worth going to the shop, on Petergate, to experience one of the greatest pork suppliers there is.

Honey-glazed Ham with Spiced Apple Sauce

SERVES 4–6

1 x 3.5kg (7 1/2 lb) boiled ham, cooled

115g (4oz) runny honey

1 tbsp English mustard

finely grated zest and juice of 1 orange

20 cloves

TO SERVE

Spiced Apple Sauce (*see* page 234)

Preheat the oven to 220°C/425°F/gas mark 7.

Score the ham fat diagonally at 2.5cm (1in) intervals, first in one direction, then another, to produce a diamond pattern.

Mix the honey, mustard, orange zest and enough orange juice to make a spreadable mixture. Smear this glaze over the ham. Stud the ham with the cloves at the points of the diamond shapes. Bake for 30 minutes, or until cooked through.

Serve the ham in slices, hot or cold, with the Spiced Apple Sauce.

Roast Leg of Lamb

I first tried this garlic, rosemary and anchovy combination with lamb while working at Antony Worrall Thompson's restaurant in the late 1980s. I was hooked; it's to die for. You might consider combining anchovies with meat curious, but somehow the anchovies make the meat meatier!

SERVES 4

1 leg of lamb

6 cloves garlic, cut into slivers

3 large sprigs fresh rosemary

1 x 75g can anchovy fillets in oil

olive oil

Preheat the oven to 180°C/350°F/gas mark 4.

Make small cuts all over the meat and insert a sliver of garlic, a small piece of rosemary and half an anchovy fillet into each cut until all the ingredients are used up.

Drizzle with a little olive oil and roast in the oven, allowing 20 minutes per 450g (1lb) for meat that is pink in the centre, 25 minutes if you prefer it more well done.

Once the joint is cooked to your liking, remove and allow to rest before you carve the meat.

Lavender Roast Leg of Lamb

Using lavender instead of rosemary contributes a subtly different flavour to your lamb.

SERVES 4

1 leg of lamb, about 2.25kg (5lb)

1 bulb garlic, cloves peeled

1 x 75g can anchovy fillets in olive oil

lots of tiny sprigs of fresh lavender

salt and pepper, to taste

about 2 tbsp lavender honey or lavender mustard

LAVENDER HONEY GLAZE
100ml (3$\frac{1}{2}$ fl oz) lavender honey

100ml (3$\frac{1}{2}$ fl oz) olive oil

Preheat the oven to 180°C/350°F/gas mark 4. Using a sharp knife, prick the leg of lamb all over, about 20 times and about 2cm (3/4 in) deep. Cut the garlic into thin strips and place one slice of garlic and a third of an anchovy fillet into each hole. Pick a sprig of lavender and place this into the holes, too. Continue until all the holes are full.

Place the joint in a roasting tray. Season with salt and pepper, and drizzle with lavender honey or spread with lavender mustard. Roast in the oven for 1 hour 20 minutes for a 2.25kg (5lb) leg of lamb, basting occasionally.

Warm the honey for the glaze in a small pan, then, with a hand blender on a high speed, pour the oil in to create a warm glaze. Pour over the lamb, and return to the oven to cook for a further 20 minutes.

When the lamb is cooked, let it rest for 15 minutes before carving.

Yeah, yeah, before we start: corn-fed and organic chickens do have a better flavour than the normal fare, but my gran didn't use them, nor did my mum or my auntie, so they should have no place in this book. (Come to think of it, we had chickens that my dad used to breed in our yard at home.) Stuffing the chicken under the skin creates flavour and helps keep the meat nice and moist.

Roast Chicken with Tapenade

SERVES 4

1 x 2kg (4 1/2 lb) chicken

175g (6oz) tapenade, bought-in or made as below

1 lemon, halved

1 bulb garlic, halved

salt and pepper, to taste

extra virgin olive oil

TAPENADE

200g (7oz) black olives, stoned

1 clove garlic

1 onion

3 tbsp capers

6 anchovy fillets

a small bunch of fresh flat-leaf parsley

juice of 1 lemon

extra virgin olive oil

Preheat the oven to 190°C/375°F/gas mark 5.

To make the tapenade, finely chop the olives, garlic, onion, capers, anchovy fillets and parsley. Mix in the lemon juice and enough oil to make a paste-like texture. Season well with salt and pepper.

Starting at the neck end of the chicken, push your fingertips between the skin and flesh to form a pocket. Spoon the tapenade between the flesh and skin, and pat down so that it spreads evenly.

Place the chicken in a roasting tin, squeeze over the lemon juice and then place the lemon halves around. Place the garlic into the body cavity. Season and drizzle with oil.

Roast in the oven for about 70–80 minutes, basting the skin every 10 minutes with its own juices. Push a skewer into the thigh at the thickest point. If the juices run clear, it is done; if not, give it another 5 minutes then test again.

Serve slices of chicken with a spoonful of tapenade on the side.

Roast Chicken with Lemon and Bacon

Roast chicken is everyone's favourite, and this is a simple recipe given an extra little kick of flavour by the lemon and bacon.

SERVES 4

1 x 1.3kg (3lb) chicken

olive oil

salt and pepper, to taste

a knob of butter

6 slices streaky bacon

2 lemons

Preheat the oven to 200°C/400°F/gas mark 6. Brush the bird all over with olive oil and season generously. Put the knob of butter inside the bird, and place the bacon over the breast part of the chicken. Place in an oven tray.

Cut the lemons in half and squeeze the juice over the bird. Place the lemon halves around the chicken, then drizzle everything with a little more olive oil.

Roast in the oven for 20 minutes per 450g (1lb), basting frequently. Push a skewer into the thigh at the thickest point. If the juices run clear, it is done; if not, give it another 5 minutes, then test again.

Leave the cooked bird to stand in a warm place for 15 minutes before carving. This standing time is vital. The bird finishes cooking while the juices are recovered and absorbed back into the meat, making every slice moist.

Spiced Pot-roasted Chicken A twist to make the standard roast chicken taste a little different.

SERVES 4

1 x 2kg (4¹/₂ lb) chicken

60g (2¹/₄ oz) butter

8 tbsp dark soy sauce

6 tbsp runny honey

2 cinnamon sticks

4 cloves garlic, halved

2 star anise

175ml (6fl oz) dry sherry

350ml (12fl oz) chicken stock

Preheat the oven to 200°C/400°F/gas mark 6.

Wipe the chicken. Melt the butter in a casserole dish, add the chicken and brown the bird on all sides. Sit breast-up in the casserole and pour over the soy sauce and honey. Add the cinnamon, garlic and star anise to the base of the pan and pour in the sherry and stock.

Place the casserole on the stove and bring to a simmer. Then cover the dish loosely with foil and put into the preheated oven. Cook for about 80 minutes, uncovering and basting with the juices every now and then. Push a skewer into the thigh at the thickest point. If the juices run clear, it is done; if not, give it another 5 minutes, then test again.

When cooked, remove the chicken and leave to rest in a warm place. Strain the juices into a clean pan and boil to reduce.

Serve the chicken, cut into pieces rather than carved, with the reduced juices, some rice and a salad.

Here's a quick and easy turkey recipe that all the family will love! The stuffing beneath the skin keeps the flesh nice and moist.

Roast Turkey Stuffed with Cream Cheese and Herbs

SERVES 10–12

1 x 4.5kg (10lb) oven-ready turkey, giblets removed

1 bunch fresh parsley, stalks removed

250g (9oz) cream cheese

1 bunch fresh coriander, stalks removed

4 tbsp olive oil

salt and pepper, to taste

Preheat the oven to 180°C/350°F/gas mark 4.

Place the turkey on a board and carefully lift the skin up at the neck. Work your hand under it to ease it away from the breast completely.

Process the parsley in a blender until chopped. Add the cream cheese and gradually add the coriander, blending between each addition until smooth. Finally, add 1 tbsp of the olive oil and blend well. Alternatively, chop the herbs as finely as you can and mix with the cream cheese and 1 tbsp olive oil.

Press the cream mixture into the space between the breast and the skin of the turkey. Pull the skin back into place over the cheese mixture, press to re-shape and smooth over.

Place the turkey in a roasting tin and drizzle with the rest of the olive oil. Season well with salt and pepper, and roast for 18 minutes per 450g (1lb), or until the juices run clear when the thickest part of the leg is pierced with a knife. Baste the turkey with the pan juices after 45 minutes.

Cover with foil and leave to stand for at least 20 minutes before carving.

Roast Turkey with Orange

The most common mistake people make when they roast turkey is the timing, especially at Christmas. With the kids running around and the gravy boiling over, you tend to forget about it! Calculate 18 minutes per 450g (1lb). Leave the turkey to rest well before you carve it, and never use an electric carving knife, as this will rip the meat and make it tough.

SERVES 10–12

1 x 4.5–5.4kg (10–12lb) turkey, giblets removed

2 oranges

24 large fresh rosemary sprigs

55g (2oz) unsalted butter, at room temperature

salt and pepper, to taste

22 streaky bacon rashers

GRAVY

600ml (1 pint) chicken stock or water

300ml (10fl oz) white wine or water

3 tbsp plain flour

2 tsp Dijon mustard

Preheat the oven to 190°C/375°F/gas mark 5. Wash the turkey inside and out and dry well with kitchen paper. Quarter 1 orange and put the quarters in the cavity with 2 rosemary sprigs. If you are stuffing the turkey (*see* page 129), put the stuffing in the neck-end only, pushing it up towards the breast (don't pull the neck skin too tightly, as the stuffing expands during cooking). Secure the neck-end with skewers crossways, then tie the turkey legs together at the top of the drumsticks for a good shape.

Weigh the turkey and calculate the cooking time at 18 minutes per 450g (1lb). Grease a large roasting tin with a little butter. Put the turkey in the tin. Melt the remaining butter. Halve the remaining orange and squeeze one-half over the turkey, then mix the remaining juice with the melted butter. Brush some of this butter over the turkey skin and season (keep the rest for basting later). Cover the turkey with foil and roast for the calculated time. Brush it every hour with the orange-butter mixture. An hour before the end of the cooking time, remove the foil. If you want, you can turn the oven up a bit higher. The turkey is ready if the juices run clear when the thickest part of the leg is pierced with a knife.

For each rosemary and bacon spike, lay a bacon rasher on the work surface with a rosemary sprig on top. Wrap the bacon around the sprig and lay it on a baking sheet with the join underneath.

Remove the turkey from the oven and transfer it to a platter, tightly cover with foil, and allow to rest for up to 30 minutes before carving, leaving the oven on. Put the bacon and rosemary spikes in the oven 20 minutes before you are ready to serve, and cook until the bacon is crisp.

While the turkey is resting, pour off all but 6 tbsp of the juices from the roasting tin into a large jug and leave them to settle. When the fat has risen to the surface, spoon it off and make the darker juices underneath up to 600ml (1 pint) with water or stock, then add the wine. Heat the juices in the roasting tin on the hob. Stir in the flour, scraping up the bits from the bottom of the tin, and cook, stirring, to a nutty brown. Slowly pour in the liquid, then bring to the boil and keep stirring until thickened. Season with the mustard and salt and pepper.

Serve the bird with the spikes, roasties, and whatever else you want.

While doing some of the photography for this book I went shooting at Jody Schekter's farm up the road from me. It was a great day and, as usual, the number of birds we said we shot was different to the number we took home. Typical men, I know! If you buy a brace of birds, or a cock and a hen, remember hens are smaller so will need to be removed from the oven before the cocks.

Pot-roast Pheasant with Cider and Calvados

SERVES 4

55g (2oz) butter

2 pheasants, cleaned

salt and pepper, to taste

1 onion, finely chopped

85g (3oz) bacon lardons

1 stick celery, chopped

1 carrot, chopped

4 sprigs fresh sage

2 Granny Smith apples, peeled, cored and cut into large chunks

50ml (2fl oz) Calvados

500ml (18fl oz) dry cider

300ml (10fl oz) chicken stock

300ml (10fl oz) double cream

BAKED APPLES

4 Cox's apples, peeled and cored

25g (1oz) butter, melted

1 tbsp soft light brown sugar

TO SERVE

kale, blanched

deep-fried sage leaves

8 slices crispy cooked pancetta

Preheat the oven to 190°C/375°F/gas mark 5. Melt the butter in a large nonstick casserole pot. Season the pheasants with salt and pepper. Place the pheasants into the casserole pot and brown over a medium heat until pale golden on all sides. Remove from the pot and set aside.

Add the onion, bacon, celery, carrot and sage sprigs to the pot and cook over a medium heat until the onion is soft and translucent and the bacon is crispy. Carefully pour off any excess fat from the lardons.

Return the pheasants to the pot and scatter over the apples. Pour over most of the Calvados and set alight. Once the flames have died down, add 300ml (10fl oz) of the cider and the chicken stock. Bring to a simmer, cover and place in the oven for about 20 minutes, until the birds are cooked through.

For the baked apples, place the apples on a baking tray that has been brushed with a little butter and sprinkle with the sugar. Bake for about half an hour, basting the apples a few times during cooking.

Remove the pheasants from the pot and place on a chopping board. Remove the thighs and breasts and set aside to keep warm. Chop the carcass into four pieces and place them back in the pot with the vegetables and the remaining cider. Bring to a boil and simmer gently for 5 minutes.

Strain the sauce into a bowl through a fine-meshed sieve. Pour the strained sauce back into the pot and add a splash of Calvados. Reduce by half. Add the cream and simmer for a further 5 minutes, or until the sauce is creamy and slightly thickened. Return the pheasant breasts and thighs to the pot to warm through and become coated in the sauce.

Remove the baked apples from the oven. Serve the pheasant on a bed of kale with a baked apple. Garnish with deep-fried sage leaves and crispy pancetta.

Mother's Pheasant with Wild Garlic Leaves, Shallots and Bacon

Wild garlic is found in damp woods and shady lanes; it has white flowers and dark green leaves, which are like a cross between dock and dandelion. If you can't find it use 450g (1lb) spinach with two cloves of garlic.

SERVES 4

2 large pheasants, cleaned

1 carrot

1/2 leek

1 onion

400ml (14fl oz) red wine

1 litre (1³/4 pints) fresh chicken stock

4 sprigs fresh thyme

salt and pepper, to taste

1 tbsp olive oil

16 rashers streaky bacon

16 shallots

40g (1¹/2 oz) butter

8 handfuls freshly picked wild garlic leaves

Remove the breasts and legs from the pheasants and leave to one side.

Preheat the oven to 220°C/425°F/gas mark 7. For the sauce, dice the carrot, leek and three-quarters of the onion and place this and the pheasant carcasses in a roasting tray. Roast in the oven for about 1 hour until nice and brown. Leave the oven on.

Remove the carcasses and vegetables from the oven and place in a large pan with the red wine, stock and half the fresh thyme. Bring to the boil and simmer gently without a lid so the liquor can reduce.

Season the pheasant legs and breasts with salt and pepper and seal in a hot pan in the olive oil. Put in an ovenproof dish in one layer and cover with the bacon. Add the shallots and remaining thyme to the dish. Place in the oven at the same heat, and roast for about 15 minutes.

Meanwhile, finely dice the remaining onion and cook in half the butter in a pan over a high heat for a few minutes. Throw in the garlic leaves and cook for about 1 minute only, until wilted. Remove from the heat.

Strain the sauce and continue to reduce over a high heat.

Remove the pheasant from the oven and leave to stand for about 5–10 minutes to rest. Add the remaining butter and some seasoning to the sauce.

Season the garlic leaves, place on the plates and put the pheasant on top with the bacon, shallots and thyme from the pan. Pour over the sauce and serve.

Honeyed Duck Confit with Crispy Seaweed and Creamy Mash

You can buy, or prepare yourself, plump, tender duck legs that have been cooked deliciously slowly in their own fat. Known as duck confit, they are ideal for many dishes.

SERVES 2

2 duck legs, confited in their own fat, homemade (*see* page 127) or from a can or jar

4 tbsp clear honey

3 tbsp olive oil

leaves stripped from 2–3 sprigs fresh thyme

300g (10½ oz) mashing potatoes, such as Maris Piper, King Edward or Desirée, peeled and chopped

salt and pepper, to taste

3 tbsp hot milk

a small knob of butter

100ml (3½ fl oz) red wine

250ml (9fl oz) fresh chicken stock (buy ready-made in a tub)

55g (2oz) crispy seaweed

Heat the oven to 180°C/350°F/gas mark 4. Scrape the fat from the duck legs and place them in a roasting pan. (Don't waste the fat – it's wonderful for frying eggs or roasting potatoes.)

Whisk the honey and oil together and smear over the duck legs. Sprinkle over the thyme leaves. Roast the legs in the oven for about 20 minutes, spooning the honey glaze over the legs two to three times.

Meanwhile, boil the potatoes in a saucepan of lightly salted water for about 15 minutes until just tender. Drain, then mash with a fork, gradually beating in the hot milk, butter and plenty of seasoning.

Place the wine and stock in a saucepan, bring to the boil and continue boiling until reduced by two-thirds. Season well.

Spoon the mashed potato on to the centre of warmed serving plates, sprinkle the seaweed round the mash and sit the duck legs on top. Scrape any meaty bits from the roasting pan and sprinkle over, then pour over the reduced red wine sauce and serve immediately.

I love 1970s food – the Berni Inn, the prawn cocktail, the chicken in a basket and *duck à l'orange*. It's fine to embrace the future, but don't ever forget the past. I cooked this recipe the other day for a dinner party, and it went down a storm. I gave them prawn cocktail to start and a Black Forest gâteau for pudding. Serve with some extra orange slices, briefly caramelized in butter, if you like, and perhaps some shreds of candied orange zest.

Duck with Orange

SERVES 2

4 tsp runny honey

40g (1¹/₂ oz) butter

2 x 200g (7oz) duck breasts

salt and pepper, to taste

caramelized orange slices, to garnish (optional)

SAUCE

40g (1¹/₂ oz) butter

1 rounded tbsp plain flour

500ml (18fl oz) hot duck, game or beef stock

2 Seville oranges, or 2 sweet oranges and 1 lemon

1 tbsp caster sugar

4 tbsp port

Make the sauce first. Melt the butter in a small pan and let it turn a delicate golden brown colour. Stir in the flour, cook for 2 minutes, then stir in the stock. Allow to simmer gently for at least 20 minutes – the longer the better. Meanwhile, preheat the oven to 200°C/400°F/gas mark 6.

To cook the duck, melt the honey and butter together in a very hot pan, then place the duck in, skin-side down. Season well with salt and pepper, and colour very well (until almost black) before turning over. Place on an oven tray and bake for 8–10 minutes, until pink. Once cooked, remove from the oven and allow to rest. Reserve any juices from the pan for use in the sauce.

Meanwhile, remove the peel from the oranges, and cut it into matchstick strips. Simmer these in boiling water for 3 minutes, then drain and add to the simmering sauce. Add the juice of the oranges (and lemon, if used) to the sauce. Stir in some sugar to taste; start with a little, and add more if necessary. Finally, pour in the reserved meat juices from the duck, which should be well skimmed of fat, then the port.

Slice the duck breast, pour the sauce over it, and serve garnished with caramelized orange slices, if you like.

Honey-roast Duck Confit with Tomato Beans

I made this dish up while doing a dinner party in Scotland, and it's now a favourite. Canned beans and canned tomatoes can taste great heated together as we all know – think of beans on toast – but this goes to another level.

SERVES 4

4 duck legs

salt and pepper, to taste

leaves from 2–3 fresh thyme sprigs

300g (10 1/2 oz) duck fat

2 tbsp clear honey

TOMATO BEANS

4 tbsp extra-virgin olive oil

1 white onion, peeled and finely chopped

4 cloves garlic, finely chopped

100ml (3 1/2 fl oz) white wine

leaves from 2 fresh thyme sprigs

1 x 400g can chopped tomatoes

6 medium tomatoes

1 x 350g can flageolet beans, drained and rinsed

55g (2oz) unsalted butter

10g (1/4 oz) fresh parsley, chopped

RED WINE SAUCE

1/2 red onion, chopped

2 tbsp extra-virgin olive oil

750ml (1 pint 6fl oz) fresh beef stock

1/3 bottle red wine

10g (1/4oz) unsalted butter

To make the duck confit, weigh the duck legs, then put them on a small tray. Sprinkle with 15g (1/2 oz) salt per kg (2 1/4 lb) and the fresh thyme leaves. Cover with clingfilm and place in the fridge overnight.

The following day, remove the legs from the tray, wipe off the salt, and put the legs in a frying pan with the duck fat. Cook slowly, covered, for about 2 1/2 hours, turning occasionally. Leave to cool in the fat.

When you are about half an hour from serving, preheat the oven to 180°C/350°F/gas mark 4.

To make the beans, heat the olive oil in a pan and sauté the onion and garlic for a few minutes. Add the wine, thyme and tomatoes, both canned and fresh, and bring to a simmer. After 15 minutes, add the beans and simmer for a further 15 minutes. Season with salt and pepper, and add the butter and parsley to finish. Keep warm.

To make the red wine sauce, sauté the onion in the oil until it is softened, about 2 minutes, then add the stock and red wine. Bring to the boil, then simmer to reduce to a good sauce consistency. Pass through a sieve, add the butter, and keep warm to one side.

Meanwhile, scrape the fat from the duck legs and place in a roasting pan. Smear the honey over the duck legs, then roast for 20 minutes, until cooked through, spooning the honey glaze over the legs at least a couple of times during cooking.

To serve, place the beans on the plates and put the duck confit alongside. Spoon the sauce around.

I bought my first goose from a butcher's shop in Malton called Derrick Fox, which used to have geese, turkey, rabbit and pheasant hung up outside. Goose is fantastic, but you must get a good bird otherwise it can be as tough as old boots. Serve the roast bird with a green vegetable, potatoes roasted in the goose fat, fried apple slices and black pudding.

Roast Goose with Stuffing

SERVES 6

1 x 4.5kg (10lb) goose with giblets (and any extra giblets you might get from your butcher if you ask nicely)

salt and pepper, to taste

about 600ml (1 pint) chicken stock

a little cornflour slaked in water

a little yeast extract

STUFFING

1kg (2¼ lb) good sausage meat

1 onion, chopped

1 clove garlic, smashed

1 medium free-range egg, beaten

freshly grated nutmeg

2 tbsp brandy

Preheat the oven to 220°C/425°F/gas mark 7.

Prick the bird all over with a fork or needle, rub generously with salt and pepper, then roast on a rack over a deep tin, starting it loosely covered with foil, for 15 minutes per 450g (1lb). From time to time, remove fat from the roasting pan and reserve. Remove the foil 30 minutes before your calculated completion time to allow the skin to brown and crisp.

While the bird is roasting, make the gravy. Chop up the neck, gizzard and heart, and simmer in the stock for about 2 hours, topping up with more stock or water as necessary. Strain. Boil to reduce a little if necessary, and thicken with the cornflour. Season and add yeast extract to taste.

About 1 hour before the bird is due to come out of the oven, make the stuffing. In a large bowl, mix all the ingredients together well and then spoon the mixture into a large nonstick loaf pan. Put in the oven with the bird and leave it in there when you take the bird out.

When the goose is cooked through, leave it to stand for 20 minutes before attempting to carve it. Transfer it to a large chopping board and sever the legs. Cut off one breast in a single piece, then the other, reversing the bird to point the other way to make this easier. Cut through the legs at the ball-socket joint to separate them into drumsticks and thighs. Lay the breast pieces skin-side down and cut into slices across and down at a 45 degree angle. Arrange the slices on a warmed ovenproof dish. Cut slices off the legs and arrange them, skin-side up, around the breast meat. Detach the wings and cut them in half across the middle joint, slicing off what meat you can. Pick over the carcass, removing any meat that is left. Just before serving, you can flash this carved meat under the grill briefly. This will crisp up the skin as well.

Turn the stuffing out of its tin, and slice it like a meat loaf. Serve the goose accompanied by slices of the stuffing, and any other chosen accompaniments. Pass the hot gravy separately.

Sausage meat, Red Pepper and Apricot Stuffing Balls

I did these for a magazine article once, and people love them with turkey. They're so simple to prepare!

MAKES 16 BALLS

450g (1lb) good sausage meat (or good sausages removed from their casings)

2 tbsp ground almonds

2 roasted red peppers (canned or bottled), finely chopped

8 dried apricots, finely chopped

1 tsp mixed dried herbs

salt and pepper, to taste

olive oil

Place the sausage meat in a bowl. Add the ground almonds, red peppers, apricots and herbs. Season with salt and pepper and mix well.

Roll into 16 balls and place on a greased baking sheet. Brush with olive oil and cook at 180°C/350°F/gas mark 4 for 30 minutes while the turkey (*see* page 119) is resting.

Chestnut Stuffing

Stuff this into the turkey as described on page 119, or bake in a separate loaf tin – or make into balls as here.

FOR A 4.5–5.4KG (10–12LB) TURKEY

25g (1oz) unsalted butter

1 large onion, finely chopped

5 juniper berries

1kg (2¼ lb) good sausage meat (or good sausages removed from their casings)

1 x 200g vacuum pack cooked, peeled whole chestnuts, roughly chopped

2 medium free-range eggs

4 tbsp chopped fresh sage

2 tbsp chopped fresh parsley

115g (4oz) white breadcrumbs

¼ tsp ground allspice

salt and pepper, to taste

In a medium saucepan, melt the butter over a gentle heat, then add the onion and juniper berries. Cook for 5 minutes, without allowing the onion to colour. Leave to cool. Remove and discard the juniper berries.

In a large bowl, mix the onion with the rest of the ingredients. To make sure you've got the seasoning right, fry a small piece of the stuffing before shaping, then taste and adjust as necessary. (You can make the stuffing a day ahead to the end of this step and keep in the fridge until ready to use. It can also be frozen.)

Shape into about 24 balls – this is easier with wet hands – and bake in a roasting tin at 180°C/350°F/gas mark 4 for 35–40 minutes while the turkey (*see* page 119) is resting.

Just look at them bubbling away in the pan: a lovely mixture of sausage and bacon to garnish roast turkey, goose or chicken. Buy dry-cured bacon so that when you fry it you don't get that weeping white liquid coming out of the bacon (from the water injected into so much bacon these days). Both sausage and bacon will end up being nice and crisp and brown.

Sausage and Bacon Wraps with Sage and Honey

SERVES 4

8 streaky bacon rashers

16 cocktail sausages

16 small fresh sage leaves

2 tbsp runny honey

Preheat the oven to 180°C/350°F/gas mark 4. Cut each of the bacon rashers in half.

Roll up the sausages in the bacon with a small sage leaf. Secure with a wooden cocktail stick if you like (it's not entirely necessary), and arrange in a shallow tin. Drizzle with the runny honey.

Place in the oven, and cook for 25–30 minutes. Turn over once or twice to brown evenly all over. Remove the cocktail sticks before serving, if necessary.

Yorkshire Pudding

Once again, this is my gran's recipe, which she used to serve with Rich Onion Gravy (*see* below). I love these with fois gras pâté in the centre, served with the same gravy. This makes a great dinner party starter, and tastes fantastic.

SERVES 4

225g (8oz) plain flour

salt and pepper, to taste

4–5 medium free-range eggs

600ml (1 pint) milk

55g (2 oz) good dripping or 50ml (2fl oz) vegetable oil

Place the flour and some seasoning in a bowl, and make a well in the middle. Add the eggs one by one, using a whisk, then whisk in the milk, mixing very well until the batter is smooth and there are no lumps. If possible, leave in the fridge for at least an hour or, even better, overnight.

Preheat the oven to about 220°C/425°F/gas mark 7. Divide the dripping or vegetable oil between four Yorkshire pudding tins (about 13cm/5in in diameter) or muffin tins, and place in the oven to get very hot.

Carefully remove the trays from the oven and, with a ladle or from a jug, fill the tins with the batter and place back in the oven straightaway. Cook for about 20 minutes before opening the door to check – otherwise they will collapse. If undercooked, reduce the heat to 200°F/400°F/gas mark 6, and cook for a further 10–15 minutes.

Rich Onion Gravy

Some of my gran's recipes are over 100 years old and have been passed down through the Yorkshire generations. This gravy is the perfect accompaniment to Yorkshire Pudding.

SERVES 4

2 white onions, sliced

15g (1/2 oz) good dripping

250ml (9 fl oz) red wine

400ml (14 fl oz) fresh beef stock

Cook the onions in a pan in the dripping for about 10 minutes, then add the wine and stock. Reduce until you have a nice thickened mixture: about another 10 minutes or so.

Season well. Serve with Yorkshire Pudding (*see* above).

stews, pots & spicy foods

How many people have eaten dumplings and thought they tasted like rubber bullets? Not if you follow this recipe! The secret to a good stew, I think, is sealing the meat well before adding the stock. This, if done properly, will give the stew increased flavour and a much better dark colour.

Beef Stew and Dumplings

SERVES 4

4 tbsp olive oil

450g (1lb) stewing beef, diced

75g (2 3/4 oz) chicken livers, cut into chunks

100g (3 1/2 oz) celery, diced

100g (3 1/2 oz) carrot, diced

1/2 leek, chopped

1 small red onion, diced

2 cloves garlic, crushed

150ml (5fl oz) good red wine

500ml (18fl oz) fresh beef stock

4 canned anchovies, diced

salt and pepper, to taste

10 baby onions

15g (1/2 oz) butter

8 sun-dried tomatoes, diced

10 new potatoes, cooked

4 tbsp fresh pesto

3 tbsp chopped fresh flat-leaf parsley

4 tbsp torn fresh basil

DUMPLINGS

125g (4 1/2 oz) plain flour

1 tsp baking powder

60g (2 1/4 oz) shredded suet

1 tbsp chopped fresh flat-leaf parsley

Preheat the oven to 140°C/275°F/gas mark 1.

Put two large pans on a high heat with a third of the olive oil in each and, when hot, brown the beef and livers in one pan and the vegetables and garlic in the other. Fry both until they are nice and brown.

Place the contents of both pans into a casserole dish and deglaze the pans with the red wine and beef stock. Add the liquid to the stewing dish.

Add the anchovies, season with salt and pepper and cook, with the lid on, in the oven for about 3 hours.

Meanwhile, make the dumplings. Sieve the flour, baking powder and a pinch of salt together into a bowl. Mix in the suet and parsley and enough water to form a slightly thick dough. Placing a little flour on your hands, roll the dough into small balls, remembering that they will swell as they cook in the stew.

At the end of the stew's cooking time, fry the baby onions in the remaining oil and the butter, season with salt and pepper and add to the stew with the sun-dried tomatoes and potatoes. Simmer for 5 minutes, then season well and add the pesto and herbs.

Remove the meat and vegetables from the liquid with the slotted spoon and keep warm in a dish, covered with foil, in the low oven.

Put the casserole over a high heat and, when bubbling, add the dumplings. Turn the heat down and poach gently for 20 minutes, as the dumplings will break up too much if they are allowed to boil.

Serve the stew with the dumplings.

Beef Stroganoff

Thinly sliced beef in a rich onion, mushroom and cream sauce, though Russian in origin, has become a classic, not just here in the UK but throughout Europe. Here, though, I've used minced beef; it's easier and less expensive – although it's a good idea to use good-quality mince for this recipe. Like the goulash opposite, this dish reminds me of my mother's food: food she placed in a big dish in the middle of the table with an even bigger bowl of pilaf rice.

SERVES 4

75g (2 3/4 oz) butter

1 tbsp olive oil

2 small onions, sliced

1 clove garlic, crushed

175g (6oz) brown mushrooms, sliced

225g (8oz) best minced beef

1 tbsp paprika

1 tbsp French mustard

75ml (2 1/2 fl oz) double cream

salt and pepper, to taste

2 tbsp chopped fresh flat-leaf parsley

TO SERVE

225g (8oz) fresh noodles, freshly cooked

a little butter

75ml (2 1/2 fl oz) soured cream

Heat a large frying pan on the stove and add the butter and olive oil. Fry the onions and garlic for about 5 minutes, until softened.

Add the sliced mushrooms, mince and paprika. Fry on a high heat to seal the mince. After 5 minutes, add the mustard and pour in the double cream. Bring to a gentle simmer before adding some salt and pepper.

At this point, remove from the heat and add the chopped parsley.

Butter the freshly cooked noodles, pile them on to plates, then spoon on the stroganoff. Serve with a dollop of soured cream on the top.

Goulash

Goulash is Hungarian in origin, and was originally a beef soup. So why is this in a book on British food? Because, like dishes such as stroganoff and satay, it's a real classic that we have been brought up with. Mum cooked this for me when I was a kid to get me used to spices and different flavours, the main spice here being paprika. Like all spices paprika has a shelf life and a use-before date on the jar. The use-before date is not, as many of us might think, when the label has changed colour in the sun....

SERVES 4

olive oil

700g (1lb 9oz) stewing steak, diced

30g (a good 1oz) plain flour

1 large onion, thinly sliced

2 cloves garlic, finely chopped

1 green pepper, deseeded and thinly sliced

1 red pepper, deseeded and thinly sliced

2 tbsp tomato purée

2 tbsp paprika

2 large tomatoes, diced

75ml (2 1/2 fl oz) dry white wine

1 1/2 x 284ml tub fresh beef stock

2 tbsp fresh chopped flat-leaf parsley

salt and pepper, to taste

150ml (5fl oz) soured cream

Preheat the oven to 160°C/325°F/gas mark 3.

Heat a little olive oil in a heavy-based saucepan. Sprinkle the steak with the flour and brown well, in batches, in the hot pan. Set the sealed meat aside.

Sauté the onion, garlic and peppers in the same pan in a little more oil. Return the beef to the pan with the tomato purée and paprika. Cook for about 2 minutes.

Add the tomatoes, white wine and stock. Cook with a lid on in the oven for 1 1/2 hours. Alternatively, cook it on the hob on a gentle heat for about an hour, removing the lid after 45 minutes.

Before serving, add the chopped parsley and season well with salt and pepper. Stir in the soured cream.

PS: Thanks for the recipe, mum!

Ham, Potato, Leek and Herb Hotpot

This is adapted from my gran's recipe. For the stock, she used the end knuckle of hams left over from the butcher's slicer, and for the meat, the bits around the bones of a carved joint. Use good-quality ham, not the sliced, processed variety bought in a packet. I use a lot of herbs because the hotpot should be like a thick stew. These serve to thicken and flavour the sauce.

SERVES 4

225g (8oz) butter

1 red onion, finely chopped

4 cloves garlic, finely chopped

2 small leeks, cleaned and sliced

200ml (7fl oz) white wine

500ml (18fl oz) fresh ham stock

450g (1lb) new potatoes, cooked

550g (1¼ lb) cooked ham, cut into chunks

salt and pepper, to taste

60g (2¼ oz) each of chopped fresh basil, parsley, chives and coriander

Using about 55g (2oz) of the butter, sauté the onion, garlic and leeks in a large pan, until soft.

Add the white wine, ham stock, potatoes and ham and cook for 5–10 minutes until everything is nice and hot.

Drain off the liquid, keeping the meat and vegetables warm. Gently simmer the liquid, adding the remaining butter bit by bit, whisking all the time to thicken the sauce. Do not boil.

Put all the ingredients back into the sauce and season. To finish, add all the chopped fresh herbs. Serve piping hot in bowls with some French bread.

Spicy Bean Stew with Sausages

Most adults and kids love this because it's so simple to make. Onions and garlic are used as a base, and good-quality sausages are the key. Cut them up into pieces, fry them all, add some canned beans and tomatoes, and stew down for about 15 minutes. Beautiful! I served this at a truckers' café once, but for breakfast, and 150 of them woofed it down!

SERVES 4

5 tbsp olive or vegetable oil

8 good free-range pork sausages

4 streaky bacon rashers, chopped

1 medium onion, chopped

2 cloves garlic, chopped

1 red chilli, chopped (or more if it is really cold!)

1 tbsp soft brown sugar

2 x 400g cans plum or chopped tomatoes

a dash of red or white wine (whatever is open)

2 x 300g cans cannellini beans, drained and rinsed

1 x 300g can kidney beans, drained and rinsed

leaves from 1 small bunch fresh parsley, chopped

salt and pepper, to taste

Place a large heavy-based saucepan on the hob and heat 3 tbsp of the oil. Add the sausages and fry over a medium heat, turning them over until they are browned on the outside. Take them out of the pan and chop them into 4cm (1½ in) pieces. Set them aside on a plate.

Add the remaining oil to the pan, turn the heat down to low, add the bacon and onion, and fry gently for around 10 minutes, stirring from time to time so that they don't catch on the bottom. They will pick up all the lovely sausagey goo in the bottom of the pan.

Add the garlic and chilli and fry for another couple of minutes, then add the brown sugar. Pour in the tomatoes, wine and 300ml (10fl oz) water, then stir in the sausage pieces along with the beans, and cook for 15–20 minutes over a low to medium heat.

Stir in the chopped parsley, salt and lots of black pepper, and serve with some nice fresh crusty bread or mashed potato.

This mutton or lamb stew made with sliced potatoes should, I think, be on every British pub menu.

Traditional Lancashire Hot Pot

SERVES 4

900g (2lb) best end and middle neck of British lamb, chopped into large bite-sized pieces

1 tbsp vegetable oil

butter

4 lamb's kidneys, cored, skinned and chopped quite small

350g (12oz) onions, cut into 1cm (1/2 in) pieces

1 tbsp plain flour

600ml (1 pint) hot lamb stock

1/2 tsp Worcestershire sauce

salt and pepper, to taste

1 bay leaf

2 sprigs fresh thyme

900g (2lb) potatoes, peeled and cut into 2cm (3/4 in) slices

Preheat the oven to 160°C/325°F/gas mark 3.

Trim the lamb of any excess fat. Heat the oil with a little butter in a large frying pan until it is very hot, then brown the pieces of lamb two or three at a time. As they cook, put them into a casserole (3.5 litre/6 pint capacity). Brown the pieces of kidney too, and tuck these in among the meat.

Fry the onions, adding a little more butter to the pan if necessary, for about 10 minutes, until they turn brown at the edges. Stir in the flour to soak up the juices and gradually add the hot stock and Worcestershire sauce, stirring or whisking until the flour and liquid are smoothly blended. Season with salt and pepper and bring it up to simmering point. Pour it over the meat in the casserole.

Add the bay leaf and thyme, then arrange the potato slices on top in an overlapping pattern. Season the potatoes and add a few dots of butter to the surface.

Cover with a tight-fitting lid and cook in the oven for 1 1/2 hours. You can remove the lid and brush the potatoes with a little more butter, then place under the grill at the end of cooking time to crisp up, if you like. Otherwise, turn the heat up during the last 15 minutes of cooking time in the oven and remove the lid. Remove the bay leaf and sprigs of thyme before serving.

Why do we now like moussaka so much in Britain? Probably because we first encountered it on holiday in Turkey or Greece, which is where I first tasted and fell in love with it. The traditional version would be cooked in a dish or a mould lined with cooked aubergine skins, and served either in the dish or turned out of the mould. Either way it's fantastic: that hot, bubbling mass of mince, aubergine and cheese. Mmm, delicious.

Moussaka

SERVES 4–6

4 aubergines

olive oil

1/2 onion, chopped

2 cloves garlic, crushed

675g (1 1/2 lb) minced lamb

3 plum tomatoes, diced

a good pinch of ground cumin

a good pinch of ground cinnamon

150ml (5fl oz) red wine

2 tbsp chopped fresh mint

150ml (5fl oz) chicken stock

200ml (7fl oz) White Sauce (*see* page 154)

2 free-range eggs, beaten

a pinch of freshly grated nutmeg

salt and pepper, to taste

50g (1 3/4 oz) mozzarella cheese, grated

50g (1 3/4 oz) Cheddar, grated

Preheat the oven to 190°C/375°F/gas mark 5.

Slice the aubergines, then fry them on both sides in a large pan with a little olive oil. Drain on kitchen paper.

To save on washing up, use the same pan with a little more olive oil to fry the onion and garlic. After 5 minutes, turn the heat up and add the lamb to brown it. Add the tomatoes.

Add the cumin and cinnamon with the wine and sauté together to break up the tomatoes. Add the chopped mint and the stock in stages.

In an ovenproof dish, place the aubergines and minced lamb mixture in alternate layers, finishing with a layer of aubergines.

Combine the white sauce with the eggs, nutmeg and some salt and pepper. Spoon over the top of the aubergines, then scatter with the grated cheeses.

Bake for 25–30 minutes to colour the cheese and cook through.

This is a classic, thought to have originated in Russia, although I doubt it somehow. Wherever it comes from, we now look on it as our own. It has great flavour, and it's a very celebratory type of dish.

Chicken Kiev

SERVES 4

4 chicken supremes

3 free-range eggs, beaten

200g (7oz) fine dry breadcrumbs

vegetable oil, for deep-frying

1 lemon, quartered lengthways

GARLIC BUTTER

3 cloves garlic, finely chopped

3 tbsp finely chopped fresh flat-leaf parsley

1 tbsp finely chopped fresh tarragon (optional)

125g (4 1/2 oz) butter, softened

salt and pepper, to taste

1 tbsp lemon juice

To make the garlic butter, put the garlic, parsley and tarragon (if using) in a blender with the butter. Season with salt, pepper and lemon juice. Blend to a smooth paste. Roll the butter in foil or clingfilm and put it in the fridge.

Remove the skin from the first chicken supreme, laying it skinned-side down. Detach the small fillet from the underside of the main fillet and cut this small fillet along its length and almost all the way through, folding it open like a book before flattening it by beating it gently with a rolling pin. Put 15g (1/2 oz) of the chilled garlic butter in the middle of the small fillet and wrap the meat around it. Repeat with the three other small fillets, returning all four to the fridge once you've finished.

Cut open each of the larger fillets in the same way, place them between plastic sheets and gently them beat out with a rolling pin. Lay a small buttered fillet in the middle of each larger fillet and wrap the escalope around it.

Dip in beaten egg and then in breadcrumbs. Repeat to give a double coating. At this point it is best to refrigerate them to allow the butter to harden again.

Heat a deep-fat fryer or a pan containing vegetable oil to high, and place the kievs in the hot oil, turning to allow 4–5 minutes' cooking time on each side. It is important to cook and handle the kievs gently to stop them from falling apart.

When the chicken is cooked and a golden-brown colour, remove and drain very well on kitchen paper.

Serve each kiev with a wedge of lemon and some salad.

When I was filming in an Indian restaurant in Birmingham this tasted so good I just had to get the recipe. The chef wouldn't cooperate at first but, after a night on the town and many beers, I got it in the end…at a cost, I might add, as my headache was unreal the day after.

Simple Lamb Curry

SERVES 4

2 tbsp vegetable oil

900g (2lb) boneless, rolled shoulder of lamb, trimmed and cut into 3cm (1¹/₄ in) cubes

2 onions, roughly chopped

4 cloves garlic, crushed

1 tbsp grated fresh root ginger

1 tbsp ground turmeric

1¹/₂ tbsp garam masala

1¹/₂ tbsp ground cumin

1 tbsp chilli powder

1 tbsp plain flour

6 large tomatoes, chopped

1 x 400g can coconut milk

600ml (1 pint) chicken stock

250g (9oz) baby spinach leaves, stalks removed

200g (7oz) plain yoghurt

salt and pepper, to taste

Heat 1 tbsp of the oil in a large pan, add the lamb and cook over a high heat to brown it quickly all over. Remove the lamb from the pan, place in a bowl and leave to one side.

Add the remaining oil to the pan, together with the onions, garlic and ginger, and cook gently for a few minutes until softened and golden brown. Add the spices and cook for a minute, then add the flour and mix well.

Add the tomatoes and coconut milk, and return the lamb to the pan. Add just enough of the chicken stock to cover the meat, and stir to release all the bits from the bottom of the pan. Cover and simmer gently for about 1 hour, until the lamb is tender, stirring occasionally.

Skim any excess fat off the surface. Stir in the spinach and cook for a few minutes until just wilted, then stir in the yoghurt and season. Serve with plain boiled basmati rice.

Coronation Chicken

A real classic that everyone must have tasted at some point, but there are loads of different recipes to choose from. I've found this one an easy and tasty way of making this dish.

SERVES 4–6

25g (1oz) butter

1/2 onion, finely chopped

3 tbsp curry paste

2 tbsp tomato purée

100ml (3 1/2 fl oz) red wine

juice of 1/2 lemon

4 tbsp apricot jam

300ml (10fl oz) mayonnaise

150g (5oz) Greek yoghurt

salt and pepper, to taste

6 chicken breasts, cooked, skins removed

In a small pan, heat the butter and then add the onion and cook for 3–4 minutes until softened. Add the curry paste, tomato purée, wine and lemon juice. Simmer, uncovered, for about 5 minutes, until the sauce is reduced. Strain and cool.

Add the apricot jam to the mixture with the mayonnaise, yoghurt and salt and pepper to taste, and mix.

At this point you can leave the mixture like this, or do as I prefer to do: blend it until smooth. But I'll leave it up to you. Mind you, I never did mind creating more washing up!

Cut the chicken into fork-sized pieces. Spoon the sauce over the chicken and serve with bread or rice and a green salad.

Quick Chicken Tikka Masala

They say this is Britain's favourite dish – which is exactly why it is here!

SERVES 4

1 x 2.5cm (1in) piece fresh root ginger, finely chopped

1 tsp ground turmeric

2 cloves garlic, finely chopped

1 red chilli, deseeded and finely chopped

1 tbsp finely chopped fresh coriander leaves

juice of 2 limes

2 tbsp vegetable oil

salt and pepper, to taste

4 chicken breasts, skinned and sliced into strips

1 onion, finely chopped

300ml (10fl oz) double cream

juice of 1/2 lemon

In a large bowl, mix the ginger, turmeric, garlic, chilli, half the coriander, the lime juice, 1 tbsp of the oil, salt and pepper. Add the chicken slices and then stir well to make sure all the pieces are coated. Put in the fridge for 10–15 minutes.

Sweat the onion in a large pan with the remaining oil. Then add the chicken slices and all the marinade ingredients. Cook on a medium to high heat for 4–5 minutes.

Add the double cream and simmer gently for 3–4 minutes, until the meat is cooked through. Season and add lemon juice to taste, together with the remaining chopped coriander.

Serve with naan bread and/or boiled rice, and a chilled beer.

pasta
& rice

Spaghetti Bolognese

This is, of course, Italian – but it is also one of the UK's most frequently cooked dishes. So, naturally, it has its place in this book – and rightly so, as the sauce is fantastic. To my mind it gets even better after a few days in the fridge before being reheated for a midnight snack.

SERVES 6

25g (1oz) butter

8 rashers streaky bacon, diced

1 large onion, diced

1 large carrot, diced

3 cloves garlic, finely chopped

500g (1lb 2oz) minced beef

600ml (1 pint) red wine

1/2 tbsp tomato purée

1 x 284ml tub fresh beef stock

400g (12oz) canned tomatoes,
or 6 fresh tomatoes, chopped

1 tbsp chopped fresh
flat-leaf parsley

a dash of Worcestershire sauce

salt and pepper, to taste

TO SERVE

325g (11 1/2 oz) spaghetti,
freshly cooked

25g (1oz) butter

Parmesan, freshly grated

Heat a really large saucepan on the stove and add the butter.

Fry the bacon, onion, carrot and garlic for a few minutes, stirring all the time. Add the beef and cook for about 4 minutes to colour well, before adding the wine and tomato purée. Simmer for about 5 minutes.

Add the stock and canned tomatoes (or fresh tomatoes if you are using them).

Simmer gently for 30–45 minutes before adding the parsley, Worcestershire sauce and plenty of salt and pepper.

Serve with freshly cooked, buttered spaghetti and some freshly grated Parmesan (not the ready-grated stuff in a cardboard tub!).

Macaroni Cheese

This is the simplest baked pasta dish of all. You could add sliced tomatoes to the mixture or put them on the top, and you can ring the changes by experimenting with different types of cheese.

SERVES 4

350g (12oz) macaroni

salt and pepper, to taste

100g (3 1/2 oz) Red Leicester cheese, grated

2 tbsp fresh breadcrumbs

a little butter

WHITE SAUCE

25g (1oz) butter

25g (1oz) plain flour

300ml (10fl oz) double cream or milk

a little freshly grated nutmeg

Preheat the oven to 180°C/350°F/gas mark 4.

Cook the macaroni in a large pan of boiling salted water for about 15 minutes. Drain well.

Meanwhile, to make the white sauce, melt the butter and then stir in the flour. Add the cream or milk gradually, stirring all the time, until you have a thick sauce. Season with salt, pepper and freshly grated nutmeg.

Add most of the cheese to the sauce, saving some for the top.

Put the cooked macaroni into a 1 litre (1 3/4 pint) serving dish. Pour over the sauce. Top with the remaining cheese and the breadcrumbs. Dot with butter and bake for 20 minutes, until golden brown.

Serve with crusty bread.

Wild garlic pesto

I made this recipe up while I was in Yorkshire at my mum's. Loads of wild garlic grows there, and you can smell it as you drive or walk past in the spring. The green leaves look similar to sorrel leaves. I have made pesto out of the pungent leaves here, but you can also add them to soups and stews, or cut them up into salads.

SERVES 4

450g (1lb) wild garlic leaves

100ml (3 1/2 fl oz) extra-virgin olive oil

salt and pepper, to taste

25g (1oz) Parmesan, freshly grated

juice and grated zest of 1 lemon

Wash and dry the garlic leaves. Place in a pestle and mortar and crush down with the olive oil and some salt and pepper.

Finish by adding the Parmesan and the lemon juice and zest. Mix well and season again to taste. Serve with freshly cooked, buttered pasta.

Green Pea and Smoked Salmon Risotto

Risotto is unashamedly Italian, but it is a dish that has become very popular with us Brits. I'm using two great British ingredients in this one. Frozen or fresh, to be honest peas are good whatever they are, as I think they're one of the few vegetables that are great from the freezer. The only thing in this recipe is to watch the seasoning – in particular, the salt – as smoked salmon is quite often salty.

SERVES 4

500ml (18fl oz) fresh fish stock

500ml (18fl oz) fresh chicken stock

25g (1oz) butter

1 shallot, chopped

1 clove garlic, chopped

250g (9oz) risotto rice (arborio or carnaroli)

50ml (2fl oz) white wine

100g (3¹/₂ oz) mascarpone cheese

225g (8oz) smoked salmon, sliced into strips

140g (5oz) frozen peas

100g (3¹/₂ oz) Parmesan, freshly grated, plus extra for serving

10g (¹/₄ oz) fresh flat-leaf parsley, finely chopped

salt and pepper, to taste

extra-virgin olive oil

Mix the two stocks and heat them in a pan on top of the stove.

Melt the butter in a separate pan and sweat the shallot and garlic for a few minutes, but don't colour. Add the rice to the pan and seal, stirring to coat it with butter, for about 30 seconds over a low heat.

Add the white wine to the pan and cook for a further few seconds, before adding the warm stocks, little by little, while stirring. Simmer for about 15–20 minutes, remembering to keep adding the stocks a little at a time, not all at once, until the rice is cooked but still has some bite.

Mix the mascarpone, salmon, peas and Parmesan into the risotto with the parsley, and season well.

To serve, put the risotto in the centre of warm plates. Top with a little extra grated Parmesan, and drizzle with a little extra olive oil.

Crab Risotto

This is one of my favourite recipes in the book – it tastes so good, and uses some of our wonderful crabs.

SERVES 4

300ml (10fl oz) fresh chicken stock

300ml (10fl oz) fresh fish stock

2 cloves garlic, finely chopped

2 shallots, finely chopped

25g (1oz) butter

280g (10 oz) risotto rice (arborio or carnaroli)

100ml (3½ fl oz) white Muscat wine

2 green chillies, deseeded and chopped

a pinch of curry powder

½ tbsp Thai green curry paste

1 stick lemongrass, crushed

3 kaffir lime leaves

2 tbsp mascarpone cheese

50ml (2fl oz) double cream

15g (½ oz) each of fresh flat-leaf parsley and coriander, finely chopped

450g (1lb) fresh white and brown crab meat

115g (4oz) Parmesan, freshly grated, plus extra for serving

juice of 1 lime

salt and pepper, to taste

chilli oil

Heat the two stocks, mixed, in a pan on top of the stove.

Meanwhile, sweat the garlic and shallots in the butter for about a minute. Add the rice, then the wine, with the green chillies, curry powder, curry paste, lemongrass and lime leaves. Stir to coat the rice with fat.

Add the warm stock, a ladle at a time, while simmering and stirring. Stir, and keep adding stock, until the rice is cooked, which should take about 15–20 minutes.

Once the rice is cooked but still with a little bite, add the mascarpone, cream, chopped herbs, crab meat and Parmesan. Adjust with more stock and cream if need be, then add the lime juice and season well.

Place the risotto in the centre of the plates and top with a little chilli oil and some extra Parmesan.

Leek and Haddock Risotto

You need the real Finnan haddock with its creamy golden flesh for this recipe, not the bright yellow, artificially dyed fish that masquerades as smoked fish. Good smoked haddock is naturally coloured through the smoking process. The fish itself is plump and moist with a wonderful salty-sweet flavour from the simple, pure brine. I like to mix flakes of this fish into a leek risotto and, as a surprise, to toss in a few cubes of crisply fried black pudding. Not only does it taste amazing, it looks so appealing. Try it for a light supper or an unusual starter.

SERVES 4

1 tbsp olive oil

175g (6oz) good-quality black pudding, cut into thick slices, then into quarters

1 smoked Finnan haddock fillet, about 300–400g (10$\frac{1}{2}$–14 oz)

25g (1oz) butter

3 shallots, chopped

2 cloves garlic, crushed

100ml (3$\frac{1}{2}$ fl oz) dry white wine

250g (9oz) risotto rice (arborio or carnaroli)

about 1.2 litres (2 pints) fresh fish or vegetable stock (buy ready-made in a tub)

2 medium leeks, thinly sliced

salt and pepper, to taste

2–3 tbsp mascarpone cheese or crème fraîche

freshly grated Parmesan, to taste

chopped fresh parsley, to garnish

Heat the oil in a wide shallow pan, add the chunks of black pudding and fry quickly for 1–2 minutes until crisp on the outside. Remove and set aside.

Skin the haddock and check carefully for any bones by running against the grain of the flesh with your fingertips. If you find any, pluck them out with your fingers or use a pair of tweezers. Cut the fish into 1cm ($\frac{1}{2}$ in) chunks and set aside.

Heat the butter in the wide shallow pan, add the shallots and garlic and sauté for about 3 minutes until softened. Pour in the wine, bring to the boil and cook until reduced by half, stirring frequently. Stir in the rice and cook for 1–2 minutes until lightly toasted.

Heat the stock until simmering and add a quarter to the rice. Simmer, uncovered, until the stock is absorbed, stirring frequently.

Add a further quarter of the stock with the leeks and continue simmering until the liquid is absorbed, stirring occasionally. Add the fish, black pudding, the remaining stock and seasoning to taste. Continue simmering, stirring occasionally, until most of the stock is absorbed and the rice grains are plump and tender yet still retain a good 'bite'. The fish should be just cooked. The whole process should take 15–20 minutes.

Stir in the mascarpone or crème fraîche and Parmesan. Check the seasoning and serve immediately, sprinkled with chopped parsley.

Mussel and Artichoke Risotto

Both mussels and artichokes are warming wintry comfort foods, so this risotto is ideal for when you just want to curl up in front of an open fire. Cook the mussels first in a little wine and butter until they open, then pull out the meat from the shells.

SERVES 3–4

1kg (2¼ lb) fresh mussels

3 cloves garlic, crushed

3 shallots or 1 onion, chopped

150ml (5fl oz) dry white wine

50g (1¾ oz) butter

2 tbsp olive oil

400g (14oz) Jerusalem artichokes, peeled and finely chopped

250g (9oz) risotto rice (arborio or carnaroli)

about 800ml (1 pint 7fl oz) fresh fish stock or chicken stock (buy ready-made in a tub)

2 tbsp mascarpone cheese

3 tbsp freshly grated Parmesan

1 tbsp chopped fresh parsley

salt and pepper, to taste

Wash the mussels in cold water, then pull away the wispy 'beards'. Place the mussels in a large pan but discard any that remain open when tapped. Add 1 crushed clove garlic, 1 chopped shallot or one-third of the chopped onion, the wine and half the butter.

Cover with a tight lid and cook over a medium heat for about 7 minutes. Uncover, strain the juices into a jug and set aside. When the mussels are cool enough to handle, pull the meat from the shells and set aside. Discard any mussels that have not opened.

Heat the oil in a frying pan, add the remaining garlic, shallots or onion and the artichokes and gently sauté for about 5 minutes until softened.

Stir in the rice and cook for 1–2 minutes until lightly toasted, then pour in all the mussel juices. Bring to the boil, stirring, and cook for about 5 minutes until the liquid is absorbed, stirring frequently.

Heat the stock until simmering and add a quarter to the rice. Simmer, uncovered, until the stock is absorbed, stirring frequently. Add the remainder of the stock a ladleful at a time in the same way until all the stock is absorbed and the rice grains are plump and tender yet still retain a good 'bite'. This should take 15–20 minutes. You may not need all the stock.

Stir in the mussels, the remaining butter, the mascarpone, Parmesan and parsley. Season well and serve piping hot and creamy.

As you might have guessed by now, I love black pudding. Funnily enough, it goes very well with the delicate sweet flavour of scallops, used together here in a delicious risotto.

Scallop Risotto with Black Pudding

SERVES 4

1 litre (1 3/4 pints) fresh fish stock

25g (1oz) butter

1 shallot, chopped

1 clove garlic, chopped

1 leek, washed and diced

250g (9oz) risotto rice (arborio or carnaroli)

50ml (2fl oz) dry white wine

85g (3oz) mascarpone cheese

100g (3 1/2 oz) Parmesan, freshly grated

4 tbsp chopped fresh parsley

salt and pepper, to taste

1 tbsp olive oil

8 slices black pudding

8 shelled scallops

Heat the stock in a large pan on the stove, but do not boil.

Melt the butter in a wide shallow pan, and sweat the shallot, garlic and leek without colouring.

Turn the heat down and add the rice, then stir to coat with butter. Add the wine and cook for a couple of minutes. Add the stock gradually, a little at a time, waiting until the last lot has been absorbed before adding the next. Simmer and cook for about 15–20 minutes or until the rice is cooked, but still retains a good 'bite'. Add the mascarpone and grated Parmesan to the risotto with the chopped parsley. Season well.

Meanwhile, in a frying pan heat the oil. When it starts to smoke, add the black pudding and cook for about 3–4 minutes. Turn over and add the scallops and cook for 1–2 minutes, turning once.

Remove the scallops, then the black pudding. Season both, arrange next to the risotto on the plates and serve.

This risotto uses my favourite British winter veg – beetroot. Served with salmon and cauliflower in a salad, or simply cooked in a risotto like this, it gives fantastic flavour and is a good way of introducing beetroot to those who think they don't like it. A mate of mine loves this risotto with a seared steak and salad.

Beetroot and Mascarpone Risotto

SERVES 4

6 raw beetroots, peeled and roughly chopped

500ml (18fl oz) fresh vegetable stock

2 cloves garlic, finely chopped

2 shallots, finely chopped

2 fresh thyme sprigs

25g (1oz) unsalted butter

225g (8oz) risotto rice (arborio or carnaroli)

100ml (3 1/2 fl oz) white wine

3 tbsp mascarpone cheese

2 tbsp chopped fresh parsley

115g (4oz) Parmesan, freshly grated

salt and pepper, to taste

Blend the beetroot in the food processor with half the stock and leave it to one side. Have the remaining stock warming in a pan on the stove.

Put the garlic, shallot and thyme in a pan in the butter and sweat for about a minute. Add the rice and stir to coat with the butter. Add the wine and cook, stirring, until it evaporates.

Add a ladleful of beetroot stock and, stirring continuously, bring to the boil. Once this has been absorbed by the rice, add another ladleful and bring to the boil again. Keep going like this until all the beetroot stock is used up. Then continue the process with the hot vegetable stock. Simmer for about 15–20 minutes in all, stirring, until the rice is cooked but still has a little bite.

Once the rice is cooked, stir in the mascarpone, parsley, Parmesan and salt and pepper. Serve hot.

fish

'Turbot and cabbage!' I hear you cry. But this works, like most fish, with Savoy cabbage. This is not like the school cabbage that scared you when you were younger. It's trendy, that's what it is. Trendy. The mustard dressing recipe below will make more than you need for this recipe, but it will keep in the fridge for a week or so.

Turbot with Savoy Cabbage and Smoked Salmon

SERVES 4

1 small Savoy cabbage, about 175g (6oz)

115g (4oz) smoked salmon

25ml (1fl oz) olive oil

salt and pepper, to taste

4 x 175–200g (6–7oz) thick turbot fillet steaks, skin on but no bones

55g (2oz) butter

MUSTARD DRESSING

4 tsp Dijon mustard

2 tbsp white wine vinegar

8 tbsp walnut oil

8 tbsp groundnut oil

For the dressing, whisk the mustard with the vinegar. Mix together the two oils and gradually add to the mustard, whisking all the time. Once everything is thoroughly mixed, season with salt and pepper.

Remove the dark outside leaves from the cabbage and cut the rest into quarters, then into 1cm (1/2 in) strips. Cut the slices of smoked salmon into pieces about the same size.

Heat a frying pan and add the oil. Season the turbot fillets, place in the pan, and add half the butter. Cook the fillets for about 3–4 minutes on either side, depending on their thickness, until cooked through.

At the same time, heat a pan and add 2–3 tbsp water and the remaining butter. Once the water and butter are boiling, add the cabbage. Season with salt and pepper, and keep turning in the pan. The cabbage will only take 1–2 minutes and it's best eaten when just becoming tender but still with some texture. Add the smoked salmon to the cabbage, check for seasoning and add 4 tbsp of mustard dressing.

To serve, simply spoon the cabbage and smoked salmon at the top of the plates, and finish with the pan-fried turbot on the side.

Brill with Peas, Pancetta and Sweet Potato Crisps

This is probably the most cheffy recipe in the book, but it tastes great. The most important thing is to use a great brill fillet – thick white flesh with the skin still on – as this will help hold it together while cooking.

SERVES 4

4 x 175–200g (6–7oz) thick pieces brill fillet, skin on

olive oil

salt and pepper, to taste

200g (7oz) warm Mashed Potatoes (*see* page 222)

8 slices pancetta, grilled until crisp

4 thin strips sweet potato, deep-fried

SAUCE

400ml (14fl oz) chicken stock

55g (2oz) pancetta, diced

15g (1oz) unsalted butter

1 small onion, finely chopped

2 cloves garlic, crushed

2 tbsp horseradish cream

a dash of white wine

150ml (5fl oz) double cream

350g (12oz) frozen peas

a pinch of caster sugar

Preheat the oven to 200°C/400°F/gas mark 6.

Start the sauce by reducing the stock. Boil until you have about 50ml (2fl oz).

Sauté the diced pancetta in the butter until crisp, then add the onion and garlic and soften without allowing them to colour.

Add the horseradish, wine and reduced stock and simmer for a few minutes. Add the cream, peas and sugar, stir and season, and simmer for a few more minutes to heat the peas through.

Brush the brill fillets with olive oil, season and pan-fry for a minute on each side. Finish by cooking for 10 minutes in the oven, or until cooked,

Place the warm mash in the centre of the plates with the brill. Put a slice of crisp pancetta and a sweet-potato crisp on top, and spoon the sauce around.

Cod with Creamy Mashed Potatoes

Sadly, cod is becoming a rarity because of over-fishing, but you can still find it at a price. Cook it carefully, please! I've made my normal mash much richer and creamier than usual here by adding double instead of single cream.

SERVES 2

1 tbsp olive oil

2 x 150–200g (5 1/2 –7oz) cod fillets

15g (1/2 oz) butter

CREAMY MASHED POTATOES

600g (1lb 5oz) Maris Piper potatoes, quartered

salt and pepper, to taste

75g (2 3/4 oz) butter, softened

100ml (3 1/2 fl oz) double cream

a little freshly grated nutmeg

Put the potatoes in a pan and cover with water. Add a good pinch of salt and bring to the boil. Cook for about 20–25 minutes.

Meanwhile, heat the oil in a pan and fry the cod, skin-side down, for about 5–7 minutes, until the flesh is about three-quarters cooked (it should feel springy). Turn over, add the butter, and turn off the heat – the fish will continue to cook in the residual heat of the pan.

Once the potatoes are cooked, drain and place back in the pan. Mash with a masher and add the butter and cream a little at a time; this will stop any lumps appearing.

Season with salt, pepper and nutmeg and serve with the cod.

All hail, Harry Ramsden! As a kid I used to love queuing outside waiting to be served with the crisp, battered fish and floppy, buttered bread on chequered tablecloths. Alas, that has all changed. I can now say without doubt that the best fish and chips on the planet are to be found at Trencher's in Whitby. Eat in or out, or do as I do and have one of each. Walk down the pier and sit on the seat at the end and, in the wind and cold, with your nose dripping on to the fish, munch away. That's how to eat fish and chips.

Deep-fried Cod

SERVES 2

vegetable oil, for deep-frying

a little plain flour

salt and pepper, to taste

2 x 200g (7oz) cod fillets, boned (haddock if you prefer)

BATTER

225g (8oz) self-raising flour, sieved

300ml (10fl oz) lager

Heat the vegetable oil in the deep-fat fryer to 180°C/350°F.

Lightly season some flour with some salt and pepper. Dip the cod fillets into the plain flour, shake off any excess and leave to one side.

To make the batter, place the sieved flour in a bowl and slowly whisk in the lager until very thick and slightly gluey in texture. Season with salt. Dip the cod fillets in, one at a time, to coat well with the batter. If the batter falls off, it is too thick.

Place the battered cod into the deep-fat fryer very slowly, literally a couple of centimetres at a time. If you drop the fish in, it will sink straight to the bottom and stick!

Allow the fish to cook for 4–5 minutes before turning over, and cook until golden brown. This should take 10–12 minutes in total.

Once the fish is cooked, drain on kitchen paper and season well. Serve with chips, mushy peas, malt vinegar and a wedge of lemon, if you wish.

Pan-fried Bream with Honey-glazed Onions
Bream is wonderful with potatoes, but fantastic spiked with the onions.

SERVES 4

6 large onions

3 cloves garlic

75g (2 3/4 oz) butter

2 tbsp runny honey

a dash of white wine vinegar

salt and pepper, to taste

1 sprig fresh thyme

2 bay leaves

1 sprig fresh rosemary

4 x 150–200g (5 1/2 – 7oz) bream fillets

Preheat the oven to 180°C/350°F/gas mark 4.

Slice the onions and garlic, and fry them together in 25g (1oz) of the butter for about 10 minutes until well caramelized. Add the honey and vinegar and season with salt and pepper.

Place the onion mixture into an ovenproof dish and top with the herbs.

Place the bream on top of the herbs and season well. Place the remaining butter in pieces on top of the bream.

Cook the dish in the oven for about 15–20 minutes, depending on the thickness of the bream.

Take the fish out of the oven and remove the herbs. Serve with the onions and a dressed salad.

Cinnamon-poached Smoked Haddock with Fried Green Tomatoes
Most people don't associate fish with spices, but fresh cinnamon and naturally smoked haddock go really well together. Try it and see.

SERVES 2

4 green tomatoes (or unripe, firm tomatoes)

300ml (10fl oz) milk

1/4 cinnamon stick

1 bay leaf

2 x 140g (5oz) pieces smoked haddock

100g (3 1/2 oz) butter

salt and pepper, to taste

1 tbsp chopped fresh parsley

juice of 1/2 lemon

Cut the tomatoes into thick slices: roughly about four slices per tomato.

Place the milk, cinnamon and bay leaf into a pan with the fish and cover with a lid. Bring to the boil and simmer slowly for about 2–3 minutes, depending on the thickness of the fish. Turn the heat off, remove the lid and leave to stand while you cook the tomatoes.

Melt half the butter in a sauté pan, add the tomatoes and season with salt and pepper. Sauté quickly until golden brown, then remove the slices from the pan and divide between two plates.

Return the pan to the heat and add the remaining butter, the chopped parsley, lemon juice and seasoning.

Remove the fish carefully from the milk in the pan, using a slotted fish slice. (Discard the milk.) Place the fish on top of the tomatoes, pour over the remaining juices from the sauté pan, and serve.

Many people don't think poached eggs can be prepared in advance, but they can: simply poach the egg, then place it into ice-cold water to cool down. When cold, pop it in the fridge. When you want the eggs, blanch them in boiling water for 30 seconds and place them on your haddock. This is particularly useful when serving breakfast for lots of people.

Smoked Haddock with Poached Egg and Horseradish Mash

SERVES 4

850ml (1¹/₂ pints) full-fat milk

juice of 1 lemon

6 black peppercorns

a few fresh parsley stalks

salt and pepper, to taste

4 x 200g (7oz) pieces natural smoked haddock

4 large free-range eggs

150g (5¹/₂ oz) fresh young spinach leaves, washed

HORSERADISH MASH

900g (2lb) King Edward or Maris Piper potatoes, peeled and chopped

100g (3¹/₂ oz) unsalted butter

approx. 200ml (7fl oz) full-fat milk, warmed

2 tbsp creamed horseradish

For the mash, cook the potatoes in boiling salted water until tender, about 15 minutes. Once cooked, drain well and, while hot but not wet, place back in the pan and return to the heat. Mash with the butter and the warm milk. Once you get the texture you want, beat in the horseradish and some salt and pepper to taste and keep warm.

Put the milk, lemon juice, peppercorns, parsley stalks and a little salt into a medium-sized flat pan, and bring to a simmer. At the same time, place a pan of salted water on to boil for the eggs.

Add the haddock pieces to the simmering milk, and cook gently for about 6–8 minutes. While this is cooking, crack the eggs into the stirred rapidly boiling water, and poach for 2–3 minutes. In another medium pan, quickly wilt the spinach in only the water clinging to the leaves. Season.

Place the spinach, then the mash, on the plates. Drain the haddock and place on the mash. Spoon a little of the flavoured milk over this and top with a soft poached egg.

I like this dish how my grandad used to have it: with spuds straight from the garden and lashings of butter! Funny, but it was the only dish my grandad would cook not just for himself, but for anybody who came to visit. From the age of five I can remember eating this waiting for what was coming next – two hours of me being batsman with him bowling Freddie Truman-style against the wall of my gran's kitchen.

Grandad's Poached Haddock with Mustard

SERVES 2

1 fillet undyed smoked haddock (my grandad used Finnan)

2 bay leaves

a few black peppercorns

1/2 onion, roughly chopped

500ml (18fl oz) milk

50g (1 3/4 oz) butter

1 tbsp plain flour

2 tbsp Dijon mustard

2 tbsp chopped fresh flat-leaf parsley

salt and pepper, to taste

Cut the haddock in half and place in a shallow pan. Add the bay leaves, black peppercorns and onion and cover with the milk.

Bring the milk to the boil and gently simmer for about 4–5 minutes to cook the fish.

Carefully remove the fish from the milk, preserving the milk, and keep the fish warm. Remove the bay leaves from the milk.

Melt the butter in a pan and then add the flour and stir over the heat for 15–20 seconds to make the base of a roux. Slowly add the warm milk, a little at a time, stirring all the time until you end up with a nice smooth sauce. You may not need all the milk. Add the mustard and parsley to taste and check the seasoning.

Place the haddock on the plate and spoon over the sauce.

Sea Bass with Onions

I go fishing with my mates Steve and Jo, and a fisherman, Rick, from Poole harbour about once a month. First, we go out and catch sand eels (they're small sardine-like fish), then we use these and live mackerel to catch the bass while drifting over ledges just off the Isle of Wight Needles. Not only is it a great day of beer, packet sarnies and chocolate bars, but also the catch is the best fish I have ever eaten. Simply cooked, fresh fish is one of the true pleasures of life, but catching your own makes the experience a little more special.

SERVES 4

3 large white onions, sliced

2 cloves garlic, crushed

olive oil

a dash of white wine vinegar

3 tbsp runny honey

salt and pepper, to taste

4 small sea bass, about 500g (18oz) each in weight, scaled and gutted

1 sprig fresh thyme

2 bay leaves

1 sprig fresh rosemary

Preheat the oven to 200°C/400°F/gas mark 6.

Fry the onions and garlic in a little oil in a hot pan. Add the white wine vinegar and honey, and cook until golden brown. Season and allow to cool.

Place the fish on an oven tray, and score the skin on top two or three times with a knife. Stuff the cavity with the onion mixture and herbs.

Season with salt and pepper, drizzle with olive oil, and roast in the oven for about 15 minutes.

Remove from the oven, and serve whole with the juices from the tray poured over the top, and a dressed salad.

Sea Bass with Mango Chutney and Red Pepper Essence

This is another great bass recipe I make with the catch we get from our fishing trips. Bass was always deemed an expensive fish in the past, but due to farming, the price has come down. This fish remains the king of the sea, though, and will always make me look forward to another day out on the boat fishing.

SERVES 4

4 x 125g (4¹/₂ oz) sea bass fillets, bones removed, skin left on

olive oil

butter

115g (4oz) beansprouts

juice of 1 lime

2 tbsp sesame oil

a small bunch of fresh coriander, chopped

8 tbsp smooth mango chutney

RED PEPPER ESSENCE

6 red peppers, stalks and seeds removed, chopped

100ml (3¹/₂ fl oz) cold water

Make the red pepper essence by placing the red peppers and water in a liquidizer and processing for 2 minutes. Tip into a clean tea-towel placed over a bowl, and squeeze out the liquid. Tip this into a pan and reduce over the heat by three-quarters, until it resembles runny honey in texture. Allow to cool.

Pan-fry the sea bass, skin-side down, in a little olive oil and butter. When the skin is crisp and brown, turn the fish over and turn off the heat.

Dress the beansprouts in the lime juice and sesame oil, and scatter the coriander over them.

Warm the mango chutney and spoon into the centre of each serving plate. Top with the beansprouts and fish, drizzle the pepper essence around the edge and serve.

Halibut is a large, sometimes massive, flat fish that is expensive because chefs love to place it on their menus. It's important that you don't overcook it, as it will become dry. The flavours of the sauce may appear strong, but halibut is a meaty fish like salmon and monkfish, and can take it. Use mussel meat if you want, as it saves a load of hassle, but I think a few mussels left in their shells look good.

Seared Halibut with Mussels and Onion Sauce

SERVES 4

1 tbsp olive oil

25g (1oz) butter

salt and pepper, to taste

4 x 175g (6oz) halibut fillets

MUSSEL AND ONION SAUCE

1.5kg (3lb 5oz) fresh mussels, beards removed, or 85g (3oz) mussel meat

2 tsp chopped fresh thyme

1 bay leaf

250ml (9fl oz) Muscat wine

25g (1oz) butter

2 onions, finely sliced

1 small leek, finely diced

1/2 fennel bulb, sliced

200g (7oz) brown chestnut mushrooms, sliced

a pinch of curry powder

25ml (1fl oz) Pernod

100ml (31/2 fl oz) double cream

40g (1 1/2 oz) fresh flat-leaf parsley, chopped

a pinch of saffron

Discard any mussels that gape or do not close when tapped on the edge of the sink – they are probably dead. Heat a large saucepan until very hot. Add the mussels, thyme, bay leaf and one-third of the wine. Cover and heat for a minute or two, then shake the pan well.

Continue to cook for a minute or two, then remove the lid. When the mussels have all opened, drain over a bowl to save the cooking liquid. Discard any mussels that are still closed, and the bay leaf. Remove some or all of the mussels from their shells, and discard the shells.

In the same saucepan, melt a little of the butter and caramelize the onions. Cook gently until the onions are soft and brown in colour, about 10 minutes. Add the leek, fennel, mushrooms, curry powder and Pernod. Cover the pan and gently sweat the vegetables for about 7 minutes, or until softened but not coloured. Add the remaining wine and bring to the boil. Cook, uncovered, until the cooking liquid has almost completely evaporated. Add the reserved mussel liquor, and cook, uncovered, for 5 minutes to reduce again.

In a nonstick pan, heat the olive oil and butter for the fish. Season the halibut and place in the hot pan. Cook for 3–4 minutes before turning over to get some nice colour on the flesh.

Meanwhile, add the cream and parsley to the sauce and bring back to the boil. Sprinkle in the saffron, heat for 1–2 minutes and season to taste. Mix the mussels in and season.

Divide the sauce between four warm plates, and serve with the halibut on the top, and a few mussels in their shells to decorate.

Hot Tea-smoked Trout with New Potatoes and Rocket

I first learned this dish while doing *Ready Steady Cook*, and I have loved it ever since. It tastes as good now as it did then. I've used trout here, but you could use salmon, chicken or duck (the meat needs to be cooked for a few more minutes than the fish). My dog Fudge loves it, but it makes his breath smell like he's been smoking ten a day....

SERVES 2

2 fresh trout, each about 280–350g (10–12 oz), gutted and heads removed

olive oil

salt and pepper, to taste

SMOKING MIXTURE

55g (2oz) demerara sugar

55g (2oz) long-grain rice

10 tea bags (any kind, but not herbal), torn open and bags discarded

TO SERVE

450g (1lb) new potatoes

115g (4oz) wild rocket

2–3 tbsp balsamic vinegar

2 tbsp chopped fresh flat-leaf parsley

55g (2oz) Parmesan, freshly grated

To make the smoking mixture, put the sugar, rice and tea leaves into a bowl and mix together. Line a deep roasting tray with foil and pour the tea mixture into the base. Cover with another layer of foil, then place on the stove to heat up.

Once it is smoking a little, add the trout on top of the foil. Drizzle with a little olive oil, making sure the fish sits in the foil. Season with salt and pepper before covering with a tight-fitting lid or another piece of foil, and leave to smoke on the stove-top over a medium heat for 15–20 minutes.

While the trout is smoking, wash and boil the new potatoes in plenty of salted boiling water for 12–15 minutes, depending on size, until cooked.

For the salad, place the rocket in a bowl with the balsamic vinegar, 6 tbsp olive oil and a pinch each of salt and black pepper, and toss.

To serve, drain the hot new potatoes and place them in a bowl with the parsley. Finish the salad with the Parmesan and place on the plate, with the hot smoked trout on the side, and the potatoes served separately.

Mackerel with Gooseberry Cream Sauce

Mackerel is such an underrated fish, but it must be eaten as fresh as possible. Just simply grilled, it has a wonderful oily taste, and goes very well with chutneys and sour fruits such as gooseberry. Don't turn the fish over while cooking; it will cook through from one side only, as it is so thin when filleted.

SERVES 4

4 large fresh mackerel, filleted

salt and pepper, to taste

olive oil

100g (3$^{1}/_{2}$ oz) mixed green leaves, dressed with balsamic vinegar and extra-virgin olive oil

GOOSEBERRY CREAM SAUCE

225g (8oz) gooseberries

25g (1oz) butter

150ml (5fl oz) double cream

granulated sugar (optional)

To make the sauce, top and tail the gooseberries. Melt the butter in a pan, add the gooseberries, cover them and leave to simmer gently until they are cooked, usually about 30 minutes. Mash them down and mix in the cream and some seasoning to soften their sharpness. Add a little sugar if the gooseberries were very young and green, but the sauce should not be sweet like an apple sauce.

Preheat the grill.

Season the mackerel to taste and brush with olive oil on both sides. Place on an oven tray, skin-side up, and grill for about 5 minutes to cook through.

Place the dressed salad leaves on the serving plates with two fillets of mackerel each and a spoonful of the gooseberry cream sauce.

This is a twist on fish pie. The cheese and the mustard are slipped in between a layer of puff pastry. Use salmon, cod, haddock or monkfish – and a handful of prawns like my gran does, if you like.

Fish Pie with Cheese and Mustard Pastry

SERVES 4

1 shallot, chopped

1 tbsp olive oil

100ml (3 1/2 fl oz) fish stock

200ml (7fl oz) double cream

salt and pepper, to taste

675g (1 1/2 lb) fish, cut into chunks

125g (4 1/2 oz) mushrooms, sliced

3 tbsp chopped fresh chives

300g (10 1/2 oz) ready-to-roll puff pastry

2 tbsp grain mustard

4 slices Emmental cheese

1 free-range egg, beaten

Preheat the oven to 200°C/400°F/gas mark 6.

Sauté the shallot in a medium pan in the olive oil. After a few minutes add the fish stock and cream and bring to the boil. Season with salt and pepper and leave to one side.

Place the fish, mushrooms and chives in an ovenproof dish. Season and cover with the shallot sauce.

Roll out the pastry until it is twice the size of your dish. Spread half of the pastry with the mustard and cheese. Fold the other half over the top to sandwich the mustard and cheese. Top the pie dish with the pastry.

Crimp the edges of the pastry and then brush it with the beaten egg. Bake for 25–30 minutes.

Once cooked, remove from the oven and serve. A good accompaniment is French beans sprinkled with some freshly cracked black pepper.

This dish is as famous as chicken in a basket. Give me this, some Tartare Sauce (*see* page 240) and a wedge of lemon, and I'm a happy man.

Goujons of Sole with Lemon

SERVES 4

450g (1lb) sole or lemon sole fillets, skinned

125g (4 1/2 oz) fine fresh breadcrumbs

1/2 tsp cayenne pepper

sunflower oil, for deep frying

50g (1 3/4 oz) plain flour

3 medium free-range eggs, beaten

salt and pepper, to taste

2 lemons, cut into wedges

Cut each sole or lemon sole fillet into strips, on the diagonal, about 1cm (1/2 in) thick. Mix the breadcrumbs with the cayenne pepper and leave to one side. Heat the oil in the fryer to 190°C/375°F.

Coat the fish in the flour, then dip first in the beaten egg and then in the breadcrumbs. Do a few pieces at a time, making sure all the fish is coated in each of the three dips.

Place a few of the goujons in the fryer at a time and cook for about 1 minute, until crisp and golden brown. Repeat until all the goujons are cooked. Once cooked, remove on to some kitchen paper to soak up the excess oil.

Pile the goujons in a dish or on plates, season, and serve with the lemon wedges. They're great with a dressed mixed green leaf salad.

Jugged Fresh Kippers with Cider Butter and Lime

When I was eight, my family had a holiday house near Whitby in North Yorkshire. Whenever we visited, I would spend the day watching the fishing boats go in and out of the harbour, and would invariably park myself next to the open window of a fish smokery. My mum would object vociferously as we travelled back in the car: I smelt like an old kipper.

SERVES 2

2 fresh kippers

100g (3 1/2 oz) butter, softened

3 tbsp chopped fresh parsley

1/4 apple, grated

50ml (2fl oz) cider

juice and finely grated zest of 1 lime

Place the kippers in a tall jug with the tails sticking out of the top, and carefully pour boiling water into the jug, up to the top.

Place the softened butter in a bowl and mix first with the chopped parsley, then more slowly with the grated apple and cider. Leave to one side.

After the kippers have been in the water for about 2–3 minutes, pour off the water and place the kippers first on kitchen paper to dry and then on plates.

Put half the butter on to each kipper along with the juice and zest of the lime. Eat as is, or with some sliced bread.

Kipper Paste

Manx kippers are the most widely known, but Whitby kippers are my favourite – not because I'm a Yorkshire man, but because I think they are the best (although hard to find if you're not local). They have a strong, smoky flavour.

SERVES 4

2 pairs Craster or Isle of Man undyed kippers

plenty of slightly salted butter

3 tbsp double cream

salt and pepper, to taste

a pinch of cayenne pepper

juice of 1 lemon

4 slices toasted brown bread, to serve

Place the kippers in a large jug or tray and immerse in boiling water. Leave for a few minutes before draining the hot water off and removing the skin and bones from the fish.

Weigh the flesh and blend, while still warm, with an equal amount of butter. Add the cream, then season with salt, pepper, cayenne and lemon juice.

Serve spread on brown toast. This mixture will keep in the fridge for up to a week in an airtight container.

Whole Poached Salmon

My mother used to do this for dinner parties at home in the 1980s, served with lemon and sliced cucumber. With buttered Jersey Royal potatoes, green salad and a glass of white wine, it's fantastic.

SERVES 8–10

1 whole salmon, about 2.5–2.7kg (5¹/₂–6lb)

2 bay leaves

1 onion, chopped

4 tbsp white wine vinegar

1 lemon, quartered

salt and pepper, to taste

TO SERVE

4–5 lemons, cut into wedges

mayonnaise

Place the salmon in a fish kettle or, if you're like me, in a large roasting tin. (I never think it's worth spending £50 on something you use only a few times, and can't even fit in the cupboard.)

Pour in enough cold water to cover the fish (it must be covered). Add the bay leaves, onion, vinegar, lemon quarters, and a good pinch of salt and a little coarsely ground black pepper.

Cover with a lid, and bring to the boil on top of the stove. It is easier and quicker to put two rings on underneath the fish. Once it is boiling, turn off the heat and allow the fish to stand in the water until cool.

Carefully remove the salmon and place on a board. Scrape off the skin, and place on a large flat serving dish. Serve with the lemon wedges and a bowl of mayonnaise.

Deep-fried Salmon Belly in Beer Batter

Many good fishmongers sell salmon belly flaps for next to nothing, or even give them away. They are the bits of the salmon that are normally cleaned off and discarded after filleting. They are full of flavour. Keep the skin on as this helps everything hold together during the cooking.

SERVES 2

vegetable oil, for deep-frying

450g (1lb) salmon belly, cut into strips

BATTER

225g (8oz) self-raising flour

2 tbsp chopped fresh mint

salt and pepper, to taste

20g (³/₄ oz) sesame seeds

350ml (12fl oz) ale or lager

Heat the oil in a deep pan to a high heat, or use a deep-fat fryer.

Place the flour in a bowl. Add the mint, salt and pepper and sesame seeds, and slowly mix in the beer. Don't worry about lumps; just make it into a thick consistency.

Mix the salmon strips into the batter. Place them, once coated, into the hot fat one by one to stop them from sticking to each other (keep shaking the basket to stop them sticking to the bottom). Cook them in two batches to speed up the cooking time.

Once they are golden brown, remove the salmon strips and place on kitchen paper to drain off any excess oil.

Pile them up in a bowl or on a plate to serve.

Baked Salmon and Dill Hash Brown with Pan-fried Tomatoes

To make it well, this dish needs lots of fresh dill and you must make sure you cook the potato through thoroughly before combining it with the salmon. I've served the dish here with pan-fried tomatoes, but a Caesar Salad (*see* page 64) makes it a good complete summer dish. The egg is used to bind the mixture during cooking.

SERVES 2

1 shallot, chopped

1 clove garlic, chopped

olive oil

1 large Estima baking potato

225g (8oz) salmon fillet (skin on but no bones)

1 free-range egg, beaten

2 tbsp fresh breadcrumbs

1 x 15g (1/2 oz) packet fresh dill, chopped

salt and pepper, to taste

3 plum tomatoes

Preheat the oven to 200°C/400°F/gas mark 6. Place the shallot and garlic in a sauté pan with 4 tbsp oil and gently start to cook.

Peel the potato and cut it into 1cm (1/2 in) dice, add to the pan and cook until the pieces are golden brown. Remove from the heat.

Cut the salmon into 1cm (1/2 in) dice and place in a bowl with the egg, breadcrumbs and chopped dill, then pour on the potato, shallot and garlic. Mix well and season with plenty of salt and pepper.

Divide the mixture between two 7.5cm (3in) stainless-steel rings placed on an oven tray, pressing it in well. Place the tray in the oven and cook for 10 minutes.

Meanwhile, cut each tomato into five slices and season with salt and pepper. Quickly seal in a hot pan with 1 tbsp olive oil to colour both sides. This should only take a minute or two.

Arrange the tomatoes on two plates, overlapping them into a circle pattern in the centre. Remove the salmon from the oven and place each ring in the middle of the tomatoes. Remove the metal rings. Drizzle with olive oil to finish the dish.

Wild Salmon with Samphire

Wild salmon is at its best in the summer, when samphire – one of the best accompaniments for it – is available. There are two types of samphire: rock and marsh. Marsh is found on tidal marshes around Britain, though it is most common in Norfolk; rock grows on – yes, you guessed it – rocky cliffs and slopes around the coast. They used to use marsh samphire as a source of soda when making glass. No glass-making here, but picked early in the season samphire can be eaten raw, blanched or pan-fried. I pickle it in vinegar in mid-season, when it is at its cheapest.

SERVES 2

500g (1lb 2oz) samphire

90g (3 1/4 oz) butter, softened

2 tbsp olive oil

4 x 175g (6oz) wild salmon fillets, bones and skin removed

freshly ground black pepper, to taste

To cook the samphire, remove any of the woody roots with a pair of scissors and wash very well. Blanch in lots of boiling water for 1 minute and then refresh in a bowl of ice-cold water to retain the colour.

Meanwhile, melt 25g (1oz) of the butter in the olive oil in a hot nonstick pan and then fry the salmon fillets over a high heat for 5–6 minutes. Do not shake the fillets.

Allow the fillets to crisp on the underside, before turning over using a palette knife. Add another 25g of the butter and remove from the heat. The residual heat in the pan will continue to cook the fish.

Drain the samphire really well before reheating in a pan with the remaining butter. Season with pepper only, as the samphire is quite salty.

Place some samphire on the plate, top with the salmon and spoon over the warm, buttery juices.

Salmon Fish Cakes with Pickled Cucumber and Ginger Relish

Fish cakes are wrongly thought to be made from poor-quality cuts of fish. But actually they should always be made using the best cuts. I've used salmon as it's readily available to us all, but fish such as haddock, smoked haddock, tuna, crab and cod are all brilliant for fish cakes.

SERVES 4

500g (1lb 2oz) King Edward potatoes, peeled and cut into large chunks

25g (1oz) butter

75ml (2 1/2 fl oz) single cream

1 tsp mild or medium curry powder

2 tbsp chopped fresh parsley

1 large green chilli, deseeded and finely chopped

1 shallot, finely chopped

salt and pepper, to taste

500g (1lb 2oz) cooked salmon, bones and skin removed

4–5 tbsp plain flour, seasoned

2 medium free-range eggs

150g (5 1/2 oz) dried breadcrumbs

sunflower oil, for frying

CUCUMBER AND GINGER RELISH

1 cucumber

25g (1oz) fresh root ginger

2 cloves garlic

juice of 2 lemons

3 tbsp groundnut oil

1 tbsp sesame oil

Boil the potatoes in a saucepan of lightly salted water for about 15 minutes, or until tender. Drain well, then return to the pan. Mash with a fork or potato masher until smooth, beating in the butter, cream, curry powder, parsley, chilli, shallot and lots of salt and pepper. Leave to cool completely.

Meanwhile, check the salmon for any remaining bones, then flake. Mix the fish with the potato and shape into eight round patties.

To coat the salmon cakes in breadcrumbs requires a methodical approach. Complete each of the three stages for all the cakes before moving on to the next stage. That way, you won't get too messy. So, first coat each cake in seasoned flour, shake well and place on a plate. Beat the eggs in a wide shallow bowl, then dip each cake into the egg to coat evenly. Place the breadcrumbs in another wide bowl and coat each cake in the crumbs, pressing the crumbs on to coat the surface evenly. Shake off any excess and place on a plate. Chill in the fridge for about 30 minutes to 'set' the crumbs.

Meanwhile, make the relish. Peel the cucumber, cut it in half lengthways and scoop out all the seeds. Slice very thinly lengthways into ribbons. Put in a bowl. Peel and grate the ginger and garlic and add to the cucumber. Mix together the lemon juice and oils and pour over the cucumber. Season with salt and pepper. Leave to marinate while you cook the first cakes.

Heat the sunflower oil to a depth of 1cm (1/2 in) in a wide, shallow frying pan until you feel a good heat rising. Slide in the cakes using a fish slice. Cook for about 3 minutes, until crisp and golden on the underside, then turn and cook the other side.

Remove and place on kitchen paper. Serve the cakes with the relish.

An odd dish, I know, but all the characteristically British flavours work really well when eaten together. You can serve it all cold, but I like the vegetables cold and the salmon hot from the pan.

Salmon with Beetroot, Cauliflower and Horseradish Cream

SERVES 4

1 large cauliflower

juice of 1 lemon

4 tbsp horseradish cream

150ml (5fl oz) double cream, semi-whipped

salt and pepper, to taste

4 x 115–175g (4–6oz) salmon fillets, skin on

olive oil

BEETROOT

8 medium beetroots, cooked

4 shallots, chopped

1 clove garlic, chopped

75ml (2¹/₂ fl oz) extra-virgin olive oil

10g (¹/₄ oz) mixed fresh chives, parsley and dill, chopped

2 tbsp balsamic vinegar

To prepare the beetroots, peel them, cut them into segments and place these in a bowl.

Sweat the shallots and garlic in a pan in a little of the oil, but don't allow them to colour. Leave to cool. Mix with the herbs, balsamic and remaining oil, pour over the beetroot and leave to one side.

Divide the cauliflower into small florets and cook these in boiling water for about 5 minutes. When just cooked, plunge into iced water, drain and leave to one side.

Make the horseradish cream by combining the lemon juice and horseradish, then adding the semi-whipped cream and some seasoning. Fold in the cauliflower and place in a serving bowl.

Season the salmon, then cook it in a hot pan in a little oil, for 3–4 minutes on both sides.

Serve the cold beetroot and cauliflower in separate containers on a plate, with the hot salmon on top of either one.

Char-grilled Smoked Salmon with Rocket and Parmesan

Smoked salmon is superb. Here I've taken an unusual approach and char-grilled it in a griddle pan, which gives it great flavour. This dish could also be served as a light main course for two people.

SERVES 4

1 x 55g (2oz) piece fresh Parmesan

olive oil

2 tbsp balsamic vinegar

salt and pepper, to taste

200g (7oz) rocket leaves

225g (8oz) sliced smoked salmon

Using a speed potato peeler, shave all the cheese into thin strips and set to one side.

Mix 4 tbsp of the olive oil and the vinegar together with some seasoning. Mix into the rocket leaves quickly and carefully, and place on the plates.

Heat a griddle pan to high. Remove the salmon from the packet, fold each slice into three to make one thicker slice. Season with black pepper and drizzle on one side with a little olive oil. When the pan is very hot, place the salmon on it, oiled-side down, and leave for about 15 seconds. Turn it 90 degrees, cook for another 15 seconds, then remove. Do not turn it over; only cook on one side.

Sprinkle the rocket with the Parmesan shavings and place the salmon, charred-side up, on top. Serve immediately.

Smoked Salmon Mousse with Cucumber

This dish is what I used to eat in Berni Inns as a kid, followed by a sirloin steak with onion rings, peas and carrots, and a jacket potato. That in turn would be followed by – but only if I sat still while my sister tormented me – jelly and ice cream with hundreds and thousands on the top.

SERVES 4

200g (7oz) smoked salmon

200g (7oz) cooked salmon, skin and bone removed

150ml (5fl oz) double cream

100g (3¹/₂oz) cream cheese

juice of 1 lemon

¹/₂ tsp horseradish cream

salt and pepper, to taste

TO SERVE

¹/₂ cucumber, finely sliced

Place the two types of salmon in a blender and blend to a paste. Remove the paste from the machine and place in a bowl. Partly whip the cream in a separate bowl.

Fold the cream cheese into the salmon mixture. Carefully fold in the lemon juice and horseradish, and finally the cream. Do not overmix, as it will split. Season and transfer to a clean bowl or individual ramekins.

Serve with the sliced cucumber, as well as some mixed leaves and thickly sliced brown bread with butter.

Gravadlax may be Scandinavian, but it frequently appears on our supermarket shelves and in our restaurants now. It should never be confused with smoked salmon as it is made in a very different way indeed. You don't need a smoker as you do for smoked salmon – all you need is time. Trust me, this stuff's worth the wait.

Gravadlax with Mustard and Dill Sauce

SERVES 6

115g (4oz) coarse rock salt

85g (3oz) caster sugar

1 tbsp white peppercorns, crushed

2 large bunches fresh dill

2 x 900g (2lb) thick salmon fillets, skin on, scaled and pin bones removed

rocket leaves, to garnish

MUSTARD AND DILL SAUCE

2 tbsp Dijon mustard

1 tbsp caster sugar

1 free-range egg yolk

150ml (5fl oz) groundnut oil

1 tbsp white wine vinegar

4 tbsp chopped fresh dill

salt and pepper, to taste

To make the salmon curing mix, place the salt, sugar and white pepper into a medium-sized bowl. Finely chop most of the dill, add to the salt mixture, and stir to combine.

Choose a large, shallow, rectangular dish that will hold the salmon fillets, and line it with clingfilm. Sprinkle a quarter of the curing mixture over the base and top with one of the salmon fillets, skin-side down. Sprinkle over half of the remaining curing mix, and top with the other half of the salmon, skin-side up. Sprinkle the remaining curing mixture on top of the fillet and wrap in the clingfilm.

Weigh the fish down with some cans or weights on top, to remove any excess liquid or moisture. Place in the fridge, turning the salmon over every 6 hours where possible, for 3–4 days.

Before serving the gravadlax, rinse the cure off the fish to remove the salt and pat dry with kitchen paper. Sprinkle the remaining finely chopped dill over one side of the salmon, then sandwich the two fillets together again. Wrap tightly in clingfilm and chill for 6 hours.

To make the mustard and dill sauce, whisk the mustard and sugar together with the egg yolk in a large bowl. Gradually whisk in the oil, making sure the oil is well emulsified. Add the vinegar, the fresh dill and some salt and pepper, and mix well.

To serve, cut the gravadlax thinly (gravadlax is traditionally served thicker than smoked salmon). Place three or four good slices on a plate along with a spoonful of the sauce, and garnish with rocket leaves. Serve with rye bread.

shellfish

Garlic Prawns

The 1970s and 1980s saw a huge rise in the popularity of garlic – from garlic prawns and garlic bread to breadcrumb-coated garlic mushrooms. Living in Hampshire, I'm lucky enough to be close to the Isle of Wight, where a lot of British garlic is grown successfully, thanks to the high density of light reflecting off the sea around the island.

SERVES 4

20 cooked tiger prawns, tails left on

4 tbsp olive oil

4 cloves garlic, crushed

2 tbsp dry white wine

salt and pepper, to taste

2 tbsp chopped fresh flat-leaf parsley

1 lemon, cut into quarters

1 loaf crusty bread, warmed

Firstly, prepare the prawns by cutting each one through the length of the back. Pull out the dark vein and discard it. It's a bit fiddly, I know, but you will thank me for this when you eat them – the gritty bit you get in your mouth if this is not removed is the remainder of the prawn's last supper.

Heat a large pan on the stove. Add the olive oil and, when it's hot, add the garlic. Sauté for a few seconds, then add the prawns and white wine. Sauté well for about 45 seconds to 1 minute. Season with salt and pepper and add the parsley.

Serve straightaway with wedges of lemon and some chunks of crusty bread so you can dunk it in the juices while eating. Oops: don't forget a bowl of warm water on the table for your fingers, as it can get a bit messy.

Oysters

Guinness was introduced to the world in 1759 by Arthur Guinness in Dublin. But now, like so many beers, it is brewed all over the world, from Jamaica and Ghana to Canada and Australia. But real lovers of Guinness, like me, will know that the best pint is always going to be in a Dublin pub – a pint poured with time and care. And the best accompaniment is an oyster.

SERVES 4

12 fresh oysters

1 lemon, quartered

a pinch of cayenne pepper

TO SERVE
brown bread and butter

4 pints Guinness

Wash and open the oysters.

Loosen the base of the oysters with a knife and arrange on crushed ice. Decorate with the lemon wedges and season with cayenne.

Serve with the bread and butter on the side and a pint of Guinness.

Tiger Prawns Steamed with Beer

I first tasted this dish a few years ago in the States, and I thought it was fantastic but lacked real flavour. I decided this was probably due to the type of beer used. So, of course, I decided to use Yorkshire bitter instead of lager, and now it's a great dish that, for me, has got even better.

SERVES 4–6

1 x 350ml bottle beer (not lager)

450–675g (1–1¹/₂ lb) raw prawns, shells on

salt and pepper, to taste

olive oil

TO SERVE

2 lemons, cut into wedges

100ml (3¹/₂ fl oz) mayonnaise

4–6 sprigs fresh flat-leaf parsley

Heat a wok to a high heat. Place a bamboo steamer base (or an ordinary steamer) in the bottom of the wok and add 200ml (7fl oz) of the beer.

Season the prawns in a bowl and drizzle with a little olive oil. Place in the steamer basket with a lid on. Reduce the heat to moderate.

Steam for 5–6 minutes, until the prawns are cooked. Tip out the prawns into a serving bowl and serve with wedges of lemon and a bowl of mayonnaise. Garnish with sprigs of flat-leaf parsley.

Potted Shrimps with Melba Toast

The first thing I look for at farmers' markets are potted shrimps. I have to – I don't know why – it's just my fix. I suppose it dates back to the days when my parents took us to Blackpool and I first tasted the shrimps from Morecambe Bay.

SERVES 4

125g (4¹/₂ oz) unsalted butter

a good pinch of cayenne pepper

a good pinch of freshly grated nutmeg

600ml (1 pint) peeled cooked shrimps

salt and pepper, to taste

TO SERVE

4 slices thin-sliced white bread

green leaf salad, dressed

1 lemon, cut into wedges

Put the butter in a pan to melt with the cayenne and nutmeg. Once it has melted, add the shrimps. Mix over the heat and season. Put the shrimps in little pots or ramekin dishes and press down. Top with butter left in the pan and chill in the fridge.

To make the Melba toast, preheat a grill until it's nice and hot. Grill the bread on both sides until golden brown. With a sharp knife, remove the crusts, then slice in half horizontally. Put back under the grill, cut side uppermost, to toast. The edges will curl up to give the traditional Melba toast effect.

Serve the shrimps with a green leaf salad, a lemon wedge and slices of Melba toast.

What a starter! Name one starter that has been on a menu in both three-star restaurants and cafés. It must be one of our all-time favourites. I remember eating this as a kid at the Berni Inn in York: defrosted prawns, iceberg lettuce, a quarter of tomato, a slice of cucumber, a wedge of lemon and Marie Rose sauce. And, of course, a must with prawn cocktail is brown bread and butter. Who said the British can't produce good food? I have brought it up to date slightly, but the taste remains much the same.

Prawn Cocktail

SERVES 6

900g (2lb) large raw prawns, shells left on

olive oil, for frying

1 lettuce, preferably cos

25g (1oz) rocket leaves

1 ripe avocado

cayenne pepper

COCKTAIL SAUCE

100ml (3½ fl oz) mayonnaise

1 tbsp Worcestershire sauce

a dash of Tabasco sauce

2 tbsp Ketchup (*see* page 241)

juice of 1 lime

To prepare the prawns, heat the oil in a large, solid frying pan and shallow-fry them for 4–5 minutes until they turn a vibrant pink. Leave them to one side to cool. Reserve six in their shells for garnish and peel the rest. Take a small, sharp knife and cut along the back of each peeled prawn to remove any black thread.

To make the cocktail sauce, mix the mayonnaise with the rest of the ingredients. Stir and taste to check the seasoning. Keep the sauce covered with clingfilm in the fridge until it is needed.

Shred the lettuce and rocket finely and divide among six plates or glasses. Peel and chop the avocado into small dice and scatter this over the lettuce. Top with prawns and then the sauce. Sprinkle a dusting of cayenne pepper on top and garnish with one unpeeled prawn per serving.

Sweet and Sour Prawns

A nod to all the Chinese who have been running restaurants in Britain since the 1950s. This dish will work with chicken, too: cut the breast into thin strips, then roll it in cornflour, blanch in boiling water for a minute or two, drain and make as described below. This will not only cook the chicken a little, but also tenderize it at the same time.

SERVES 4

1¹/₂ tbsp groundnut oil

1 tbsp coarsely chopped garlic

2 tsp chopped fresh root ginger

4 spring onions, cut into 2.5cm (1in) pieces diagonally

450g (1lb) raw prawns, shelled and deveined

115g (4oz) red and green pepper, cut into 2.5cm (1in) squares

225g (8oz) canned water chestnuts, drained and sliced

SAUCE

150ml (5fl oz) chicken stock

2 tbsp rice wine or dry sherry

3 tbsp light soy sauce

2 tsp dark soy sauce

1 tbsp tomato paste

3 tbsp Chinese white rice vinegar or cider vinegar

1 tbsp caster sugar

1 tbsp cornflour, blended with 2 tbsp water

Heat a wok over a high heat, then add the oil. When it is very hot and slightly smoking, add the garlic, ginger and spring onions, and stir-fry for a couple of seconds.

Add the prawns and stir-fry them for 1 minute. Next add the pepper and water chestnuts, and stir-fry for another 30 seconds.

Now add all the sauce ingredients except for the cornflour mixture, then turn the heat down and simmer for 3 minutes.

Add the cornflour to thicken the sauce, stir-fry for 2 minutes more, and serve with plain or egg-fried rice.

Crab Cakes
A fabulous taste of the sea and another twist on the traditional British fish cake. Serve these crab cakes piping hot.

SERVES 4

500g (1lb 2oz) King Edward potatoes, peeled and cut into large chunks

salt and pepper, to taste

25g (1oz) butter

2 tbsp double cream

1 tsp mild or medium curry powder

2 tbsp chopped fresh coriander

1 large green chilli, deseeded and finely chopped

1 tbsp grated red onion

500g (1lb 2oz) flaked crab meat, preferably white meat

2–3 tbsp plain flour, seasoned

2 medium free-range eggs, beaten

100g (3 1/2 oz) dried breadcrumbs

corn or sunflower oil, for frying

Boil the potatoes in a saucepan of lightly salted water for about 15 minutes, or until tender. Drain well, and then return to the pan. Mash with a fork or potato masher until smooth, beating in the butter, cream, curry powder, coriander, chilli, onion and lots of salt and pepper. Leave to cool completely.

Meanwhile, check the crab meat carefully for any flecks of shell and discard these. Mix the crab meat with the potato mixture, and then shape into eight neat round patties. If the mixture sticks to your hands, simply dip them in cold water.

Coat the crab cakes with seasoned flour, egg and breadcrumbs as described on page 191, then chill in the fridge for about 30 minutes to 'set' the crumbs.

Heat the oil to a depth of 1cm (1/2 in) in a wide, shallow frying pan until you feel a good heat rising. Carefully slide in the crab cakes using a fish slice. Cook for about 3 minutes, until crisp and golden brown on the underside, then carefully turn and cook the other side. Remove and place on kitchen paper. (If you have a medium-sized frying pan, you may find it best to fry the crab cakes in two batches).

If you're not serving the crab cakes immediately, place them uncovered in a warm oven so that the coating stays crisp.

Potted Crab

Potted shrimps are familiar to most of us, in particular shrimps from Morecambe Bay, which come in small buttered pots and are served with lemon and brown bread and butter (a must with all potted fish for me). Crab makes a nice change, as it's quite difficult to find the small brown shrimps in this country.

FILLS 12 RAMEKINS

400g (14oz) white crab meat

400g (14oz) brown crab meat

400g (14oz) best unsalted butter

a good pinch of ground mace

a good pinch of freshly grated nutmeg

$1/3$ tsp cayenne pepper

salt and pepper, to taste

lemon juice

Preheat the oven to 150°C/300°F/gas mark 2. Put the crab meats into separate bowls. Have ready 12 ramekins.

Clarify 225g (8oz) of the butter by melting it gently, then pouring it carefully into another pan, leaving behind the milky, curd-like solids (which you should discard). Add the mace, nutmeg and cayenne to the clear butter, then pour the spiced butter into the bowl with the white crab meat. Amalgamate well, and season with salt, pepper and a squeeze of lemon juice to taste.

Fill each ramekin with a layer of the buttered white crab meat, followed by a layer of brown meat. Finish with a layer of the white meat. You will just have enough room at the top of the ramekin for a final layer of clarified butter (which you will add after the poaching). Place the ramekins in a roasting tin, pour boiling water to come halfway up the sides, and place in the oven for 25 minutes.

Remove the ramekins from the oven, and leave to cool. Clarify the rest of the butter as above, and pour the clear liquid over the ramekins, rather like sealing wax. Place in the fridge to set.

The ramekins should be removed from the fridge before serving. Then slip a slim knife blade all the way around the girth of each ramekin right to the bottom, turn the potted crab out on to the palm of your hand, and put each one, butter-side up, on individual plates.

Serve with warm toasted brown bread and dressed salad leaves.

Thyme-steamed Mussels

Here is a dish that is a bit like *moules marinières*, but with fresh thyme. Hot sourdough (or rye) bread is great to dunk in the juices afterwards. Mussels should be bought as fresh as possible. A mussel that is dead or even slightly bad can cause unpleasant side-effects. Check them before cooking and discard any whose shells refuse to close when tapped briskly, as these are likely to be dead. Once they are cooked, throw away any that have not opened as they might also be bad. Also, avoid frozen mussels.

SERVES 2

900g (2lb) fresh mussels

25g (1oz) butter

1/2 red onion, roughly chopped

3 cloves garlic, roughly chopped

250ml (9fl oz) white wine

4 sprigs fresh thyme

250ml (9fl oz) double cream

salt and pepper, to taste

1 x 20g (3/4oz) packet fresh flat-leaf parsley, roughly chopped

TO SERVE

1 medium sourdough loaf

butter

Wash the mussels in a colander to remove any dirt or grime. Pick through the mussels and remove the stringy bits from the edges; this is what the mussel uses to hold on to rocks or its mates before being taken from the sea. Discard any that do not close when tapped briskly.

Wrap the bread in foil (to prevent it from drying out) and place it in a low oven – about 150°C/300°F/gas mark 2 – to warm up slowly while you cook the mussels.

Place the butter in a large pan and sauté the onion and garlic for 1 minute before adding the wine. Bring to the boil and add the fresh thyme and mussels. Place the lid on the pan and cook for 3–4 minutes, until the mussels start to open.

Add the cream, salt, pepper and parsley, stirring the ingredients with a spoon. Heat through, making sure all the mussels are open (discard any that are not).

Divide the mussels between two bowls and pour the sauce left in the pan over them. Remove the bread from the oven and break into large chunks. I like to eat all the mussels first, and dunk the bread (with loads of butter on it) in at the end.

vegetarian

Love it or loathe it, the British cauliflower is a great vegetable. Chefs love to cook with it, but other people are still divided, probably due to the school dinners we used to have – that dreaded grey stuff that was kept warm for hours in steaming trays with lids on. Overcooked cauliflower still scares me to this day.

Cauliflower Cheese

SERVES 4

1 large cauliflower, divided into florets, or use individual baby cauliflowers

salt and pepper, to taste

butter

CHEESE SAUCE

1 clove

1 bay leaf

1 small onion

600ml (1 pint) milk

25g (1oz) butter

25g (1oz) plain flour

freshly grated nutmeg

150ml (5fl oz) single cream

1 tsp English mustard

250g (9oz) mature Cheddar, grated

To make the sauce, first stud the clove through the bay leaf into the peeled onion, and place in a saucepan with the milk. Warm the milk slowly to allow the flavours to impregnate the milk.

Melt the butter in a saucepan. Once melted, add the flour and cook on a low heat for a few minutes, stirring from time to time. Add the simmering milk, a ladle at a time, and stir to a smooth sauce. Bring to a simmer and cook for about 8–10 minutes.

Remove the onion and season the sauce with salt, pepper and nutmeg. Add the cream, which will loosen the sauce slightly. Add the mustard and 200g (7oz) of the grated Cheddar. Once completely melted into the sauce, taste again for seasoning and strength. Do not boil. Strain through a sieve.

Cook the cauliflower florets in a pan of salted water until just tender, a few minutes. Drain. (The cauliflower can be cooked ahead of time and refreshed in ice water. To reheat, either microwave or plunge back into boiling water. If using baby cauliflower, you could keep it whole, as in the photograph.) Warm a knob of butter in a frying pan and add the florets. Roll these, without colouring, in the butter and season with salt and pepper.

To finish, preheat the oven to 200°C/400°F/gas mark 6 or preheat the grill. Spoon a little cheese sauce into an ovenproof dish, arrange the cauliflower on top and coat with more of the sauce. Sprinkle the last of the grated Cheddar on top and place in the oven or under the grill to melt and colour for 10–15 minutes.

Baked Cheese in a Box

Pubs are a great showcase for British food, and that's where I got the idea for this. The Red Lion Pub in Stourbridge, Kent, serves fantastic food and great British beers. I had this baked cheese there with a loaf of bread to dunk into it, and it was well worth the 200-mile round trip!

SERVES 4

1 Bonchester or English Camembert cheese in a box

salt and pepper, to taste

extra-virgin olive oil

1/2 tsp chopped fresh thyme

TO SERVE
fresh crusty bread

Preheat the oven to 190°C/375°F/gas mark 5.

Remove the cheese from the box and, if the box is held together only with glue, staple it together as the glue will melt in the oven.

Take a sharp knife and cut the top off the cheese – just the skin. Then place the cheese back in the box, cut-side up.

Season, drizzle with olive oil and sprinkle with fresh thyme.

Put in the oven for 10–15 minutes until cooked through and brown on top.

Remove from the oven and serve with warm, crusty bread. It's a bit like a dip really; sort of a fondue thing.

Stilton Fondue with Pears

This is a Swiss concept, using very British ingredients. If you don't have a fondue set you can improvise with an oven-to-table dish on a rack over nightlights.

SERVES 4

150g (5 1/2 oz) Stilton cheese, diced

85g (3oz) mascarpone cheese

75ml (2 1/2 fl oz) double cream

a drizzle of vodka

salt and pepper, to taste

3 pears, cored and sliced

1/2 walnut bread loaf, in chunks

Place the Stilton, mascarpone and double cream in a pan and warm over a low heat until the cheeses have melted.

Add the vodka, remove from the heat and season.

Place the pears and bread in separate dishes. Serve the fondue warm in the middle of the table. Dip the pear slices and bread chunks into the fondue, and enjoy!

I know it doesn't have vegetables in it, but humour me! This recipe provides the ideal centrepiece for vegetarians.

Double-baked Cheese Soufflés

SERVES 6

unsalted butter

250g (9oz) ground almonds

40g (1 1/2 oz) plain flour

300ml (10fl oz) hot milk

160g (5 3/4 oz) Emmental cheese, grated

5 medium free-range egg yolks

salt and pepper, to taste

500ml (18fl oz) free-range egg whites

3 tbsp lemon juice

SAUCE

1.3 litres (2 1/4 pints) double cream

250ml (9fl oz) Kirsch

140g (5oz) Emmental cheese, grated

Preheat the oven to 180°C/350°F/gas mark 4. Butter six small soufflé moulds, then dust with ground almonds. Put the moulds in a roasting tray.

To make the béchamel base of the soufflés, melt 40g (1 1/2 oz) butter in a pan, add the flour and stir until smooth. Add the hot milk gradually, stirring, until smooth. While it is still hot, stir in the grated cheese until melted. Leave to cool. Stir in the egg yolks and season.

Whisk the egg whites with the lemon juice until firm. Add a quarter of this to the cheese béchamel and fold in. When smooth, slowly fold in the rest. Fill the moulds with this. Pour enough boiling water into the roasting tray to come halfway up the moulds, then put the tray in the oven for 10 minutes. Allow the soufflés to cool. (You could freeze them at this stage.) Reduce the oven temperature to 160°C/325°F/gas mark 3.

Remove the soufflés from the moulds, and place in a baking dish. For the sauce, mix the cream and Kirsch, pour over the soufflés, and top with the grated Emmental. Bake in the cooler oven for 8 minutes. Serve the soufflés hot, with their sauce.

Aubergines are not really English, but I'm growing them in my greenhouse and they taste wonderful. Simply pan-fry slices of aubergine, top with mozzarella cheese and Parmesan, place under the grill and serve with a tomato sauce. This is a real classic Italian dish that we Brits have learned to love.

Grilled Aubergine with Tomato Sauce

SERVES 4

plain white flour

4 medium free-range eggs, beaten with a pinch of salt

2 aubergines, cut into 8mm (3/8 in) rounds

olive oil

salt and pepper, to taste

300g (10 1/2 oz) buffalo mozzarella cheese, sliced

100g (3 1/2 oz) Parmesan, freshly grated

TOMATO AND BASIL SAUCE

extra-virgin olive oil

1 medium onion, finely chopped

2 cloves garlic, finely chopped

1kg (2 1/4 lb) tomatoes, diced

1/4 tsp dried oregano

8 fresh basil leaves, torn

To make the sauce, heat 4 tbsp of olive oil in a pan and fry the onion and garlic for 4–5 minutes. Add the tomatoes and oregano, bring to the boil, then reduce the heat and cook for 10–15 minutes. Halfway through the cooking, add the basil leaves. Season and blend to a smooth sauce, then leave to one side.

Preheat two frying pans on the stove, and preheat the grill.

Put the flour and beaten eggs in separate shallow bowls. Dip the aubergine slices first in flour and then in beaten egg, and fry in shallow olive oil until golden on both sides. Put each slice on absorbent kitchen paper.

Place the drained aubergine slices on a grill tray and season. Top with the sliced mozzarella and grated Parmesan.

Grill until the cheeses have melted and started to brown, then serve immediately with the heated tomato and basil sauce.

Quick Onion Bhajias

This recipe isn't really mine, as it comes from one of my boys in the bistro kitchen. I promised him I'd put it in the book. I hope you like these as much as I do. I know bhajias are not really British, but we've kind of adopted them. To make a good dip for them, mix some ground cumin, lime juice and chopped mint into some Greek yoghurt.

MAKES 8–10

2 onions, thinly sliced

70g (2½ oz) self-raising flour

1 tsp medium curry powder

½ tsp ground cumin

2 tsp turmeric powder

½ tsp salt

150g (5½ oz) plain yoghurt

vegetable oil, for deep-frying

Place the onions, flour, spices and salt in a bowl and then stir in the plain yoghurt.

Divide the mixture into small balls in the palm of your hands.

Heat the oil to 180°C/350°F, then deep-fry the bhajias for 1–2 minutes, to colour and cook. Drain on kitchen paper and cool for a while.

Serve as required, with either a spiced yoghurt dip (*see* recipe introduction) or some mango chutney.

Garlic Mushrooms

There was a time when to eat anything with garlic in it was considered a bit 'daring'. Now we just enjoy it, and it goes fantastically with mushrooms. Try different types of mushrooms: buttons would be good, too, as would some of the exotic cultivated varieties, such as oyster mushrooms.

SERVES 4

600g (1lb 5oz) chestnut or brown cap mushrooms

25ml (1fl oz) extra-virgin olive oil

4 cloves garlic, finely diced or crushed

30g (1¼ oz) butter

juice of ½ lemon

salt and pepper, to taste

2 tbsp chopped fresh flat-leaf parsley

Clean the mushrooms. Heat the oil in a large frying pan and add the mushrooms. Fry for about 2–3 minutes over a high heat, stirring all the time.

Add the garlic and butter and cook for a further 2–3 minutes.

Finish by quickly stirring in the lemon juice and salt and pepper to taste and the chopped parsley.

Serve in a bowl with some lovely warm, crusty bread.

I love a fry-up, and this is simply a more elegant way of serving the classic, ever-popular 'bubble and squeak'.

Bubble and Squeak Cakes

MAKES 4

500g (1lb 2oz) floury potatoes, such as King Edward, Maris Piper or Desirée, peeled and chopped

125g (4 1/2 oz) shredded green cabbage

olive or sunflower oil, for frying

3 rashers smoked bacon, rinded and chopped

1 shallot, chopped

2 cloves garlic, crushed

3 tbsp chopped mixed fresh herbs, such as parsley, dill or coriander

salt and pepper, to taste

seasoned flour, for coating

Boil the potatoes in lightly salted water for about 15 minutes until just tender, then drain well and mash in the pan. Leave in the pan.

Blanch the cabbage in a little boiling water for 2 minutes, then drain, rinse under cold running water and pat dry with kitchen paper.

Heat a trickle of oil in a frying pan, add the bacon and fry until crisp. Remove and drain on kitchen paper. Add 1 tbsp of oil to the pan, add the shallot and garlic and sauté for 3 minutes until softened.

Add the shallot and garlic to the mashed potato with the cabbage, bacon, chopped herbs and seasoning. Set aside to cool.

Shape the mixture into four cakes. Toss in seasoned flour to coat, shaking off any excess. Heat oil to a depth of 1cm (1/2 in) in a large frying pan. Lower the cakes into the hot oil using a fish slice and cook for about 3 minutes on each side, turning them carefully. Remove and drain on kitchen paper.

The pizza may not be traditionally British, but it's up there in our favourite things to eat, so it had to be in the book. I love it with some salami milano and cooked chicken but, whatever your taste, use this as a base and you won't go wrong. You can make the pizzas larger if you wish and, of course, they can be any shape you fancy.

Pizza Margherita

MAKES 4 X 25CM
(10IN) PIZZAS

olive oil

3 cloves garlic, finely chopped

1kg (2 1/4 lb) vine-ripened tomatoes, skinned, deseeded and roughly chopped

salt and pepper, to taste

1 tbsp chopped fresh oregano

500g (18oz) buffalo mozzarella cheese, thinly sliced

a large handful of basil leaves, torn into pieces

PIZZA BASE

550g (1 1/4 lb) strong white flour, plus extra for dusting

4 tsp easy-blend yeast

2 tsp salt

450ml (16fl oz) hand-hot water

4 tsp olive oil

4 tbsp polenta or semolina

For the base, sift the flour, yeast and salt into a bowl, and make a well in the centre. Add the warm water and olive oil, and mix together to a soft dough. Tip the dough out on to a lightly floured surface and knead for 5 minutes, or until smooth and elastic. Return it to the bowl, cover with clingfilm and leave in a warm place for approximately 1 hour, or until doubled in size.

Meanwhile, for the topping, heat 6 tbsp of the oil and cook the garlic in a large, shallow pan. As soon as the garlic starts to sizzle, add the tomatoes and some salt and pepper, and simmer quite vigorously for 7–10 minutes, until reduced to a thickish sauce. Season again if necessary.

Put a large baking tray into the oven and heat the oven to its highest setting. Knock the air out of the dough and knead it briefly once more on a lightly floured surface. Divide into four pieces, and keep the spare ones covered with clingfilm while you shape the first pizza.

Sprinkle a spare baking sheet or a pizza peel with some of the polenta or semolina. Roll the dough out into a disc approximately 25cm (10in) in diameter, lift it on to the baking sheet and reshape it with your fingers into a round. Spread one-quarter of the tomato sauce to within about 2.5cm (1 in) of the edge. Sprinkle with some of the oregano, then cover with a quarter of the mozzarella cheese slices.

Drizzle with a little olive oil, then open the oven door and quickly slide the pizza off the tray on to the hot baking sheet on the top shelf. Bake for 10 minutes, or until the cheese has melted and the crust is crisp and golden. Repeat the assembling and cooking process with the remaining pieces of dough, cooking individually.

To serve, scatter with the basil leaves and serve hot.

vegetables

Roast Potatoes

Everyone has a different recipe for roast potatoes; this is mine. It was my gran's first, then my mother's, and it's still the best. Use lard or dripping for the cooking fat (or vegetable oil if you don't have either), but best of all use some goose fat.

SERVES 6

10 medium King Edward, Maris Piper or Desirée potatoes

salt

50g (1 ³/₄ oz) fat (*see* above)

Preheat the oven to 200°C/400°F/gas mark 6. Peel the potatoes and cut each one in half (into three if large). Place in a saucepan, cover with cold water and add a good pinch of salt. Bring to the boil and simmer for a maximum of 3–4 minutes. Put into a colander and allow to drain well.

Heat the lard or dripping in a roasting tray on the stove, and fry the potatoes until they start to brown. Turn them occasionally. Sprinkle generously with salt, then roast for about 25 minutes.

Remove from the oven and turn the potatoes in the tray to prevent them from sticking. Roast for another 25 minutes and remove. Serve immediately. (I also love roast potatoes cold – which is why I always make bucketloads of them! I eat them with cold meat and a good wodge of butter.)

Roast Parsnips

I love these, at Christmas or any other time of the year.

SERVES 6

900g (2lb) parsnips, peeled and quartered

2 tbsp olive oil

leaves from 2 fresh thyme sprigs

salt and pepper, to taste

40g (1 ¹/₂ oz) unsalted butter

4–6 tbsp runny honey

Preheat the oven to 200°C/400°F/gas mark 6. If the parsnips are large and have woody centres, cut these out before cooking. The parsnips can be boiled in salted water for 2 minutes before roasting.

Preheat a roasting tray on the stove and add the oil. Fry the parsnips until golden on all sides, allowing burnt tinges on the edges. Add the thyme and then roast, turning every 10 minutes, for 20–30 minutes.

Remove from the oven and season. Add the butter and honey. Return to the oven for 5–10 minutes. Place in a serving dish and spoon over the juices.

Mashed Potatoes
How fantastic does good mashed potato taste? It goes with anything: it can top fish pies or it can simply be served with sausages and onion gravy. I could eat this just with cold roast lamb – that's my favourite.

SERVES 4

900g (2lb) large Maris Piper potatoes, peeled and quartered

115g (4oz) unsalted butter

125ml (4fl oz) single cream

salt and pepper, to taste

freshly grated nutmeg

Boil the potatoes in salted water until cooked, about 20–25 minutes, depending on size.

Drain off all the water, replace the lid and shake the pan vigorously, which will start to break up the boiled potatoes. Add the butter and single cream, a little at a time, while mashing the potatoes.

Season with salt, pepper and some nutmeg according to taste. The potatoes will now be light, fluffy, creamy and ready to eat.

Dauphinoise in a Pan
Yes, this dish is French, and purists will complain that traditionally it's cooked in layers raw in the oven, and not with cheese. But I'm all for making life easier, and this recipe takes a quarter of the time to cook. When working in France at a three-star Michelin restaurant, this is all I ate, and it now features on many of my menus.

SERVES 6

900g (2lb) King Edward potatoes

25g (1oz) unsalted butter

2 cloves garlic, chopped

2 shallots, peeled and chopped

150ml (5fl oz) milk

600ml (1 pint) double cream

salt and pepper, to taste

55g (2oz) Cheddar, grated

100g (3 1/2 oz) mozzarella cheese, crumbled

Peel and slice the potatoes as thinly as possible (preferably using a mandolin). Melt the butter in a medium heatproof dish or in a large pan, and sauté the garlic and shallot lightly. Add the milk and cream and bring to a simmer. Add the sliced potato, and cook on a gentle simmer for about 8–10 minutes to just cook the potato.

Preheat the grill to medium-hot.

Season the potatoes well, and either leave in the dish to serve or ladle carefully from the pan into six small heatproof dishes. Top with the cheeses, spreading them evenly. Place under the grill for a couple of minutes until brown, then serve.

Parsley and Mozzarella Croquettes

This is party food without the mess, as the cheese will melt inside – and a great side dish, too.

MAKES 24

1kg (2 1/4 lb) potatoes, peeled

a pinch of freshly grated nutmeg

salt and pepper, to taste

25g (1oz) unsalted butter

200g (7oz) mozzarella cheese, finely diced

2 medium free-range egg yolks

15g (1/2 oz) fresh parsley leaves, chopped

plain flour

2 medium free-range eggs, beaten

140g (5oz) fresh white breadcrumbs

vegetable oil, for deep-frying

Place the potatoes in salted water, bring to the boil and simmer until they are tender.

Drain and return to the pan. Place over a low heat and mash-fry with a potato masher. Season with the nutmeg, salt and pepper, then beat in the butter and leave to cool.

Once the mash is cold, add the diced mozzarella, the egg yolks and the chopped parsley.

Divide the mixture into 24 pieces. Roll these into cylinder shapes on a lightly floured surface.

With the beaten eggs in one bowl and the breadcrumbs in another, coat the croquettes first in the egg, then in the crumbs. Repeat to give them a double coating.

Preheat the oil to 190°C/375°F and deep-fry the croquettes until golden brown, about 5–6 minutes. Drain on kitchen paper and serve straightaway.

Salt-baked Baby Potatoes with Taleggio and Bacon

I loved baby jacket potatoes at Hallowe'en or Bonfire Night as a kid. There are many cheeses available now – you could use dolcelatte torta or my favourite, Taleggio.

SERVES 6–8

140g (5oz) sea salt flakes

16–20 baby roasting potatoes

140g (5oz) Taleggio cheese, grated

4 streaky bacon rashers, rinded, chopped and blanched in boiling water

Preheat the oven to 230°C/450°F/gas mark 8.

Cover a baking tray with a layer of sea salt flakes. Lay the potatoes on the salt and bake for 30–40 minutes, or until cooked through.

Cut a slit in the top of each potato and stuff with the cheese and bacon.

Place the stuffed potatoes back in the oven or put under a well preheated grill for a few minutes, until the cheese has melted and the bacon is cooked through and golden.

Serve immediately, while still hot.

Chips and French Fries
Nothing can beat chips – whether fat or thin – with a little salt and ketchup.

SERVES 4–6

vegetable oil, for deep-frying

4–6 large potatoes, about 1.5kg (3lb 5oz)

salt

Heat the oil in a deep-fat fryer or a deep, heavy-based pan to 95°C/200°F for blanching.

For good large chips, peel then trim the potatoes into rectangles. Now cut into 1cm (1/2 in) thick slices, then cut again to give chips 1cm (1/2 in) wide. If you want French fries, then simply halve the thickness, making them 5mm x 6–7.5cm (1/4 x 2 1/2 –3in).

The chips now need to be blanched in the preheated fryer. This is very important, as it guarantees the chips will be totally cooked before serving. Frying them at 95°C/200°F will cook them without allowing them to colour. The large chips will take up to 10 minutes before becoming tender; the smaller fries will need only 6–8 minutes.

Once cooked, check with a knife. When ready, remove from the oil and drain. The chips or fries can be left to cool on greaseproof paper and even chilled before finishing in the hot fryer.

To finish, preheat the oil in the fryer to 180°C/350°F. Once hot, place the chips in the fat. These will now take around 2–3 minutes to become golden brown and crispy. Shake off any excess fat and sprinkle with salt before serving.

Jacket Potatoes
Sometimes a little of what hurts you does you good – and a good knob of butter melting into jacket potatoes tastes fantastic.

SERVES 4

4 large baking potatoes

olive oil

rock salt or sea salt flakes

75g (2 3/4 oz) butter

Preheat the oven to 180°C/350°F/gas mark 4. Wash and dry the potatoes and prick each one about eight times all over with a fork. Rub with olive oil and sprinkle with rock or sea salt.

Bake the potatoes in the oven for 1 1/2 –2 hours, until cooked. They should be crisp on the outside and soft in the middle.

Cut a cross in the top, then, using your fingers, squeeze in the middle to push the top out. Spoon on a good knob of butter.

Roasted Vegetables with Rosemary and Honey

This is a fab way to serve veg at a dinner party or Sunday lunch. It's a bucket-load less stressful than five pans of boiling water with overcooked roots inside!

SERVES 6

450g (1lb) each of new potatoes, parsnips and carrots

225g (8oz) fennel bulbs

225g (8oz) red onions

6 cloves garlic

6 lemon slices

6 tbsp olive oil

75ml (2 1/2 fl oz) clear honey

25g (1oz) unsalted butter

1 fresh rosemary sprig, torn into 4 pieces

salt and pepper, to taste

juice of 1 lemon (optional)

Preheat the oven to 220°C/425°F/gas mark 7.

Wash the potatoes, parsnips, carrots and fennel, but don't peel them, then slice into large chunky pieces. Cut the red onions into quarters.

Place all the vegetables into an oven tray with the garlic and lemon slices, and drizzle with olive oil and honey. Add the butter in knobs and sprinkle on the rosemary. Season well. Roast for 30–40 minutes.

Remove from the oven and coat all the vegetables in the glaze in the base of the pan. Serve with some lemon juice squeezed over if you like.

Celeriac Rémoulade

This French salad has become popular over here. You can serve celeriac raw, although some people prefer it blanched in boiling water for 1 minute. The sauce is a mustard mayonnaise livened up with my special touches.

SERVES 4

500g (1lb 2oz) celeriac

1 red onion, thinly sliced

250ml (9fl oz) thick mayonnaise

3 tbsp coarse-grain mustard, such as Pommery or Gordons

finely grated zest and juice of 1 lemon

a dash of Worcestershire sauce

salt and pepper, to taste

2 tbsp chopped fresh parsley

Peel the celeriac, then slice it as thinly as possible (use a mandolin if you have one). Stack the slices three or four at a time on top of each other and cut into long, thin julienne or matchsticks.

Place in a bowl and mix with the onion. (If you prefer a milder flavour, first soak the onion in a large bowl of cold water for 1 hour.)

Beat the mayonnaise with the mustard, lemon zest and juice, Worcestershire sauce and seasoning. Combine with the celeriac and onion. If you find the sauce a little too thick, thin it with 1–2 tbsp milk. Check the seasoning, stir in the parsley and serve in an attractive bowl.

Roast Squash, Lemon and Mustard Purée

This is a good dish to serve with roast meat, poultry or game, and makes a nice change from mashed spuds every time.

SERVES 6–8

2 butternut squashes, about 650g (1lb 7oz) each

2 cloves garlic, crushed

2 lemons, each cut into 4 slices

1 tbsp olive oil

leaves from 1 sprig fresh thyme

90g (3 1/4 oz) unsalted butter

3 tbsp coarse-grain mustard

5 tbsp double cream

salt and pepper, to taste

Preheat the oven to 190°C/375°F/gas mark 5.

Cut the squashes in half, scoop out the seeds, then peel and chop the flesh into even-sized chunks. Place the squash in a bowl with the garlic, lemons, oil and thyme.

Melt 55g (2oz) of the butter and add half of this to the bowl. Toss together, then spread out in a roasting tin and roast for about 20 minutes, until the squash feels tender when pierced with a knife.

Scoop the squash into a food processor with the remaining melted butter, the mustard, cream and seasoning. Whizz to a smooth purée. Alternatively, mash the squash and stir in the other ingredients.

Reheat and dot with the remaining butter when ready to serve.

Caramelized Beetroot
A speedy, simple serving idea for cooked beetroot. You can use ready-cooked beets from a pack but be sure to avoid the variety contained in that awful vinegar. But better still, cook and peel your own fresh beetroot.

SERVES 4

3 tbsp runny honey

25g (1oz) butter

4 whole cooked beetroots, cut in half

juice of 1 lemon

salt and pepper, to taste

1 tbsp chopped fresh parsley

Heat a large nonstick frying pan until you feel a good heat rising. Spoon in the honey and swirl in the butter.

When you have a golden brown glaze, add the beetroot halves with the lemon juice and cook for 3–5 minutes, spooning the honey juices constantly over the beetroot.

Season well and tip into a warmed serving dish. Scatter over the parsley and serve.

Mushy Peas

Fish and chips can't be without them. There are so many recipes for mushy peas, but the old ones are still the best.

SERVES 6

225g (8oz) dried marrowfat peas

1 tsp bicarbonate of soda

30g (1 1/4 oz) butter

salt and pepper, to taste

In a large bowl, soak the peas in three times their volume of water with the bicarbonate of soda for at least 4 hours or, if you have the time, overnight.

Drain the peas, rinse under the tap, place on the stove in a large saucepan and cover with water. Cover and bring to the boil and, once boiled, reduce the heat and simmer the peas for 1 1/2 – 2 hours, stirring from time to time.

The peas should be soft and mushy in texture but not too dry. If they are too wet, continue cooking over the heat with the lid off to dry out a little. Beat in the butter, season and serve.

Butter Bean and Rosemary Purée

Use Spanish butter beans if you can, but otherwise French haricots are a good alternative. You can make the purée in advance and simply reheat it before serving.

SERVES 4

175g (6oz) dried white beans (*see* above)

1 tbsp olive oil

3 shallots, chopped

3 fat cloves garlic, crushed

3 rashers smoked bacon or pancetta, rinded and chopped

leaves from 1 sprig fresh rosemary, chopped

1 sprig fresh thyme

150ml (5fl oz) dry white wine

400ml (14fl oz) fresh chicken or vegetable stock (buy ready-made in a tub)

salt and pepper, to taste

2–4 tbsp double cream or crème fraîche

Soak the beans in water overnight, then drain and rinse them. Place in a saucepan, cover with cold water and bring to the boil. Continue to boil for 5 minutes, then drain.

Meanwhile, heat the oil in a frying pan, add the shallots, garlic and bacon or pancetta and sauté for 5 minutes. Add the blanched beans with the rosemary, thyme, wine and stock. Bring to the boil, then season with pepper only.

Cover and simmer for about 30 minutes until the beans are softened. Remove the lid, add salt to season and boil again to evaporate any remaining liquid. Remove the thyme sprig and transfer the bean mixture to a food processor or blender. Add the cream or crème fraîche and whizz to a purée.

To make a quicker version of this dish, use 2 x 400g cans butter beans in place of the dried beans. Simply rinse and drain the beans, then add them to the sautéed shallots, garlic and bacon or pancetta with the herbs and wine, but without the stock. Simmer for 15 minutes, then blend with the cream or crème fraîche to make a purée.

Buttered Brussels Sprouts

The old days of putting the Brussels on at the same time as the turkey have, thankfully, long gone. Sprouts cooked properly with lots of melted butter can be a real joy to eat.

SERVES 4

1kg (2¼lb) Brussels sprouts

salt and pepper, to taste

butter

Trim off the outer leaves of the Brussels sprouts.

Bring a large saucepan of salted water to the boil. Place the sprouts in the water and bring back to the boil as quickly as possible. Simmer for 3–4 minutes, until just cooked but still with a bit of crunch.

Drain into a colander and place in a bowl with a knob of butter and a good twist of freshly ground black pepper.

Brussels Sprouts with Chestnuts and Bacon

A simple way to make Brussels taste more interesting – although if you use Brussels still on the vine (much more readily available now), the sprouts don't dry out so much and are fresher in flavour. Chestnuts are readily available vacuum-packed from delis and supermarkets.

SERVES 10–12

1.3kg (3lb) Brussels sprouts, or 2 stems Brussels sprouts, trimmed

salt and pepper, to taste

a large knob of unsalted butter

12 smoked streaky bacon rashers or dry-cured ham, rinded and cut into thin matchsticks

1 x 200g vacuum-pack cooked, peeled whole chestnuts

Bring a large pan of salted water to the boil, add the sprouts and cook until just tender, 8–12 minutes, depending on their size. Drain well.

Meanwhile, melt the butter in a large frying pan or wok and fry the bacon until crisp. Add the chestnuts and cook for about a minute, to heat through.

When warm, tip in the drained Brussels sprouts. Mix well and season with salt and pepper.

sauces

Apple Sauce

The Americans eat apple sauce by itself. I like it best with cold pork and stuffing. Mmm – delicious.

SERVES 4

225g (8oz) Bramley apples

4 tbsp water

1 tbsp brown sugar

a pinch of freshly grated nutmeg

25g (1oz) butter

Peel, core and thinly slice the apples and put them in a pan with the rest of the ingredients.

Cook over a gentle heat and simmer, stirring all the time, until the apples have reduced to a pulp.

Allow to cool before chilling in the fridge until you're ready to use the sauce.

Spiced Apple Sauce

A change from the normal apple sauce, this goes very well with roast pork and ham, especially the Honey-glazed Ham on page 110.

SERVES 6

500g (1lb 2oz) Bramley Seedling apples

25g (1oz) butter

2 tbsp water

2 tbsp white wine vinegar

1/4 tsp freshly grated nutmeg

1/4 tsp ground cinnamon

1/4 tsp freshly ground black pepper

25g (1oz) soft dark brown sugar

Peel, core and cut up the apples.

Put them in a pan with the butter, water, vinegar and spices. Cover and cook gently until soft enough to beat to a purée.

Add sugar to taste, and more spices if you like.

Real Mint Sauce

This was my gran's mint sauce recipe. She never had a sharp knife, so she had to resort to chopping the mint in a grinder – this white plastic thing which you feed the leaves into while turning the handle. It did it in the end, but took about an hour to wash up.

SERVES 4

1 bunch fresh mint

a pinch of salt

1 level tbsp caster sugar

4 tbsp boiling water

4 tbsp white wine vinegar

Strip the mint leaves off the stalks, sprinkle the leaves with the salt, and chop finely.

Place in a jug, add the sugar and pour over the boiling water. Stir and leave to cool.

Stir in the vinegar and taste. Add more water or vinegar, and adjust the seasoning to suit your taste.

Horseradish Sauce

The best accompaniment to any roast beef or, indeed, steak.

MAKES 200ML (7FL OZ)

85g (3oz) fresh horseradish, peeled and finely grated

1 tsp Dijon or English mustard

1 tbsp white wine vinegar

1 tsp caster sugar

175ml (6fl oz) double cream, whipped

salt and pepper, to taste

Place all the ingredients except the seasoning in a bowl, and whisk together to a soft peak consistency. Season with salt and pepper.

The sauce is best served chilled.

Mum's Gravy
Thanks, mum, for the best gravy recipe I know.

SERVES 4–6

100ml (3 1/2 fl oz) vegetable cooking water

2 white onions, sliced

25g (1oz) butter

4 tsp gravy powder

150ml (5fl oz) red wine

3/4 tsp mustard powder

1 tsp cornflour

1 tsp yeast extract

Remove the roasted meat from the roasting tray and pour off any excess fat. Add the vegetable water to the remaining juices in the tray and slowly simmer over a low heat on the stove top.

In a separate pan, fry the onions in the butter to give a lot of colour. Dissolve the gravy powder in 600ml (1 pint) of hot water. Pour this into with the roasting tray with the red wine and add the onions.

In a small dish, stir the mustard powder and cornflour into a little water to make a paste. Whisk or stir into the simmering gravy. Add the yeast extract and stir in well. Pour into the sauce boat and serve as required.

Bread Sauce
My grandmother left me an old Be-Ro flour book in her will, which had been passed down from my great-great-grandmother. In it there were alternatives and variations to classic recipes, written in pencil by my great-grandmother: the pages were full of crossings out, and notes. This recipe is based on one in that book.

SERVES 8

225g (8oz) stale French stick

700ml (1 1/4 pints) full-fat milk

1 small onion, studded with 6 cloves

1 bay leaf

a good knob of unsalted butter

a pinch of ground allspice

about 200ml (7fl oz) double cream

salt and pepper, to taste

Shave the light-brown crust from the French stick with a bread knife and discard it. Cut the bread centre into 5cm (2in) cubes.

In a saucepan, bring the milk, onion, bay, butter, allspice and 3 tbsp of the cream to the boil. Reduce the heat, then add the bread. Gently simmer, uncovered, for 5 minutes. Add a little seasoning and then cool. Remove the onion and bay.

The sauce can be refrigerated in a covered container overnight. To serve, warm through gently in a pan, adding enough double cream to give a light consistency. Grind over some black pepper and serve.

This is one of the first sauces you learn to make as a chef, and although it's French in origin, us Brits have fallen in love with it. It should never be overheated, otherwise the butter will split. Asparagus is great with this, as are poached eggs. Clarified butter is what you get when it separates from the whey. To do this, place the butter in a small pan and leave it over a very low heat until it has melted. Skim off any scum from the surface, and pour off the clear (clarified) butter into a bowl, leaving behind the milky white solids that will have settled on the bottom.

Hollandaise Sauce

SERVES 4

2 tbsp water

2 free-range egg yolks

225g (8oz) clarified butter, warmed

juice of 1/2 lemon

a good pinch of cayenne pepper

1/2 tsp salt

Put the water and egg yolks into a stainless-steel or glass bowl set over a pan of simmering water, making sure that the base of the bowl is not touching the water. Whisk until voluminous and creamy.

Remove the bowl from the pan and gradually whisk in the clarified butter until thick. Then whisk in the lemon juice, cayenne pepper and salt.

This sauce is best used as soon as it is made, but will hold for up to 2 hours if kept covered in a warm place, such as over a pan of water.

Béarnaise is French as well, not British, but we have taken it to our hearts. It's one of what they call the 'mother sauces', the basis for others such as 'Choron' and 'Maltaise'. It's closely related to Hollandaise, based on butter and egg yolks, and has as many uses. It's wonderful with any fish dish and with meat (especially steak) and vegetables. In the best kitchens it's made with clarified butter and by hand – but my version is much easier. The secret of this Béarnaise is to make sure that the butter is bubbling when it is added to the egg yolks for the sauce to thicken.

Béarnaise Sauce

SERVES 4

2 tbsp tarragon vinegar

50ml (2fl oz) white wine or water

1 tsp crushed white peppercorns

200g (7oz) unsalted butter

4 free-range egg yolks

2 tbsp chopped fresh tarragon

salt and white pepper, to taste

a squeeze of lemon juice

In a pan, heat the vinegar and wine or water with the peppercorns and bring to the boil. Simmer rapidly until the liquid has reduced by half. Strain out the peppercorns, return the liquid to the pan and bring back to the boil.

In another pan, gently melt the butter. Add the reduced liquid and bring to a rolling boil.

Place the egg yolks in a liquidizer and blend. Then, with the motor running slowly, pour the hot vinegar and butter mixture into the liquidizer in a thin stream through the lid.

Pour the sauce into a bowl and leave for 3 minutes, stirring occasionally. If the sauce has not thickened enough, pour it back into the pan and stir constantly over the lowest possible heat until it thickens.

Add the chopped tarragon and season with the salt, pepper and lemon juice. Serve immediately.

Tartare Sauce

Tartare sauce is a classic accompaniment for any fish – grilled, baked or fried. It's much better if you make it yourself rather than buy it in a jar. In fact, you could make the mayonnaise yourself too, but perhaps that's a culinary step too far!

SERVES 4

200ml (7fl oz) mayonnaise

1 tbsp each of chopped capers and gherkins

1 tbsp each of chopped fresh parsley, tarragon and dill

juice of 1/2 lemon

salt and pepper, to taste

Combine all the ingredients together and season to taste.

Chill in the fridge until ready to use.

Barbecue Sauce

If people knew barbecue sauce was this easy to make, they wouldn't be buying ready-made stuff in bottles. Use as a marinade, a basting sauce *and* a serving sauce.

SERVES 4–6

1 onion, chopped

3 cloves garlic, crushed

2 tbsp olive oil

1 fresh red chilli, deseeded and finely chopped

1 tsp fennel seeds, crushed

55g (2oz) dark brown sugar

50ml (2fl oz) dark soy sauce

300ml (10fl oz) tomato ketchup

salt and pepper, to taste

Fry the onion and garlic in the olive oil with the chilli, fennel seeds and sugar.

Add the soy sauce and ketchup (you could use homemade, *see* page 241), and season with salt and pepper. Bring to the boil and simmer for a few minutes to amalgamate the flavours.

Homemade Salad Cream

I know what you're all thinking. Why should I make my own when I can buy it in a bottle? But like the homemade tomato ketchup on page 241, don't make that decision until you have tried making it – they are *so* much more delicious. If refrigerated, this sauce will keep for a minimum of 1–2 weeks.

MAKES 200–300 ML
(7–10 FL OZ)

1 tbsp plain flour

4 tsp caster sugar

2 tsp mustard powder

a pinch of salt

2 free-range eggs

100ml (3 1/2 fl oz) white wine vinegar

150ml (5fl oz) double cream

a squeeze of lemon juice

Mix together the flour, sugar, mustard and salt in a bowl. Beat in the eggs and white wine vinegar.

Place the bowl over a pan of simmering water – the base of the bowl must not touch the water – and stir until warmed and thickened. This will take only 4–5 minutes. Once 'cooked', remove the bowl from the heat and leave to cool.

Now it is time to add the cream. With this you can be as generous as you wish. A minimum of 100ml (3 1/2 fl oz) will be needed. Finish with a squeeze of lemon juice and the salad cream is ready.

Ketchup

Tomato ketchup is a tradition in British cooking. The homemade stuff tastes great. Give it a go: you may be surprised.

SERVES 4–6

1 tsp ground allspice

250ml (9fl oz) cider vinegar

8 tbsp demerara sugar

1.5kg (3lb 5oz) ripe tomatoes, diced

1 bay leaf

1 tsp English mustard

1 clove garlic, chopped

1 tbsp tomato purée

a dash of Worcestershire sauce

a dash of Tabasco sauce (optional)

Put all the ingredients into a large pan and bring to the boil, stirring all the time. Reduce the heat and simmer for about 40 minutes, stirring occasionally to make sure it doesn't stick to the bottom of the pan.

Blitz in a liquidizer and pass through a fine sieve. Pour into a sterilized bottle (*see* page 368 for sterilizing instructions), and keep in the fridge.

sweet pastries & fritters

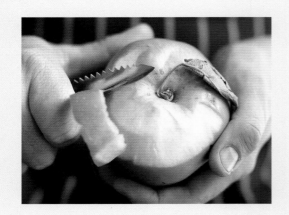

Sweet Shortcrust Pastry
Making pastry may seem like hard work, but it's worth it. It's not just that the flavour and texture are better than that of the shop-bought stuff – but it makes you feel good, too.

MAKES ABOUT
325G (11OZ)

115g (4oz) cold unsalted butter, cubed

225g (8oz) plain white flour

a pinch of salt

2 tbsp caster sugar

2 tbsp ground almonds

1 free-range egg, lightly beaten, plus extra to glaze

Place the butter, flour, salt, sugar and almonds in a food processor. Blitz until you have a fine breadcrumb texture, but do not overwork. Add the egg and 1/2 an egg-shell full of cold water and mix well, using the pulse button until the pastry balls; again, do not overwork.

Turn the pastry out of the processor and knead very gently, just to bring it together. Flatten the dough slightly (this makes it easier to roll when chilled) and wrap in clingfilm, then chill in the fridge for at least 20 minutes – an hour or two would be better.

Grease a 23cm (9in) diameter, 4cm (11/2 in) deep flan ring. Lightly flour the work surface. Roll the pastry out so you end up with a circle about 4cm (11/2 in) larger in diameter than the flan ring. Carefully roll the pastry on to the rolling pin and then unroll it over the flan ring, taking care not stretch the pastry too much.

Immediately ease the pastry into the ring and use your thumb to gently push it into the bottom and corners; do not leave any creases in the outside or air between the pastry and the ring. Leave about 1cm (1/2 in) overhanging the top edge of the ring. Then trim off with a sharp knife or roll a rolling pin over the top to remove the excess. Use your thumb to squeeze up the top edge again (the pastry will shrink back a little during cooking), and pinch with your thumb and forefinger to make the edge more decorative. Using a piece of well-floured leftover pastry, push the bottom of the flan into the corners so it's flush. Chill for 30 minutes. Preheat the oven to 200°C/400°F/gas mark 6.

Cut out a round piece of greaseproof paper 4cm (11/2 in) larger than the flan and place it inside the pastry-lined flan tin. Fill with baking beans and bake blind for 15 minutes, or until the top edge is slightly brown. Remove the paper and beans, turn the oven down to 160°C/325°F/gas mark 3, and cook for a further 10 minutes, until the pastry is set but has taken no colour. Remove from the oven, brush with extra beaten egg (to stop the pastry getting soggy when you add the filling), and then put it back in the oven for 2 minutes to seal. Cool for a little while before adding the filling.

What can I say? Just look at the photograph and give it a go. I promise you won't be disappointed.

Apple Pie and Custard

SERVES 4–6

675g (1 1/2 lb) ready-made shortcrust pastry

700g (1lb 9oz) Bramley apples

100g (3 1/2 oz) caster sugar, plus extra for sprinkling

finely grated rind and juice of 1/2 lemon

25g (1oz) butter, plus extra for greasing

ground cinnamon (optional)

1 free-range egg, beaten

CUSTARD

1 vanilla pod

300ml (10fl oz) milk

300ml (10fl oz) double cream

6 free-range egg yolks

100g (3 1/2 oz) caster sugar

Butter a 22cm (8 1/2 in) pie dish and preheat the oven to 190°C/375°F/gas mark 5.

Roll out two-thirds of the pastry on a floured work surface and carefully line the pie dish.

Peel, quarter and core the apples, then slice them thickly into a bowl to which three-quarters of the sugar and all the lemon juice and rind have been added. Stir gently to mix.

Put the apple slices and sugar into the pastry-lined pie dish. Dot with a little butter and a sprinkling of cinnamon.

Roll out the remaining pastry and put it on top of the apples. Seal and crimp the edges well and then make a small hole in the top to allow the steam to escape.

Make decorations from any pastry trimmings (I like to do a few leaves) and seal them with a little water. Brush with the beaten egg, dredge with the remaining caster sugar and then bake for 35–40 minutes, until the fruit is tender and the top is golden brown.

For the custard, split open the vanilla pod and scrape the seeds out into a heavy-based saucepan. Add the vanilla pod, milk and cream and bring slowly to the boil.

Place the egg yolks and sugar in a bowl and whisk together until they lighten in colour.

Pour the infused milk and cream on to the eggs, whisking well. Return the mixture to the pan. Place the pan over a low heat and cook the custard for about 5 minutes, stirring all the time, until it thickens slightly and coats the back of the spoon. Do not boil or the custard will curdle. Strain through a sieve and serve with the warm apple pie.

This is a great dish! Roughly puréed Bramleys (the king of British apples) form the base, and are topped with slices of Cox's. Custard is poured on the top. Don't rush cooking the custard, as you'll risk it 'souffléing' and so splitting on the surface. If you are unsure, cook the tart for a bit longer and pop it in the fridge to firm the custard before you serve it.

Bramley Apple, Custard and Honey Tart

SERVES 4–6

1 x 23cm (9in) Sweet Shortcrust Pastry case, baked blind (*see* page 245)

FILLING

2 large Bramley apples

caster sugar, to taste

1 large Cox's apple

20g (³/₄ oz) unsalted butter

4 medium free-range egg yolks

2 medium free-range eggs

2 tbsp clear honey

700ml (1¼ pints) double cream

a pinch of saffron strands (optional)

TO SERVE (OPTIONAL)

1 large Cox's apple

icing sugar

a little whipped double cream

Preheat the oven to 160°C/325°F/gas mark 3.

Peel, core and roughly slice the Bramleys. Put them in a pan with a little water, and cook over a medium heat for 5–10 minutes, until soft. Add some sugar to taste and beat to a purée.

Peel and core the Cox's apple, and cut it into neat 5mm (¼in) slices. Fry gently in the unsalted butter until softened and lightly coloured. Place the apple purée in the bottom of the pastry case and overlap the apple slices on top.

In a bowl, beat together the egg yolks, eggs and honey. Place the cream and saffron (if using) in a small pan and bring to the boil. When boiling, whisk the cream into the egg mix, beating all the time. Pour into the pastry case, over the apple, and bake for 20 minutes, until the mixture has set and is golden brown.

If you want to garnish with caramelized apple, peel and core the Cox's apple and cut it into slices, 3cm (1¼ in) thick. Sprinkle with icing sugar and toast under a hot grill until caramelized.

Serve the tart warm or at room temperature with a few pieces of caramelized apple and a dollop of cream on each slice.

This is a twist on a prune and almond tart, but it works better as the plums stew down while the tart is cooking. Use dark plums to give the frangipane a rich colour. Fluff the butter and sugar for the frangipine together well before adding the eggs and flour, as this will create a much lighter filling – and never put the cooked tart in the fridge.

Plum and Almond Tart

SERVES 4–6

butter, for greasing

1 recipe Sweet Shortcrust Pastry (*see* page 245)

plain flour, for dusting

900g (2lb) plums, dark if you can get them

icing sugar

FRANGIPANE

225g (8oz) unsalted butter

225g (8oz) caster sugar

4 free-range eggs, beaten

4 tbsp brandy

115g (4oz) ground almonds

4 tbsp plain flour

TO SERVE

100ml (3 1/2 fl oz) double cream

Cassis to taste (optional) or 4 tbsp ready-made custard (bought or homemade, *see* page 246)

a few blackberries (optional)

Preheat the oven to 200°C/400°F/gas mark 6.

Grease and line a 34cm (13 1/2 in) round fluted or rectangular tart tin. Roll out the pastry on a lightly floured surface, press it into the tin, trim the edges and prick the base lightly with a fork. Cover and chill.

Meanwhile, make the frangipane. Using an electric whisk, beat together the butter and sugar until pale and creamy. Gradually beat in the eggs. Stir in the brandy, almonds and flour. Spread the frangipane evenly over the base of the pastry case.

Remove the stones from the plums and cut into quarters. Gently push the plum quarters vertically into the frangipane.

Place the tart on a baking sheet and bake for 10–15 minutes, or until the pastry is beginning to brown. Reduce the oven temperature to 180°C/350°F/gas mark 4 and continue to bake for 35 minutes.

Remove the tart from the oven and leave to cool slightly, then remove from the tin and dust lightly with icing sugar.

Serve the tart at room temperature. Cut it into wedges and serve it warm with plain, thick double cream, double cream flavoured with Cassis, or custard, and perhaps a few blackberries.

I find this quite hard to cook, as it appears to be cooked long before it is. If you're unsure, turn the oven a bit lower and cook for a while longer or else the nuts will burn.

Pecan Pie

SERVES 4–6

350g (12 oz) pecans (or walnuts)

55g (2 oz) bitter chocolate, grated

1 tsp vanilla extract

2 pinches salt

350ml (12fl oz) good maple syrup

4 large free-range eggs

300g (10 1/2 oz) granulated sugar

115g (4oz) unsalted butter, melted

1 x 23cm (9 in) Sweet Shortcrust Pastry case, baked blind (*see* page 245)

Preheat the oven to 160°C/325°F/gas mark 3.

Place the nuts, grated chocolate, vanilla extract, salt and maple syrup in a bowl. Beat the eggs in a separate bowl, then stir into the nut mixture together with the sugar. Finally add the melted butter and stir well.

Pour into the prepared pastry case and bake for 55–60 minutes, or until set in the middle. Allow to cool completely before cutting.

Bakewell Tart

Bakewell tart and Bakewell pudding are more or less the same, but the original did not contain almonds, and was more like a custard tart. One tip for this is to mix the ingredients well at the start, as this will make the mixture lighter and give a nice texture.

SERVES 6

115g (4oz) caster sugar

55g (2oz) ground almonds

125g (4 1/2 oz) plain flour, plus extra for dusting

100g (3 1/2 oz) butter, finely diced

1 large free-range egg, plus 1 extra free-range egg yolk

finely grated zest of 1 small lemon

a pinch of salt

FILLING

85g (3oz) butter

85g (3oz) caster sugar

2 medium free-range eggs

3 drops almond essence

55g (2oz) fresh white breadcrumbs

85g (3oz) ground almonds

8 tbsp raspberry jam

20g (3/4 oz) flaked almonds

First, make the pastry. Put the sugar, almonds and flour into a food processor, and turn on to full speed for a few seconds. Add the butter and work again until just blended in. The mixture will resemble fine breadcrumbs.

Add the egg and extra yolk, the lemon zest, 2 tsp water and a tiny pinch of salt. Work again until the pastry balls. Wrap in clingfilm and refrigerate.

Preheat the oven to 190ºC/375ºF/gas mark 5.

Roll out the chilled pastry on a flour-dusted surface and use to line a 20cm (8in) loose-bottomed tart tin. If it breaks it can be repaired by pressing with your fingers. Make the shell as even as possible, and ensure that around the edges it is pushed right up to the top, as it will shrink as it bakes. Be careful to press into the bottom edges to eliminate air between the tin and pastry. Chill.

To make the filling, put the butter and sugar in a blender, and blend until light and fluffy. With the machine running on full speed, add the eggs and almond essence until combined to a smooth paste, then fold in the breadcrumbs and ground almonds.

Put the pastry shell on a baking tray, prick the base with a fork and line with foil. Fill with baking beans and bake blind for 10 minutes. Remove the foil and beans, and leave to cool slightly, then spread the base with a layer of raspberry jam. Cover this with the almond filling. Scrape the surface smooth and level, and sprinkle with the flaked almonds.

Return the tart to the oven and bake for 25–30 minutes, until risen and lightly browned.

Yorkshire Curd Tart

My auntie's favourite, and a tart that is famous all over the country. Thought to originate from the 13th century, this is otherwise known as cheesecake. You can make small tarts as well: cook these for slightly less time.

SERVES 4–6

1 x 23cm (9in) Sweet Shortcrust Pastry case, baked blind (*see* page 245)

FILLING

500ml (18fl oz) whipping cream

8 free-range egg yolks

75g (2 ³/₄ oz) caster sugar

1 tsp ground allspice

Preheat the oven to 120°C/250°F/gas mark 1.

To make the filling, put the cream into a saucepan over a medium heat and bring to the boil. Mix the egg yolks with the caster sugar and half the allspice in a bowl. Pour the cream on to the egg mixture, being careful not to let the yolks curdle, then pass through a sieve. Pour into the cooked pastry case.

Sprinkle the curd tart with the remaining allspice and bake in the oven for 23–45 minutes, until the custard is set. Remove from the oven and allow to cool.

Serve at room temperature.

Syrup and bread in pastry…whoever invented this? But whoever you are, what a combination! I feel, though, that you must eat this warm and never place it in the fridge. Serve with double cream, ice cream, whipped cream or with fruit. I'll leave it up to you.

Treacle Tart

SERVES 6–8

butter, for greasing

500g (18oz) ready-made sweet shortcrust pastry

plain flour, for rolling

FILLING

400g (14oz) golden syrup

125g (4 1/2 oz) fresh breadcrumbs

2 free-range eggs, lightly beaten

finely grated zest and juice of 1 lemon

Preheat the oven to 180°C/350°F/gas mark 4, and butter a 35cm (14in) ovenproof tart tin.

Roll out the pastry on a floured surface until very thin and, using the tart tin as a template, cut around the dish, allowing enough to go up the sides of the tin. Place the disc of pastry in the bottom of the dish and up over the sides. Prick the base with a fork, line with foil and fill with baking beans. Bake for 10–12 minutes, until lightly golden. Remove from the oven, and lower the oven temperature to 140°C/275°F/gas mark 1. Remove the foil and beans.

In a bowl, mix together the golden syrup, breadcrumbs, eggs and lemon juice and zest. Once combined, spoon into the pastry case and bake at the reduced temperature for 50–60 minutes.

Trim off the edges of the pastry, and cut the tart into portions. Allow the tart to cool slightly before serving. It is best eaten warm, with a spoonful of whipped cream.

Chocolate and Raspberry Tarts with Fennel

This is on my restaurant menu. It might seem peculiar to put fennel with chocolate, but it's a combination I love. You can use fennel, aniseed or Pernod.

SERVES 4

butter, for greasing

1/2 recipe Sweet Shortcrust Pastry (see page 245)

plain flour, for dusting

FILLING

350g (12oz) bitter chocolate, broken into pieces

4 medium free-range eggs

55g (2oz) caster sugar

75ml (2 1/2 fl oz) double cream

200g (7oz) raspberries

GARNISH

cocoa powder

vanilla ice cream

4 fresh mint sprigs

fennel oil (see below)

Preheat the oven to 190°C/375°F/gas mark 5, and grease eight 7.5cm (3in) plain-edged tart tins.

Roll out the pastry on a lightly floured surface and use to line the tins (see page 245). Prick the bases with a fork, line with foil and fill with baking beans. Bake for about 15–20 minutes. Allow to cool and then keep in the tins. Remove the foil and beans.

For the filling, melt the chocolate carefully in a bowl over simmering water. In another bowl, whisk up the eggs and sugar, then fold in the cream and melted chocolate.

Spoon this mixture into the baked pastry cases and sprinkle with the raspberries. Bake for 10 more minutes, until just lightly cooked.

Serve warm with a dusting of cocoa powder, a scoop of vanilla ice cream, a sprig of fresh mint and some fennel oil drizzled around the edge.

Fennel Oil

I used to make this with a stock syrup and blended fennel through it, but it works better with olive oil.

MAKES 300ML
(10FL OZ)

salt

30g (1 1/4 oz) fresh flat-leaf parsley leaves

1 large fennel bulb, finely chopped

300ml (10fl oz) good olive oil

Bring a pot of salted water to the boil. Place the parsley leaves in a strainer and dip them into the water for 10–15 seconds, keeping the water at a strong boil. Remove the strainer and plunge the blanched parsley into an ice-water bath to chill. Drain the cold parsley and squeeze as dry as possible.

Place all the parsley and chopped fennel in a blender with enough of the oil just to cover. Turn on the blender to medium speed and blend for a minute. Turn the speed to high and continue to blend for 2 minutes.

Pass the finished oil through a fine sieve or a clean tea-towel. Store the oil in the refrigerator or freeze. Use as required.

Chocolate and Marron Glacé Tart

Sugared marrons glacés and roasted fresh chestnuts are a must at Christmas. You might stuff fresh chestnuts inside your turkey, but you could try the sugared ones in this quick and simple dessert. This is one of those puds that gets a little better after a day in the fridge.

SERVES 8

75ml (2 1/2 fl oz) dark rum

55g (2oz) caster sugar

200g (7oz) marrons glacés, chopped

400g (14oz) good-quality chocolate cake

375g (13oz) good dark chocolate, broken into pieces

560ml (20 1/2 fl oz) double cream

good cocoa powder

100ml (3 1/2 fl oz) pouring cream or double cream, semi-whipped

Heat the rum and 50ml (2fl oz) water in a pan with the sugar. When hot, remove the pan from the heat. Allow to cool, then add the chopped marrons glacés.

Slice the chocolate cake and use it to line the base of a 25cm (10in) flan tin. Scatter an even layer of the rum and marron glacés mixture over the top, using up all the mixture.

Melt the chocolate in a bowl over a pan of hot water. Allow to cool slightly before adding the cream. The mixture should go smooth and glossy. Spoon this over the surface of the marrons and cake.

Place the tart in the fridge to set for a few hours or overnight before serving.

Dust with cocoa powder, then serve sliced with a drizzle of pouring cream or a spoonful of the semi-whipped cream on the side.

Bitter Chocolate Tart

You need the best chocolate for pastries, but don't listen to chefs who tell you to use over 70 per cent cocoa solids. The maximum you need is 70 per cent, otherwise you can't eat the stuff. Serve this tart warm and never refrigerate it once cooked. To make it even more special, make a chocolate pastry case: substitute 30g (1¼oz) of the flour with cocoa powder.

SERVES 6–8

200g (7oz) bitter chocolate, 70 per cent cocoa solids (no more)

100g (3½ oz) milk chocolate

2 large free-range eggs, plus 2 large free-range egg yolks, at room temperature

60g (2¼ oz) caster sugar

150g (5½ oz) unsalted butter, melted

1 x 23cm (9in) plain or chocolate Sweet Shortcrust Pastry case, baked blind (*see* page 245)

icing sugar

COFFEE BEAN SYRUP

2 tbsp liquid glucose

10 fresh coffee beans, crushed

200g (7oz) caster sugar

juice of ½ lemon

Preheat the oven to 220°C/425°F/gas mark 7.

Break the two chocolates into pieces, and melt together in a heatproof bowl over a pan of gently simmering water.

Place the eggs, egg yolks and sugar in the bowl of a food mixer and whisk at high speed until very thick. Remove the bowl from the machine and carefully stir in the melted chocolate, taking care not to knock too much air out of the eggs. Fold in the melted butter, again very carefully.

Place the blind-baked flan case on a baking sheet, pour the chocolate mixture into the pastry shell, and bake for 7–8 minutes, or until just set – do not let the edges soufflé up. Remove from the oven and leave to cool on a wire rack.

Meanwhile, make the coffee bean syrup. Place 225ml (8fl oz) cold water, the glucose, coffee beans and sugar in a pan and bring to the boil. Remove from the heat, cover and allow to cool. Finally, add lemon juice to taste to the cooled syrup, then strain to remove the coffee beans.

Eat the tart at room temperature, cut into wedges, dusted heavily with icing sugar, accompanied by the coffee syrup.

Quick Chocolate Tart

As you can see by the number of chocolate tarts I've included in this book, it's one of my favourite things to eat! This one is quite quick to prepare, but looks and tastes no less special because of that.

SERVES 6–8

PASTRY

250g (9oz) unsalted butter, softened, plus extra for greasing

40g (1 1/2 oz) icing sugar

1 medium free-range egg

500g (1lb 2oz) plain flour, sifted

CHOCOLATE FILLING

350ml (12fl oz) double cream

150ml (5fl oz) full-fat milk

400g (14oz) dark chocolate (70 per cent cocoa solids), broken into pieces

3 medium free-range eggs, beaten

Preheat the oven to 180°C/350°F/gas mark 4. Place a baking sheet on the middle shelf in the oven.

Cream the butter and sugar in a food mixer, or in a bowl with a wooden spoon, until pale and fluffy, then add the egg. Turn the food mixer to its lowest setting and add the plain flour. Mix until the pastry comes together. Wrap in clingfilm and chill for at least 30 minutes.

Grease a 20cm (8in) tart ring or loose-bottomed tart tin. Roll out the pastry into a circle 3mm (1/8 in) thick and about 5cm (2in) bigger than the tart ring. Line the tart ring with the pastry, pressing it down gently and leaving a 2.5cm (1in) overhang.

Prick the base with a fork, line with foil and fill with baking beans. Bake for 20 minutes, or until starting to brown. Remove and trim the overhanging pastry level with the top of the ring, using a sharp, heavy knife. Remove the foil and beans.

Turn the oven down to 120°C/250°F/gas mark 1/2. To make the filling, in a saucepan heat the cream and milk until trembling, just under boiling point. Take off the heat. Add the chocolate to the cream and milk and stir until fully blended, then add the beaten eggs and mix again.

Pour the chocolate mixture into the tart case and bake for about 1 hour. The tart is done when it is still a bit wobbly in the middle. Leave to set for at least 45 minutes before serving.

I know you're going to look at this mincemeat recipe with horror because of the raw mince I've used in it. But this is the traditional way of making mincemeat. Most bought mincemeat doesn't have meat in it, of course, but I thought it would be interesting to explore. You can easily omit the steak if you want to. The recipe makes far more than you need for the pies, so perhaps use some in the Real Christmas Bread on page 365.

Traditional Mince Pies

MAKES 24

1 recipe Sweet Shortcrust Pastry (*see* page 245)

butter and flour, for greasing and dusting

milk and icing sugar, for finishing

TRADITIONAL MINCEMEAT

225g (8oz) seedless raisins

350g (12oz) currants

175g (6oz) minced rump steak

350g (12oz) beef suet, chopped

225g (8oz) dark brown sugar

15g (¹/2 oz) candied citron peel, chopped

15g (¹/2 oz) candied lemon peel, chopped

15g (¹/2 oz) candied orange peel, chopped

¹/4 small nutmeg, grated

finely grated zest and juice of ¹/2 lemon

350g (12 oz) peeled and cored apples, finely chopped

75ml (2 ¹/2 fl oz) brandy

Make the mincemeat at least two weeks in advance of making the mince pies. Mix all the ingredients together in the order given, pouring in the brandy when everything else is well mixed together. Press closely into sterilized jars to exclude the air (*see* page 368 for sterilizing instructions). Cover and leave for at least a fortnight. You'll need about 450g (1lb) for the mince pies.

Grease two 12-hole patty tins. Have ready a 7.5cm (3 in) pastry cutter and a 6cm (2 ¹/2 in) pastry cutter, either plain or fluted. Preheat the oven to 200°C/400°F/gas mark 6.

Roll out just over half of the pastry on a lightly floured board to about 3mm (¹/8 in) thick. Cut out 24 larger circles, gathering up the scraps and re-rolling if necessary. Cut the remaining pastry into 24 circles, using the smaller cutter.

Line the patty tins with the larger circles, and then fill, not quite to the top, with the mincemeat. Dampen the edges of the pastry with water, and press on the smaller circles. Crimp to seal, and make a couple of holes in the top with scissors. Brush with milk.

Bake near the top of the oven for 25–30 minutes, until golden brown. Cool on a wire rack, and dust the tops with icing sugar.

Chocolate Profiteroles

Chocolate eclairs and profiteroles were my downfall, causing me to get to nearly 20 stone while I was working as a pastry chef in a hotel. I used to eat about 20 of them before 11 in the morning. What a pig I was!

MAKES ABOUT 40

CHOUX PASTRY

200ml (7fl oz) cold water

4 tsp caster sugar

85g (3oz) unsalted butter

115g (4oz) plain flour

a pinch of salt

4 medium free-range eggs, beaten

vegetable oil, for greasing

CREAM FILLING

600ml (1 pint) double cream

CHOCOLATE SAUCE

175g (6oz) good-quality plain chocolate, broken into pieces

5 tbsp water

15g (½ oz) unsalted butter

Preheat the oven to 200°C/400°F/gas mark 6. To make the choux pastry, place the water, sugar and butter in a large saucepan. Place over a low heat to melt the butter. Increase the heat and add the flour and salt all in one go. Remove from the heat and quickly beat the mixture vigorously with a wooden spoon until a smooth paste is formed, stirring continuously to dry out the paste. Once the paste curls away from the side of the pan, transfer the mixture to a large bowl and leave to cool for 10–15 minutes.

Beat in the eggs, a little at a time, until the paste is smooth and glossy. Continue adding the eggs until you have a soft dropping consistency. It may not be necessary to add all the eggs. The mixture will be shiny and smooth, and will fall from a spoon if it is given a sharp jerk.

Lightly oil a large baking tray. Dip a teaspoon into some warm water and spoon out 1 tsp of the profiterole mixture. Rub the top of the mixture with a wet finger and spoon on to the baking tray. This ensures a crisper topping. Cover the whole of the tray with dollops of pastry, working as swiftly as you can. Place the tray in the oven and, before closing the door, throw a little water into the bottom of the oven. Shut the door quickly. This will make more steam in the oven and make the choux pastry rise better. (Top pastry chef tip there!)

Bake for 25–30 minutes, until golden brown. Remove from the oven and prick the base of each profiterole. Place on to the baking tray with the hole facing upwards and return to the oven for 5 minutes. The warm air from the oven helps to dry the middle of the profiteroles.

To prepare the filling, lightly whip the cream until soft peaks form. Do not overwhip. When the profiteroles are cold, use a piping bag with a plain nozzle to pipe the cream into the holes of the profiteroles.

To make the sauce, melt the chocolate with the water and butter in a bowl over a pan of boiling water. Stir without boiling until smooth and shiny. Arrange the buns on a dish and pour over the hot sauce. Eat hot or cold.

Baby Coffee Eclairs
This is the kind of party food that always impresses: delicious éclairs packed with thick pastry cream.

MAKES ABOUT
40–50 ECLAIRS

butter, for greasing

**1 quantity choux pastry
(*see* page 263)**

1 free-range egg, beaten

COFFEE PASTRY CREAM

300ml (10fl oz) whole milk

10g (1/4 oz) freshly ground coffee

4 large free-range egg yolks

**60g (2 1/4 oz) unrefined
caster sugar**

**60g (2 1/4 oz) plain white
flour, sifted**

**300ml (10fl oz) double cream,
lightly whipped**

ICING

5 tsp instant coffee

3 tbsp boiling water

**about 250g (9oz) fondant
icing sugar**

Preheat the oven to 220°C/425°F/gas mark 7. Lightly grease two baking sheets. Spoon the choux pastry into a large piping bag fitted with a 1.5cm (5/8in) nozzle. Pipe the pastry on the baking sheets into 4cm (13/4in) long éclairs. Brush with beaten egg and refine the shape at the same time. Bake for 15–20 minutes, or until well risen and golden.

Once the éclairs are fully formed and golden, turn the oven down to 160°C/325°F/gas mark 3 and cook the éclairs for a further 5–10 minutes to dry them out until they are very crisp. The crisper they are, the easier they are to pipe and ice. Remove from the oven and cool completely – don't store them in an airtight container as this makes the pastry soggy.

Meanwhile, make the coffee pastry cream: bring the milk and ground coffee to the boil in a pan, stirring all the time. Remove from the heat and leave to infuse for 10 minutes.

Meanwhile, whisk the egg yolks and sugar together. Add the flour and mix well. Strain the milk and coffee mixture through a fine sieve on to the egg and sugar mixture and stir well. Return to the pan and bring to the boil slowly, stirring all the time in a figure of eight so it doesn't catch. Once boiling, remove from the heat and pour into a clean bowl. Cover with clingfilm and leave to cool.

Whisk the cooled coffee pastry cream to loosen and break it down, then add the whipped cream and whisk together. Spoon into a piping bag fitted with a 5mm (1/4 in) nozzle. Using a little knife, make small incisions in the base of each éclair large enough to fit the nozzle. Pipe the coffee cream into the éclairs one by one, until they feel heavy and full.

For the icing, mix together the instant coffee and boiling water, then gradually add enough fondant icing sugar to make an icing of coating consistency. Dip the éclairs into the icing one at a time and smooth off with your finger. Leave to set for 15 minutes and then serve piled high.

Choux Pastry

Don't be put off making choux pastry by rumours of it being difficult. It's not that hard – honest – and well worth it!

MAKES ENOUGH FOR
ABOUT 50 BABY ECLAIRS

115g (4oz) unsalted butter, cubed

a pinch of sugar

a pinch of salt

140g (5oz) plain white flour, sifted

3–4 free-range eggs, beaten

Bring the butter and 300ml (1/2 pint) of cold water to the boil in a pan. Add the sugar and salt, and then immediately add the flour and beat well until the mixture comes away from the pan. Allow to cool completely (more egg is absorbed when the mixture is cold).

Gradually add 3 of the beaten eggs to the cooled pastry, a little at a time (it's best to do this in a food mixer or food processor) and then beat small amounts of the last egg into the mixture until you get the right consistency. The reason for only adding 3 eggs at the start is that the mixture needs to be quite tight; if you add too much egg, the end product will not rise correctly and, of course, you can always add the extra egg but you can't take it out. The finished paste should just fall off the paddle on the machine. It's best to use choux dough straight away, but it will keep for a couple of days in the fridge.

Puff Pastry Hearts

Such a simple idea, this, using ready-made puff pastry. Don't refrigerate the pastry once cooked as it will become too hard. Glazing it in this way with icing sugar requires a very hot oven.

MAKES 15–20 HEARTS

300g (10 1/2 oz) ready-rolled puff pastry

plain flour, for dusting

8 tbsp caster sugar

1 tbsp ground cinnamon

150ml (5fl oz) double cream

85g (3oz) raspberry or strawberry jam

If necessary, roll out the pastry on a floured work surface until it is about 5mm (1/4 in) thick. You should have a rectangle of about 30 x 20cm (12 x 8 in).

Mix the caster sugar and cinnamon together in a bowl. Brush the pastry with some water, then sprinkle some of the spiced sugar liberally over the top. Fold each long side over to meet in the middle.

Brush the top with water again, then sprinkle again with some of the spiced sugar, then repeat the above, folding the long sides over to meet in the middle. Brush with water and sprinkle with the sugar again, and fold over. You should have eight layers. Place in the fridge to chill.

Meanwhile, preheat the oven to 200°C/400°F/gas mark 6. Using a sharp knife, cut the pastry into strips about 5mm (1/4 in) wide and place on an oven tray with the cut-side up. Bake for 10–15 minutes to open to a heart shape and take on a golden brown colour. Remove the hearts from the oven and allow to cool completely.

While cooling, whip up the double cream until stiff, and place in a piping bag with a plain or starred nozzle. Take one of the pastries and add a spoon of the jam in the middle. Pipe the double cream on top. Add another piece of pastry on top – at a slant so you can see the filling inside – and serve.

Jam or Marmalade Roly Poly

You may have been put off these types of homely desserts by those served at school. But try this one or, better still, serve it at a smart dinner party, and everyone will love it. Let's face it, what could be better?

SERVES 4–6

225g (8oz) self-raising flour

1 tsp baking powder

a pinch of salt

finely grated zest of 1 lemon or orange

140g (5oz) vegetarian or beef suet, chopped

100–150ml (3 1/2 – 5fl oz) milk, plus extra for brushing

140–175g (5–6oz) orange marmalade or raspberry jam

Sift together the flour, baking powder and salt into a bowl. Add the lemon or orange zest, and suet, and rub the mixture gently with your fingertips until it resembles breadcrumbs. Add the milk a little at a time, and squeeze with your hands until a soft texture is formed. Wrap in clingfilm and allow to rest in the fridge for 20–30 minutes.

Roll the dough into a rectangle approximately 35 x 25cm (14 x 10in). Spread the marmalade or jam on the dough, leaving a border of 1cm (1/2 in) clear. Brush the border with extra milk or water.

Roll the dough from the shorter edge and pinch at either end to retain all of the marmalade or jam. Wrap the roly poly loosely in greaseproof paper, followed by loose foil, and tie with string at either end.

Steam the pudding in a steamer for 2 hours, topping up with hot water, if necessary, during cooking. Once cooked, unwrap, slice and serve (it's great with custard or ice cream).

Apple Fritters

Whichever way you do fritters, they are always a winner.

SERVES 6

6 large Cox's Orange Pippins, or other firm eating apples

caster sugar, to taste

a good dash of brandy

vegetable oil, for deep-frying

vanilla ice cream, to serve

BATTER

115g (4oz) plain flour

1 free-range egg plus 1 free-range egg yolk

1 tbsp oil or clarified butter

up to 300ml (10fl oz) milk

a pinch of saffron strands (optional)

Peel, core and slice the apples thickly. Put them into a dish, sprinkle with sugar and pour on the brandy. Leave them to one side for an hour or so, turning occasionally in the liquid.

Meanwhile, for the batter, mix the flour, egg, egg yolk and oil or clarified butter. Beat in about half the milk. Pour 3 tbsp of almost boiling water over the saffron, if using, and leave to steep for a little while. When the water is a good crocus yellow, strain it into the batter. Add more milk if the batter is too thick.

Drain the apple slices well and coat them with the batter. Heat the vegetable oil in a deep-fryer to 180°C/350°F. Dip the coated apple slices into the batter, and fry them in hot oil until golden brown. Drain on kitchen paper and serve sprinkled with sugar, with a scoop of vanilla ice cream.

fruit puds

This can also be made as individual trifles. Use four medium ramekins, and just make the trifles in miniature, cutting the Swiss roll slices smaller, if necessary.

White Chocolate and Raspberry Trifle

SERVES 4

175g (6oz) white chocolate

2 medium free-range egg yolks

25g (1oz) caster sugar

300ml (10fl oz) milk

700ml (1¼ pints) double cream

8 x 4cm (1½ in) slices Swiss roll (bought or homemade)

2 tbsp Kirsch

600g (1lb 5oz) raspberries

4 fresh mint sprigs

Put a 55g (2oz) piece of white chocolate in the fridge – this will make it easier to grate later. Break the remainder into small pieces.

Cream the egg yolks and caster sugar together in a large bowl. Whisk for about 2–3 minutes, until the mixture is pale, thick and creamy and leaves a trail.

Pour the milk and 175ml (6fl oz) of the cream into a small, heavy-based saucepan and bring to the boil. Pour this on to the egg mixture, whisking all the time, then pour it back into the pan and place over a moderate heat. Stir the mixture with a wooden spoon until it starts to thicken and coats the back of the spoon. Add the broken-up pieces of chocolate and stir in until completely incorporated. Remove the pan from the heat and allow to cool slightly. Cover the custard with clingfilm to stop a skin forming.

Place half the Swiss roll slices in a large glass bowl and sprinkle with half the Kirsch. Scatter over a third of the raspberries, then repeat. Pour the white chocolate custard over the top and leave to set in the fridge.

To serve, whip the remaining double cream. Top the custard with the whipped cream, scatter over the remaining raspberries, grate over the chilled white chocolate and place the mint sprigs on top.

Sherry Trifle with Raspberries

Trifles are ancient – they go back to medieval times. Some contained jelly and some used syllabub as a topping instead of cream. You can also use sponge fingers or macaroons instead of the sponge cake.

SERVES 6

70g (2½ oz) raspberry jam

225g (8oz) plain sponge cake, sliced

150ml (5fl oz) sherry

200g (7oz) fresh raspberries

Custard made with 600ml (1 pint) milk (double the quantity on page 246)

finely grated zest of 2 oranges

400ml (14fl oz) double cream

25g (1oz) flaked almonds, toasted

Spread the jam over the slices of sponge cake and place in the bottom of a large glass dish, or divide evenly among six glasses or glass dishes.

Pour the sherry over the cake and sprinkle the fresh raspberries evenly over the top.

When you have made the custard, pass it through a sieve, add the orange zest and allow to cool. Pour over the sponge and fruit.

Whip the double cream and either pipe it over the top of the trifle or, if you are like my mother, whose piping bag is collecting dust at the back of a drawer in the kitchen, spread it on and spike it with a fork.

Cover and refrigerate overnight, and sprinkle with the toasted flaked almonds just before serving.

Raspberry Pavlova

Named after a ballerina, this is a national dish in both New Zealand and Australia, but we love it here as our own. I have made the pavlova in a slightly different way, in what is called boiled or Italian meringue; I think this is the best way to make a pavlova. My top tip with a pavlova is to fill it full of seasonal fruit.

SERVES 4

280g (10oz) caster sugar

5 free-range egg whites

TO SERVE

100g (3 1/2 oz) white chocolate, melted

250ml (9fl oz) double cream, whipped

350g (12 oz) fresh raspberries

icing sugar, for dusting

4 mint sprigs, to garnish

Preheat the oven to 120°C/250°F/gas mark 1/2 , and cover a large tray with nonstick baking parchment. In a pan, boil 100ml (3 1/2 fl oz) water and the sugar to the soft ball stage (115°C/239°F). Remove from the heat.

Whisk up the egg whites in a food mixer bowl, and pour in the liquid sugar while still beating. Keep on beating until the mixture is cool. Spoon the mixture on to the tray, and spread it out into four circles. Using a spoon, mould the centres into a pavlova shape, with an indentation. Place the tray in the oven and cook for 3–4 hours, or overnight.

Remove from the oven, cool, then arrange on a plate. Spread the melted white chocolate across the top of each meringue (this will stop the cream softening it). Leave to set.

Fill the indentation with double cream, top with raspberries, a little dusting of icing sugar and a sprig of mint, and serve.

Eton Mess

A dessert that is said to originate at Eton College, and which is a mixture of fruit, cream and crushed meringue. My variation contains a little balsamic vinegar to boost the flavour of the fruit. It's an economical dish, particularly if you get the meringues from discount shelves at a supermarket – where they come ready crushed – and strawberries that are marked down in price because they are nearly past their best.

SERVES 4

500g (1lb 2oz) strawberries

400ml (14fl oz) double cream

3 x 7.5cm (3in) meringue nests, crushed into small chunks

1 tbsp balsamic vinegar

Grand Marnier (optional)

Hull the strawberries (remove the green tops) and purée half in a blender. Chop the other half into small dice.

Whip the double cream until stiff, and fold in the strawberry purée and crushed meringue. Mix the chopped strawberries in the vinegar and fold them in as well. Stir in a tbsp or so of Grand Marnier to add a bit of orangey spice, if you like.

Divide between cold wine glasses and serve, or keep in the fridge until needed (but for no longer than a couple of hours).

Strawberry and Vanilla Soft Iced Terrine

This is based on a *semifreddo*. You can use most soft fruits that are in season, and nougat or meringue added to the mixture is also really nice. A simple, great-tasting dessert that you can make, keep in the freezer and take a slice of whenever you fancy.

SERVES 4–6

4 free-range eggs, separated

4 tbsp caster sugar

1 vanilla pod, split

400g (14oz) mascarpone cheese

200g (7oz) strawberries, diced

olive oil

STRAWBERRY SAUCE

300g (10 1/2 oz) strawberries, diced

50ml (2fl oz) water

2 tbsp icing sugar

STRAWBERRY COMPOTE

115g (4oz) strawberries, diced

50ml (2fl oz) strawberry sauce (*see* above)

4 fresh mint leaves, finely chopped

TO GARNISH

2 tbsp caster sugar

1 tsp ground cinnamon

4 small doughnuts (the mini supermarket ones are fine)

4 sprigs fresh mint

Put the egg yolks in one bowl, and the whites in another. Add the sugar to the egg yolks, along with the seeds from the vanilla pod, and whisk until very light and frothy. Add the mascarpone and keep mixing.

Whip up the egg whites to stiff peaks, then fold them into the mascarpone mixture carefully, along with the strawberries.

Grease a 450g (1lb) loaf tin with olive oil, then line with clingfilm. Pour the mixture into the mould, and freeze until set, overnight if possible.

For the strawberry sauce, blend all the ingredients together, then pass them through a sieve. For the strawberry compote, mix all the ingredients together.

Mix the caster sugar and cinnamon powder together in a bowl, and add the doughnuts one at a time to coat them.

Tip the iced terrine from the tin and slice. Place a slice on each plate, with a doughnut alongside. Put a little strawberry compote in the doughnut hole, garnish with a sprig of fresh mint and pour around some of the remaining strawberry sauce.

Summer Fruit Pudding

This is another classic pud, but most people are put off making it as they think it needs to be kept in the fridge for a fortnight with a brick on the top. This alternative recipe is a tribute to my mother. It can be eaten straightaway.

SERVES 4–6

1/2 punnet each of strawberries (hulled), blackberries and redcurrants

400g (14oz) mixed frozen fruit, defrosted

approx. 125g (4 1/2 oz) caster sugar

vegetable oil, for greasing

15 slices white bread

Quarter half of the fresh strawberries and add to three-quarters of the frozen fruit. Add 50g (1 3/4 oz) caster sugar. Place the rest of the frozen fruit in the blender and purée for the sauce. Add more sugar to taste.

Line four to six small moulds with a little oil and then with clingfilm. Remove the crusts from the bread. Cut a bread circle for the base, slices for the sides and a circle for the top, dipping the bread in the fruit purée sauce on one side before placing it, purée-side out, in the mould.

Fill the centre with the strawberry mixture, blackberries and redcurrants, and press well. Top with bread. Remove each pudding from the mould and place on a plate. Remove the clingfilm. Spoon over the fruit purée sauce and garnish with the remaining strawberries.

Spun Sugar

Sugar work was probably my trademark on *Ready Steady Cook*. It looks really impressive.

SERVES 4–6

200g (7oz) caster sugar

In a very clean pan heat the sugar until it turns a deep brown and becomes a caramel. Cool slightly.

Using a clean small metal spoon and a knife-sharpening steel, dip the spoon into the caramel and lift it out again. Move backwards and forwards over the steel until a candyfloss-type texture is achieved.

Place the spun sugar on top of the dessert you wish to decorate in a tall pile.

Gooseberry Fool

In my garden these are one of the first fruits of the spring, but the British seem to be the only people to embrace this fantastic fruit. Other than with mackerel, I feel the gooseberry should just be used for puddings and puddings alone. It is good in a pie and in a fool, or it can be simply served with vanilla ice cream.

SERVES 6–8

55g (2oz) butter

500g (1lb 2oz) young green gooseberries, topped and tailed

caster sugar, to taste

300ml (10fl oz) double cream, or half each single and double cream

juice and finely grated zest of 1 orange

Melt the butter in a large pan, add the gooseberries, cover and leave to cook gently for about 5 minutes. When the fruit looks yellow and softened, remove the pan from the heat and crush the fruit with a wooden spoon, then a fork. Do not try to produce too smooth a purée by sieving or liquidizing the gooseberries; they should be more of a mash. Sweeten with sugar to taste. Allow to cool.

Whip the cream(s) until you have half-whipped but soft peaks, and fold in the cooled fruit, orange juice and most of the zest. Taste and add more sugar if necessary, but do not make the fool too sweet.

Serve lightly chilled, sprinkled with the remaining orange zest, and accompanied by almond biscuits or shortbread.

Rhubarb Fool with Toasted Oatmeal

Yorkshire is fab for a lot of foodie things, but in the area of Bradford, Leeds and Wakefield the most famous ingredient is rhubarb. These three cities form the area of the 'Rhubarb Triangle', which is where the best rhubarb in England, and indeed the world, comes from.

SERVES 4

500g (1lb 2oz) forced rhubarb

4 tbsp caster sugar

3 free-range egg whites

250ml (9fl oz) double cream

juice and finely grated zest of 2 oranges

TO SERVE

55g (2oz) toasted cracked oatmeal

4 strawberries, hulled

4 sprigs fresh mint

Preheat the oven to 200ºC/400ºF/gas mark 6. First, wash and cut the stems of rhubarb into 5cm (2in) pieces. Place in an ovenproof dish and sprinkle with the sugar and 4 tbsp water. Bake for about 20 minutes, until soft. Remove from the oven and allow to cool.

Meanwhile, whip up the egg whites and cream – separately – to soft peaks. Fold the rhubarb into the cream, together with the orange juice and zest, then fold in the whipped egg whites.

Spoon the mixture into four glasses and chill, before serving each one topped with the toasted oatmeal, a strawberry and a sprig of mint.

Baked Bananas with Toffee Sauce

Bananas and rosemary are like pineapple and black pepper, pears and saffron, and apples and tarragon: a weird combination, but one that is literally made in heaven.

SERVES 4

4 large bananas

4 sprigs fresh rosemary

TOFFEE SAUCE

85g (3oz) butter

600ml (1 pint) double cream

85g (3oz) dark brown sugar

2 tbsp golden syrup

2 tbsp black treacle

TO SERVE

600ml (1 pint) vanilla ice cream

Preheat the oven to 200°C/400°F/gas mark 6.

Do not peel the bananas. Using a sharp knife, make a slit in the top of each banana and insert a sprig of rosemary. Place the bananas on a baking tray and bake in the oven for about 10 minutes until they are brown in colour and soft inside.

While the bananas are cooking, put the butter, cream, sugar, golden syrup and treacle into a pan, bring to the boil and keep warm.

Remove the bananas from the oven and cut lengthways, skin and all. Place on plates, pour the sauce over and spoon lots of vanilla ice cream on the side!

Poached Pears with Cinnamon and Goat's Milk Sauce

The more you cook the sauce in this recipe, the better it is (it should be a dark caramel colour). Cook it in a large pan because when you add the baking powder it will boil all over the place.

SERVES 4

1 vanilla pod, split in half lengthways

200g (7oz) caster sugar

4 Comice pears

juice and finely grated zest of 1 lemon

1 x 200g tub good vanilla ice cream

SAUCE

600ml (1 pint) goat's milk

200g (7oz) caster sugar

50ml (2fl oz) golden syrup

1 cinnamon stick

1 tsp baking powder

Start the sauce by putting the milk, sugar and golden syrup in a pan. Bring to the boil. Crumble the cinnamon stick into the milk and add the baking powder. Take the pan off the heat and stir well as the mix will rise quickly. Continue to whisk the mixture until it stops rising.

Place the sauce on the heat again and bring back to the boil, whisking all the time. Turn down the heat and simmer for about 45 minutes, stirring from time to time to prevent the mixture from burning. When the sauce is ready it should be a caramel colour. Burnt or black is no good. Strain out the cinnamon.

Meanwhile, place the vanilla pod in a pan with the sugar. Peel the pears, leaving the stalks on, and use the peeler to remove the core from the bottom of the pears. Place in the pan with the sugar and vanilla, and cover with hot water. Pour in the lemon juice and zest, and cover. Bring to the boil with the lid on. Turn down the heat and simmer for 20–30 minutes, until the pears are cooked, testing them with a knife.

Remove the pears from the pan and drain for a minute on kitchen paper. Using a sharp knife, fan the pears by cutting five slits in each of them. Place the pears on serving plates, pour the hot sauce over the top and serve with vanilla ice cream.

The original Pêche Melba was created by the great Savoy chef, Escoffier, for Dame Nellie Melba. I have made a few changes, for a much simpler version.

Peach Melba

SERVES 2

1 small can peach halves

2 tbsp apricot coulis

2 brandy snap baskets

2 scoops vanilla ice cream

4 tbsp raspberry coulis

25g (1oz) fresh raspberries

a sprig of mint

2 chocolate cigarette curls

Drain the peaches. Pour 1 tbsp apricot coulis on to the centre of each of two plates and add a brandy snap basket to each, pressing it down to secure it in place. Top with a scoop of ice cream and a peach half.

Pour 2 tbsp raspberry coulis around each peach half. Garnish with fresh raspberries, mint and a chocolate curl.

These are like crumpets, but easier and quicker to make. They will freeze well, but must be layered between sheets of greaseproof paper or else they'll all stick together. Warm them up on a tray in a low oven.

Risen Pancakes with Fresh Fruit and Maple Syrup

SERVES 8

175g (6oz) self-raising flour

1 tbsp baking powder

100g (3 1/2 oz) caster sugar

2 medium free-range eggs, beaten

275ml (9 1/2 fl oz) milk

unsalted butter

TO SERVE

200g (7oz) mixed fresh fruit (strawberries, raspberries, and blueberries)

100ml (3 1/2 fl oz) maple syrup

To make the pancakes, sift the flour into a bowl with the baking powder and caster sugar. Add the eggs and milk and whisk together, but be careful not to over-mix.

Heat a little butter in a nonstick pan, then add 2 tbsp of batter for each pancake. Once golden brown, turn over and cook on the other side, about 2 minutes in all. Repeat, using a little more butter, until you have used all the batter.

Serve the pancakes with the fresh fruit on top. Drizzle with maple syrup.

While filming, I visited the famous 'Rhubarb Triangle', which is located between Leeds, Wakefield and Bradford. It is well worth a visit, as you can see rhubarb growing in forcing sheds. The plants grow in complete darkness for about six to eight weeks, and you can actually hear the rhubarb growing; it sounds like two wellies rubbing together. Harvesting is the best bit: it is done, by candlelight, by hand to give the stalks their unique colour and flavour. Sadly, forced rhubarb production has declined, as it is so labour-intensive and expensive. But if you see it growing and taste it, you will be a rhubarb convert for life.

Rhubarb and Ginger Crumble

SERVES 6

10 sticks young forced rhubarb

4 tbsp water

115g (4oz) caster sugar

3 tbsp stem ginger in syrup, chopped

CRUMBLE

100g (3 1/2 oz) butter, softened

100g (3 1/2 oz) demerara sugar

175–200g (6–7oz) plain flour

Preheat the oven to 180°C/350°F/gas mark 4.

Cut the rhubarb into 5cm (2in) slices and place on a baking tray. Sprinkle with the water and caster sugar and roast for 10 minutes.

Once the rhubarb is cooked, remove it from the oven and sprinkle the ginger over it. Mix together and place in an ovenproof dish about 3–4cm (1 1/4 –1 1/2 in) deep.

In a separate bowl, mix the butter and demerara sugar together until the mixture resembles breadcrumbs. Then mix in the flour to make the crumble.

Sprinkle the crumble over the rhubarb and bake for 10 minutes. Remove and allow to cool slightly before serving with ice cream or double cream.

Apple Charlotte

This is a classic that never fails to impress. It has to be made with Bramley apples. If you don't want to use apples, try rhubarb or a mix of apples and rhubarb. You could make it in one large dish (when it would take 30–40 minutes to cook) or four small ones, as here. Chuck custard, double cream or ice cream on it and dive in.

SERVES 4

1kg (2 1/4 lb) Bramley apples

juice of 1 lemon

175g (6oz) unsalted butter

125g (4 1/2 oz) caster sugar

4 tbsp smooth apricot jam

10 thin slices white bread, crusts removed

Preheat the oven to 180°C/350°F/gas mark 4.

Peel, core and slice the apples, place them in a bowl and pour over the lemon juice.

In a large pan, melt 25g (1oz) of the butter, then add the sugar, apples and any lemon juice. Put the lid on and cook over a gentle heat for about 10 minutes, stirring occasionally.

Remove the lid and cook for a further 5–10 minutes, until you have a smooth purée. Add the apricot jam and allow to cool.

Meanwhile, melt the remaining butter. Cut the slices of bread in half, and then cut each half into four slices to get small fingers. Dip each piece of bread into the melted butter and use to line four small dariole moulds about 6cm (2 1/2 in) wide. Reserve some slices, dipped in butter, for lids.

Once the moulds are lined, spoon in the apple purée and top with the remaining bread slices. Bake for 15 minutes, or until golden on top.

Remove from the oven and allow to cool slightly. Carefully turn out and serve immediately.

Warm Blackberries with Cheat's Brown Bread Ice Cream

When in season, blackberries are one of my favourite foods. I like them best with nothing much done to them – as here. brown bread ice cream is traditional (well, since Victorian times), but this is the quick, 'cheat's' way to make it.

SERVES 4

500g (1lb 2oz) fresh blackberries

1 1/2 tbsp caster sugar

sprigs of fresh mint

ICE CREAM

2 slices brown bread

150ml (5fl oz) vanilla ice cream

Preheat the oven to 200°C/400°F/gas mark 6. Place the sliced bread in a blender and reduce to crumbs, then place on an oven tray and bake for 10 minutes. Allow to cool and rub together in your hands to break up the larger pieces.

Heat a small pan on the stove, then add the blackberries and sugar. Sauté for about 1 minute, until the berries are warm but not too mashed. Spoon the berries into the serving bowls, top with a scoop of vanilla ice cream, then sprinkle the breadcrumbs over the ice cream. Serve with a sprig of mint on top of the ice cream.

Spiced Oranges

This sweet and spicy orange accompaniment is simple to prepare and has the versatility to complement a wide range of sweet (and savoury) dishes.

SERVES 4–6

8 oranges

100ml (3 1/2 fl oz) water

100g (3 1/2 oz) caster sugar

1 cinnamon stick

3 large pinches ground allspice

Remove the zest from four of the oranges using a swivel vegetable peeler and place in a large saucepan with the water, the sugar and spices. Bring to the boil, then reduce the heat and simmer for 15 minutes.

Meanwhile, cut away the pith from all eight fruits. Cut between the membranes to remove the orange segments, working over a bowl to catch the juice. Add the juice to the pan. Place the orange segments in a heatproof bowl.

Strain the contents of the pan over the orange segments and leave to cool. When cool, transfer to the refrigerator to chill.

steamed & sponge puds

Syrup Sponge with Custard

Purists will say, 'Steamed pudding in a microwave? You've got to be joking!' But if, like me, you can't wait to taste your pud, then try this recipe. It takes a few minutes to cook, a few to prepare and a few to eat.

SERVES 4

150g (5 1/2 oz) plain flour

1 tsp baking powder

125g (4 1/2 oz) butter, melted

125g (4 1/2 oz) caster sugar

2 free-range eggs

finely grated zest and juice
of 2 small lemons

milk

vegetable oil, for greasing

TO SERVE

4 tbsp golden syrup or jam

Custard (*see* page 246)

Sieve together the flour and baking powder.

Tip the butter, sugar, eggs and flour and baking powder mix into a food processor and mix to a paste.

Add the lemon juice and zest and continue to mix, adding enough milk to make a dropping consistency.

Spoon the mixture into a greased 1.2 litre (2 pint) basin (suitable for the microwave). Cover and microwave on full power for 4 minutes, or until the sponge begins to shrink from the side and is springy to the touch.

Leave to stand for 2–3 minutes before turning out and serving with golden syrup or jam, and custard.

Spotted Dick and Custard

This dessert should always be made with lemon and currants. The 'spotted' refers to the currants dotted through the sponge.

SERVES 4

butter, for greasing

350g (12oz) plain flour

2 tbsp baking powder

150g (5 1/2 oz) shredded suet

75g (2 3/4 oz) caster sugar

125g (4 1/2 oz) currants

75ml (2 1/2 fl oz) milk

75ml (2 1/2 fl oz) single cream

25g (1oz) butter, melted

juice and finely grated zest
of 2 lemons

TO SERVE

Custard (*see* page 246)

Butter a 1 litre (1 3/4 pint) pudding basin.

Place all the dry ingredients in a bowl. Separately, mix together the milk and cream. Add the melted butter to the dry ingredients and then stir in the lemon juice and zest. While stirring, slowly add enough of the milk and cream mixture to create a dropping consistency.

Pour the mixture into the prepared pudding basin, cover and place in a colander over a pan of boiling water for about 1 hour, until cooked.

Turn the pudding out of the basin and serve it, cut into wedges, with hot custard.

Sticky Toffee Pudding with Toffee Sauce

This is the king of all puddings, and my recipe is well over a hundred years old. It's not very slimming, mind you, but forget about diets and just enjoy yourself. It can be made either in one 13cm (5in) pudding basin or, better still, two to three small 7.5cm (3in) metal pudding basins.

SERVES 2–3

85g (3oz) butter, softened

25g (1oz) plain flour

175g (6oz) dark brown demerara sugar

200g (7oz) pitted dried dates

300ml (10fl oz) water

1 tbsp golden syrup

2 tbsp black treacle

2 free-range eggs

1/2 tsp vanilla essence

200g (7oz) self-raising flour

1 tbsp bicarbonate of soda

TO SERVE

Toffee Sauce (*see* page 280)

vanilla ice cream

Preheat the oven to 200°C/400°F/gas mark 6. Take 25g (1oz) of the soft butter and butter the mould(s) very well. Scatter the plain flour over the buttered inside to coat it thoroughly. Discard any excess flour.

Using a food mixer with a bowl and a whisk attachment, blend the remaining butter and the demerara sugar.

While mixing, bring the dates and water to the boil in a small pan.

Add the golden syrup, treacle, eggs and vanilla essence to the butter mixture and carry on mixing. Then slowly add the self-raising flour on a slow setting. Once mixed together turn off the mixer.

Purée the water and date mixture in a blender, add the bicarbonate of soda, and quickly stir this, while hot, into the egg and butter mix.

Once combined, pour into the mould(s) and bake in the oven for 20–25 minutes until the top of the pudding is just firm to the touch.

Remove the pudding(s) from the mould(s) and place on a plate with lots of toffee sauce on top. Vanilla ice cream is a must when eating this dish.

Sussex Pond Pudding

One of the best desserts ever, but be warned that it takes a while to make. This is not a dish ever likely to appear at a Weight Watchers' convention dinner, as the amount of butter and sugar is frightening! But you'll forget all about that when you pour double cream over it and have a spoon in your hand....

SERVES 4–6

225g (8oz) self-raising flour

115g (4oz) shredded beef suet

75ml (2 1/2 fl oz) milk

200g (7oz) slightly salted butter, diced

200g (7oz) soft light brown or caster sugar

2 large lemons

Mix the flour and suet together in a bowl. Combine the milk with 75ml (2 1/2 fl oz) water in a jug. Mix enough of the wet ingredients into the dry ingredients to make a dough that is soft, but not too soft to roll. Roll this dough out into a large circle, then cut out a quarter of the circle to be used later as the lid of the pudding.

Butter a 1.5 litre (2 3/4 pint) pudding basin. Drop the three-quarter circle of pastry into it and press the cut sides together to make a perfect join.

Put 100g (3 1/2 oz) each of the butter and sugar into the pastry-lined basin. Prick the lemons all over with a larding needle so the juices can escape, then put them on to the butter and sugar. Fill the rest of the cavity with the remaining butter and sugar, adding more if you wish to.

Lay the reserved pastry on top of the filling and press the edges together so the pudding is sealed in. Put a piece of foil right over the basin with a pleat in the middle. Tie it in place with string and make a string handle over the top so the pudding can be lifted out easily.

Put a large pan of water on to boil and lower the pudding in, sitting it on a trivet (or upturned saucer). The water must be boiling, and it should come halfway, or a little further, up the sides of the basin. Cover and leave to boil for 3–4 hours. If the water gets low, replenish it with boiling water.

To serve, remove the basin from the pan and take off the foil lid. Put a deep dish over the basin and quickly turn the whole thing upside down. It is a good idea to ease the pudding from the sides of the basin with a knife first. Put on the table and serve immediately, making sure everyone gets a bit of lemon.

Make Christmas pudding at least a month in advance – ideally in August or September – and allow it to sit in the fridge or larder like my grandmother used to, with an old fly net over the top to stop flies nibbling. I like to make this recipe in two 1.5 litre (2 3/4 pint) bowls rather than one large one, as I find this makes a better-tasting pudding.

Christmas Pudding

SERVES 10

350g (12oz) sultanas

350g (12oz) currants

150g (5 1/2 oz) dried figs, chopped

115g (4oz) mixed candied peel, chopped

100g (3 1/2 oz) dried apricots, chopped

75g (2 3/4 oz) glacé cherries, halved

150ml (5fl oz) brandy

115g (4oz) stem ginger in syrup, chopped, plus 3 tbsp of the syrup

2 Bramley apples, peeled, cored and grated

juice and finely grated zest of 2 oranges

6 medium free-range eggs, beaten

250g (9oz) shredded suet

350g (12oz) soft muscovado sugar

250g (9oz) fresh white breadcrumbs

200g (7oz) self-raising flour

1 tsp ground mixed spice

unsalted butter, for greasing

In a large bowl, soak the sultanas, currants, figs, peel, apricots and cherries in the brandy, covered, overnight if possible – or for at least a few hours.

In a larger bowl mix the ginger and syrup, apple, orange juice and zest, eggs, suet, sugar, breadcrumbs and flour. Using a wooden spoon or your hands, stir in the soaked fruit and mixed spice and mix well.

Butter the bowls, and divide the mixture between them. Cover with circles of greaseproof paper with a folded pleat down the centre to allow the pudding to expand. Tie in place with some string and make a string handle over the top so each pudding can be lifted out easily. Steam as described on page 295 for 3 hours.

Let the puddings cool before removing the paper. Cover them with clingfilm over the top of pudding and bowl, and store in a cool, dry place if you aren't using them straightaway. You can soak them with more booze in the run-up to Christmas, if you like.

To reheat, steam the puddings for 2 hours before turning out and flaming with hot brandy.

Quick Christmas Pudding with Baked Ice Cream

This is a great way of saving time on Christmas Day. The ice cream parcels are better made in advance (at least the day before) and placed in the freezer. The icing sugar on the top caramelizes to create a lovely crunchy garnish for the hot Christmas pudding.

SERVES 4

8 ready-made filo pastry sheets

1 medium free-range egg, beaten

4 scoops bought or homemade vanilla ice cream

icing sugar

4 x 115g small bought Christmas puddings

200ml (7fl oz) brandy sauce (*see* opposite)

4 fresh mint sprigs

Preheat the oven to 220°C/425°F/gas mark 7.

Unroll the filo and cut into 12 x 10cm (4in) squares. Layer three of the squares at slight alternate angles and brush with some beaten egg.

Place a scoop of the ice cream in the centre of each filo square, and bring up the sides of the pastry to stick together. Brush with beaten egg.

If cooking straightaway, dust with icing sugar, place on an oven tray and bake for about 3–4 minutes. Alternatively, place in the freezer until ready to use (much better).

Meanwhile, place the puddings in the microwave to cook (follow packet instructions) and warm the brandy sauce through on the stove.

Spoon the warm sauce into the centre of the plates, and place a Christmas pudding in the middle. Remove the ice cream parcel from the oven and place on top of the pudding.

To finish, simply dust the top with icing sugar and garnish with a sprig of mint. Serve immediately.

Brandy Sauce

This is one of the few recipes I use granulated sugar in. As you can probably imagine, it was used in my grandmother's recipe (although she had to grate sugar from a large lump or chop sugar cubes). I remember her bringing this sauce back home to the farmhouse, and me fighting with my sister to remove the greaseproof paper from the top.

SERVES 4–6

200ml (7fl oz) double cream

600ml (1 pint) full-fat milk

25g (1oz) cornflour, slaked with 4 tbsp cold water

55g (2oz) unrefined granulated sugar

55g (2oz) unsalted butter, cubed

brandy, to taste

Bring the cream and milk to the boil together, and then stir in the slaked cornflour. Bring back to the boil, stirring, to thicken.

Remove from the heat and stir in the sugar and butter, until dissolved. Finally, stir in brandy to taste.

Cover to stop a skin forming, and keep warm.

cream, eggs & vanilla

Hot Chocolate Fondants

Hands up all those who love a dark and delicious hot chocolate soufflé? Almost everyone, I bet. Well, this recipe is sure to please. If you've ever wondered how chefs manage to bake a pudding with a rich sauce that oozes out, then follow these simple instructions. You can cook the mixture as soon as you've finished making it, but it also freezes brilliantly and can be baked once it has thawed.

SERVES 8

225g (8oz) dark chocolate with at least 60 per cent cocoa solids

4 tbsp double cream

100g (3 1/2 oz) unsalted butter

35g (1 1/4 oz) ground almonds

2 large free-range eggs, separated

30g (1 1/4 oz) cornflour

85g (3oz) caster sugar

Finely grate 40g (1 1/2 oz) of the chocolate and set aside. Gently melt a third of the remaining chocolate with the cream in a small saucepan, stirring well to mix. Remove and leave to cool.

Line a small plate with clingfilm and pour on the mixture. Place in the freezer for about 8 hours until set hard, then stamp out eight small rounds using a 3cm (1 1/4 in) round cutter. Set aside.

Melt half the butter and brush liberally all over the inside of eight small ramekins. Dust well with the grated chocolate, shaking out any excess. Set aside on a baking sheet.

Melt the remaining chocolate (including any shaken-out excess) and butter in a small heatproof bowl over a pan of barely simmering water, or in a microwave-proof bowl in the microwave on high for 2–3 minutes, stirring once. Do not overheat or the chocolate will 'seize', or turn solid. Scrape this mixture into a bigger bowl, then beat in the ground almonds, egg yolks and cornflour.

Whisk the egg whites in a separate bowl until they form stiff but not dry peaks. Gradually beat in the caster sugar. You may like to use a hand-held electric whisk for this.

Fold this meringue mixture into the melted chocolate mixture. Spoon half the combined mixture into the base of the ramekins to half fill them, place a chocolate disc on top, then fill each ramekin with the remaining mixture. Smooth the tops of the fondants and chill in the refrigerator while you heat the oven to 180°C/350°F/gas mark 4.

Bake the fondants in the oven for 10–15 minutes until risen and slightly wobbly, then remove and eat as soon as possible.

Baked Chocolate Mousse

This mousse-cake contains no flour and needs to be baked and eaten fresh. As it starts to cool it will collapse, but don't worry – it still eats well, so long as you don't put it in the fridge.

SERVES 6–8

300g (10 1/2 oz) dark bitter chocolate, broken into pieces

140g (5oz) unsalted butter, diced

6 free-range eggs, separated

55g (2oz) caster sugar

double cream, to serve

Line the base and sides of a 20cm (8in) loose-bottomed cake tin with greaseproof paper, and preheat the oven to 180°C/350°F/gas mark 4.

Melt the chocolate and butter in a metal bowl over a pan of simmering water (the bowl must not touch the water). Whisk the egg yolks with 2 tbsp of the sugar. Stir in the melted chocolate and mix well.

Beat the egg whites with the remaining sugar until very stiff. Quickly stir one-third of the whites into the chocolate mix, then gently fold in the remainder and pour the mix into the prepared cake tin. Place on the middle shelf of the oven and bake for 20 minutes.

Remove from the oven and leave to cool slightly, before serving with the double cream poured over.

Cranachan

I bet that no more than a few weeks after this book's out some Scot will come up to me to say this recipe is all wrong. It's great, but then how could it not be? Cream, whisky and raspberries – it's one of the few cold desserts I know that will warm your cockles on a winter's day.

SERVES 8

85g (3oz) pinhead oatmeal

3 tbsp whisky

600ml (1 pint) double cream

85g (3oz) caster sugar

450g (1lb) raspberries

Put the oatmeal on a baking tray and toast briefly under the grill, taking care not to burn it. Remove and, while still warm, sprinkle over the whisky and leave to stand for 10 minutes.

While the oatmeal is absorbing the whisky, whip the double cream, adding the caster sugar as it starts to hold, and continue to whisk until it forms soft peaks. Be careful not to take it too far, or the cream will split.

Fold the oatmeal into the cream and spoon the mixture into some large wine glasses.

Divide the raspberries between the glasses, sitting them on top of the cream. Chill for 30 minutes to firm up before serving.

Angel Delight, blancmange, strawberry and orange jelly and chocolate mousse – all great foods we used to eat as kids. I remember the blancmange my gran used to make. It was bright pink and was made in those old jelly moulds. I'm not giving you the recipe for that, as the best is out of a packet. Another great treat, of course, was chocolate mousse. This, I suppose, is the grown-up version.

Chocolate Mousse

SERVES 6

200g (7oz) dark chocolate (70 per cent cocoa solids), broken into pieces

125ml (4fl oz) warm water

3 large free-range eggs, separated

40g (1 1/2 oz) golden caster sugar

TO SERVE
a little whipped cream

Place the broken-up chocolate and warm water in a large, heatproof bowl and sit it over a pan of barely simmering water, making sure the bowl doesn't touch the water.

Keep the heat at its lowest setting and allow the chocolate to melt slowly – it should take about 6 minutes.

Remove it from the heat and stir thoroughly until the chocolate is smooth and glossy. Let the mixture cool before adding the egg yolks. Mix them in thoroughly with a wooden spoon.

In a clean bowl, whisk the egg whites to the soft-peak stage. Whisk in the sugar gradually, then continue whisking until the whites are glossy. Using a metal spoon, fold the egg whites into the chocolate mixture. Take care not to knock the air out of the egg whites.

Divide the mousse between six ramekins or glasses and chill for at least 2 hours. Serve with a dollop of whipped cream on top.

Bananas and Custard Soufflé

Bananas and custard was the best dessert ever when I was growing up, but when you reach a certain age you never seem to eat it again, apart from when you're ill. I've played around here with a real British classic – and it's a great dish to serve as a bit of fun at a dinner party, or just for a cosy dinner for two.

SERVES 2

50g (1 3/4 oz) butter

3 tbsp caster sugar

4 free-range egg whites

finely grated zest of 2 oranges

8 tbsp fresh custard (bought-in or homemade, *see* page 246)

3 medium bananas

TO SERVE

100ml (3 1/2 fl oz) vanilla ice cream (optional)

Preheat the oven to 180°C/350°F/gas mark 4.

Rub two ramekin dishes with half the butter and sprinkle with 1 tbsp of the caster sugar. Whisk the egg whites and, when they are stiff, beat in another tbsp of the caster sugar.

Mix the orange zest into the custard and then gently fold in the whisked egg whites. Spoon the mixture into the prepared ramekins and place on an oven tray. Bake for 15–20 minutes.

While the soufflés are cooking, peel the bananas and cut in half lengthways.

Heat up a wide nonstick pan and add the remaining butter. When it's nut-brown, add the remaining sugar and the halved bananas. Fry them on both sides, taking care not to break them, to give them a nice golden colour.

To serve, place the warm bananas on the plate, serve the soufflé on the side and, if you dare, a dollop of vanilla ice cream on the side, too!

Baked Cheesecake

Americans have mastered the art of making cheesecakes, but they started in the UK and were taken across the Atlantic. This is a great recipe, light in texture and delicious served with caramelized bananas.

SERVES 6

a little butter, for greasing

1 x 25cm (10in) bought sponge flan case

200g (7oz) caster sugar

finely grated zest of 3 lemons

4 tbsp cornflour

3 tbsp sultanas, soaked in a little bourbon

850g (1lb 14oz) full-fat soft cream cheese

3 medium free-range eggs

1 vanilla pod

50ml (2fl oz) Jack Daniels or bourbon, to taste (optional)

375ml (13fl oz) double cream

TO SERVE

10 small bananas

25g (1oz) butter

2 tbsp caster sugar

caramel sauce or maple syrup

Preheat the oven to 180°C/350°F/gas mark 4.

Butter a 25cm (10in) loose-bottomed cake tin. Cut the sponge horizontally into two discs. Use one to line the buttered cake tin (I'd suggest using the other to line a trifle).

In a bowl, mix together the sugar, lemon zest, cornflour and sultanas using a wooden spoon, then beat in the cream cheese. Add the eggs, one by one, beating constantly until all of them are well incorporated.

Slice open the vanilla pod, remove the seeds with a sharp knife, and place them in the cream cheese mixture. Add the Jack Daniels or bourbon, if using, and mix everything together well. Add the cream and beat well until the mixture is smooth. Pour gently over the sponge base in the cake tin.

Sit the tin in a baking tray filled with 2–3mm ($1/8$ in) of warm water to help create steam during cooking. Bake for 50 minutes, until the top is golden. Remove from the oven and leave to cool and set completely before removing from the tin.

Just before serving, peel the bananas and fry in the butter and sugar until brown and slightly caramelized.

Serve the cheesecake cut into wedges, with the bananas and a drizzle of caramel sauce or maple syrup.

How can I describe this dish? Well, it's like a custard tart and lemon meringue pie rolled into one. I remember my auntie used to make it, along with stuff like pink blancmange, jam tarts – oh, and Dripping Cake (*see* page 342). They all tasted good then, and they taste even better now, as they bring back so many memories.

Queen of Puddings

SERVES 6–8

250ml (9fl oz) milk

250ml (9fl oz) double cream

1 vanilla pod, split

100g (3¹/₂ oz) caster sugar

6 medium free-range egg yolks

140g (5oz) fresh breadcrumbs

finely grated zest of 2 lemons

200g (7oz) raspberry jam

MERINGUE

4 medium free-range egg whites

115g (4oz) caster sugar

1 tbsp icing sugar

To make the custard, pour the milk and cream into a pan and add the split vanilla pod. Bring to the boil over a medium heat.

In a bowl, whisk the sugar into the egg yolks until it is well dissolved and the mixture is light and creamy. Slowly pour in the hot milk and cream, whisking all the time. Remove the vanilla pod.

Mix in the breadcrumbs and lemon zest, then pour into an ovenproof glass or ceramic baking dish of about 20 x 25 x 5cm (8 x 10 x 2in). Allow to stand for 10–15 minutes.

Meanwhile, preheat the oven to 150°C/300°F/gas mark 2, and have a roasting tin ready, half-full of boiling water (a bain-marie).

Place the baking dish in the bain-marie in the centre of the oven and bake for 25–30 minutes, until the custard is still slightly wobbly in the centre. Remove and allow to cool.

Whack the oven temperature up to 190°C/375°F/gas mark 5.

For the meringue, whisk the egg whites until stiff, then whisk in the caster sugar – apart from 1 tbsp.

Melt the jam in a pan and spread it over the custard. Cover the pudding with the meringue mix, sprinkle with the remaining caster sugar and the icing sugar, and bake for 10–15 minutes, until the top is crisp and lightly browned. Serve straightaway.

School dinners always seemed to include a milk pudding such as rice pudding, tapioca or sago, which will probably have put you off them for life. But rice pudding is great, its reputation only knocked by a lack of thought and care put into making it over the years. Try this one, and you'll be a convert.

Baked Rice Pudding

SERVES 4

25g (1oz) butter, plus extra for greasing

100g (3 1/2 oz) short-grain pudding rice

450ml (16fl oz) milk

450ml (16fl oz) double cream

1 vanilla pod, split (optional)

75g (2 3/4 oz) caster sugar

a little freshly grated nutmeg

Preheat the oven to 180°C/350°F/gas mark 4.

Lightly butter a pudding basin or ovenproof dish about 1–1.8 litres (2–3 pints) in capacity.

Wash the rice under cold water and allow to drain.

Bring the milk and cream to the boil with the vanilla pod (if using) and add the rice and sugar. Stir well.

Pour into the oven dish and grate a little nutmeg over the top. Dot with knobs of butter.

Bake for about 15 minutes, then lower the temperature to 150°C/300°F/gas mark 2, and bake for a further 1 1/4 hours. It should be golden brown on top and creamy underneath.

Classic Lemon Posset

Simple is always the best, and this is incredibly simple! For something extra special, place some crushed biscuits and a dollop of homemade lemon curd (but it must be homemade, or the stuff you get at a WI stall in the market) in the bottom.

SERVES 6

600ml (1 pint) double cream

140g (5oz) caster sugar

juice of 2 large lemons and finely grated zest of 4 large lemons

Put the double cream in a large pan and add the sugar. Bring this slowly to the boil, boil for 3 minutes, then leave to cool.

Add the lemon juice and half the lemon zest and whisk well until thickened. Pour into six large serving glasses and refrigerate for 3 hours.

Sprinkle with the remaining lemon zest before serving.

Lemon Syllabub

Not a real syllabub made with egg yolks and sugar, this was invented when I was filming *Housecall* for the BBC. I think it is a fantastic recipe, quick to make and really tasty to eat.

SERVES 4–6

100g (3 1/2 oz) caster sugar

juice and finely grated zest of 2 lemons

2–3 tbsp brandy

600ml (1 pint) double cream

Whisk together the caster sugar, lemon juice, lemon zest and brandy.

In another bowl, whisk the cream until thick, then slowly whisk in the lemon mixture. Pour into wine glasses and refrigerate overnight.

Serve with ratafia biscuits or brandy snaps.

Lemon Verbena Crème Brûlée

I grow lemon verbena in my garden – it is so nice, even the dog likes eating it. You have to get some of this herb for your garden at home, as its smell and flavour are different to any other herb. I use it mainly for desserts, as the flavour lends itself well to being infused in a liquid, as in this crème brûlée.

SERVES 4–6 DEPENDING ON SIZE OF RAMEKINS

250ml (9fl oz) milk

5 sprigs fresh lemon verbena, chopped

10 free-range egg yolks

175g (6oz) caster sugar

750ml (1 pint 6fl oz) double cream

55g (2oz) demerara sugar

Preheat the oven to 120°C/250°F/gas mark 1/2 . Heat the milk in a pan with the lemon verbena until just boiling, then remove from the heat to cool and allow the flavours to blend.

Place the egg yolks in a bowl, add the caster sugar and whisk together until combined. Add the milk and cream, and whisk well. Pass through a sieve to remove any egg shell and the lemon verbena.

Ladle the cream mixture into small ramekins, and place on a baking tray. Bake in the oven for 1 1/2 – 2 hours, until set. Remove and allow to cool. Either refrigerate or use straightaway.

When ready to eat, sprinkle the demerara sugar over the top and caramelize with either a blow torch or by putting under a hot grill.

ices

Blood Orange Ice Cream

The custard base here could be used for other ice creams: add a little vanilla extract for vanilla or some other fruit flavourings. You could also add some brandy to this custard for a brandy sauce for Christmas pud.

SERVES 6

500g (1lb 2oz) blood oranges, preferably unwaxed

350g (12oz) caster sugar

6 medium free-range egg yolks

200ml (7fl oz) double cream

400ml (14fl oz) full-fat milk

Finely grate the orange zest into a bowl, then quarter the fruits. Put the quarters into the bowl as well, and pour over 250g (9oz) of the caster sugar. Refrigerate, covered, for a day or so.

Squeeze the juice from the mixture – start by using your hands, then press through a nylon sieve. Measure the juice and discard the pulp.

Make the custard for the ice cream by whisking the egg yolks and remaining sugar together until thick and pale. This should take 10 minutes in a food mixer.

Bring the cream and milk to the boil in a heavy-bottomed pan, then whisk this into the eggs. Return the pan to the heat and cook gently, stirring constantly, until the custard begins to thicken. Do not allow the mixture to boil or it will scramble. (If you prefer, you can cook the custard in a bowl set over a pan of simmering water.) Check whether it is thick enough by coating the back of a wooden spoon with it; if, when you slide your finger through it, it leaves a trail, it is ready. Remove from the heat and cool.

Whisk the juice with 1½ times its volume of cooled custard, then churn in an ice-cream maker. Alternatively, pour the mixture into freezerproof containers and half-freeze, then whisk again to remove the ice crystals. Return to the freezer.

Arctic Roll

I spoke to a load of chefs one day, while cooking, about food for this book. When asked what dessert they used to eat as kids, this was the one that brought back the best memories. The hardest thing was trying to replicate that frozen pud your mother used to buy from the shops, and the best way that I have found of doing this is to use a piece of drainpipe. Yes, a piece of drainpipe! I'll say no more; just read on and have a go.

SERVES 4–6

1 x 500ml tub vanilla ice cream

about 150g (5 1/2 oz) fresh raspberries

3–4 tbsp raspberry jam

2 tbsp chopped fresh mint

icing sugar

SPONGE

butter, for greasing

3 free-range eggs

75g (2 3/4 oz) caster sugar, plus extra for sprinkling

75g (2 3/4 oz) plain flour, plus extra for dusting

Preheat the oven to 190°C/375°F/gas mark 5. Start the sponge by lining a 30 x 20cm (12 x 8in) shallow Swiss roll tin with butter and greaseproof paper. Whisk together the eggs and caster sugar until they reach ribbon stage, then sift in the flour and gently fold it in. Once the mixture is well blended, pour it into the tin and push it to the edges, levelling with a palette knife. Bake in the preheated oven for 8–10 minutes, until golden brown. Once cooked, you should be able to test it with your finger by pressing lightly on the top; if it springs back, then it's cooked.

Remove from the oven and tip out on to a clean tea-towel sprinkled with caster sugar. Remove the greaseproof paper from underneath the sponge, cover with a dampened tea-towel and allow to cool.

For the ice cream, you need a piece of clean drainpipe, 30cm (12in) long and 12–15cm (4 1/2 – 6 in) in diameter. Place the ice cream in a bowl and fork in the raspberries, leaving half a punnet for garnish. Fill the drainpipe with ice cream. Press down well, then put in the freezer.

Spread the sponge evenly all over with jam, then sprinkle over the mint. Use a hot cloth to remove the ice cream from the drainpipe, by wrapping the cloth around the outside and then pushing the ice cream out from one end. Place the ice cream on the sponge and roll the sponge around it by pulling the tea towel towards you.

Once the sponge covers all the ice cream, trim off any excess sponge and put the roll on a plate, seam-side down, with a dusting of icing sugar, the remaining raspberries and a sprig of mint.

To serve, cut into slices. I bet you never thought you'd be able to make this one at home!

I made this while playing with my new ice-cream machine, and it works, but be careful with the sugar in the recipe. Standard recipes for ice cream say 225g (8oz) of sugar per litre (1¾ pints) of liquid, but sugar will act as a de-icer, and the ice cream won't freeze properly if there is too much. The same applies to alcohol, so remember to reduce the quantity if making a high-sugar or alcoholic ice cream. This ice cream is great served with seasonal fresh berries or with a toasted croissant and some hot chocolate sauce.

Orange Marmalade Ice Cream

SERVES 4–6

1 vanilla pod

250ml (9fl oz) milk

750ml (1 pint 6fl oz) double cream

175g (6oz) caster sugar

10 free-range egg yolks

6 tbsp orange marmalade

Taking a sharp knife, cut the vanilla pod in half lengthways, and scrape out and retain the seeds.

Place the milk, cream, vanilla seeds and pod, and caster sugar in a pan, and bring to the boil.

In a separate bowl whisk the egg yolks. When the cream mixture has boiled, pour the mixture slowly on to the eggs, whisking all the time. Pour into a clean pan and mix quickly over a gentle heat until the mixture has thickened. Pass through a sieve.

Place the mixture into an ice-cream machine and churn until the ice cream is nearly set. Add the marmalade and continue to churn. Once set, transfer the ice cream from the machine into a container, and place in the freezer.

This is a simple way of using leftover Christmas pudding. Please invest in a decent ice-cream maker, which blends while the ice cream is freezing. Make sure Father Christmas comes down the chimney with one! Serve the ice cream with a large glass of brandy and some brandy snaps.

Christmas Pudding Ice Cream

SERVES 4–6

85g (3oz) leftover Christmas pudding, chopped into small pieces

2 tbsp brandy

140g (5oz) caster sugar

1 cinnamon stick

1/2 tsp ground mixed spice

225ml (8fl oz) custard base for ice cream (*see* opposite)

150ml (5fl oz) double cream

Soak the Christmas pudding in the brandy.

To make the stock syrup, heat 150ml (5fl oz) water and the sugar together in a heavy-based pan until the sugar has melted, then simmer to reduce to 185ml (6 1/2 fl oz). Transfer to a small pan and add the cinnamon stick and mixed spice. Remove from the heat and leave to cool and infuse for 15 minutes.

Mix the custard with the cream. Strain the stock syrup to remove the cinnamon and add to the cream mixture. Mix in the Christmas pudding and brandy.

Churn in an ice-cream maker until thick and frozen, then transfer to a freezerproof container. Store in the freezer for up to a couple of weeks.

I know what you're thinking, squash in an ice cream? Sounds weird, but trust me:
I won't let you down. It really is a delight!

Ginger and Butternut Squash Ice Cream

SERVES 4–6

450ml (16fl oz) double cream

2 tbsp peeled and chopped fresh root ginger

4 medium free-range egg yolks

100g (3 1/2 oz) caster sugar

150g (5 1/2 oz) cooked, cooled and puréed butternut squash

a dash of lemon juice

Bring the cream and ginger to the boil together. Cover, remove from the heat and leave to steep for 30 minutes.

Return the cream to the boil. Whisk together the egg yolks and sugar in a jug and pour in some of the hot cream mixture. Mix quickly, then pour into the cream mixture left in the pan. Continue cooking over a gentle heat for 3–4 minutes, or until the mixture coats the back of the spoon. Cool over ice, stirring occasionally, until cold.

Mix the cooked and cooled squash purée into the cooled custard, add lemon juice to taste, and strain through a fine sieve. Freeze in an ice-cream machine or in a freezerproof container. Keep frozen until ready to use.

Apricot Yoghurt Ice Cream

This is such a great idea. It's so quick and easy, and works with most puréed fruit. Strawberries work best after apricots, I think, as the orange juice complements their taste.

SERVES 20

650g (1lb 7oz) apricot purée

350g (12oz) icing sugar

2 vanilla pods

1 tbsp Amaretto

50ml (2fl oz) liquid glucose

90ml (3fl oz) orange juice

300g (10¹/₂ oz) Greek yoghurt

250ml (9fl oz) crème fraîche

Slowly stir the apricot purée into the icing sugar to form a paste.

Using a sharp knife, split the vanilla pods lengthways and scrape the seeds out into the apricot purée. Mix in the remaining ingredients, and whisk them until smooth.

Churn in an ice-cream machine until it is just set, then place in a container in the freezer. Allow to defrost a little before serving.

Vanilla Ice Cream

Here's a real vanilla ice cream recipe if you want to have a go at making it yourself.

SERVES 4–6

500ml (18fl oz) milk

500ml (18fl oz) double cream

2 vanilla pods, split

225g (8oz) caster sugar

10 free-range egg yolks

Place the milk and cream in a saucepan and add the seeds from the vanilla pods. Slowly bring to a simmer. Meanwhile, whisk the sugar and egg yolks together in a large bowl.

Pour the hot milk and cream mixture on to the eggs, whisking all the time. Return the pan to a very low heat and keep stirring until the mixture coats the back of a wooden spoon. (A quick chef's tip: keep stirring until most of the bubbles disappear, do not boil. The bubbles disappearing is a sign that the mixture is starting to thicken.)

Freeze in an ice-cream machine or a metal container. If you use the latter, freeze for about 1 hour, then take out of the freezer and beat with a whisk to break up the ice crystals and re-freeze for at least 3 hours.

Cheat's Raspberry and Cassis Ripple Ice Cream

When serving this, hide the ice-cream cartons to make it look like you did it all yourself. It tastes fantastic!

SERVES 8

2 litres (3½ pints) vanilla ice cream, partly thawed in the fridge until just soft

CASSIS SAUCE

300g (10½ oz) frozen raspberries

25g (1oz) caster sugar

juice and finely grated zest of ½ lemon

3 tbsp Cassis

To make the cassis sauce, blend the raspberries, sugar, lemon juice and zest and Cassis. Pass it through a sieve to remove the raspberry seeds.

Drizzle the sauce over the ice cream and quickly marble it through, using a folding motion with a spoon.

Place the ice cream in a freezerproof container and freeze it for 3–4 hours before serving.

Instant Banana Ice Cream

This may be instant, but it is one of the most delicious ice creams around.

SERVES 4

4 bananas

¼ tsp vanilla essence

3–4 tbsp caster sugar, to taste

150ml (5fl oz) buttermilk

Peel the bananas, cut them into chunks and place in a single layer on a freezerproof dish or tray, as you would if freezing raspberries, then freeze so that you have separate pieces.

Tip the frozen banana chunks into the food processor. Add the vanilla essence, sugar and half the buttermilk.

Turn on the processor and let it run for a few moments. Then, while it is still running, pour in the remaining buttermilk in a thin, steady stream. Let the machine run until the mixture is smooth and creamy. Serve at once.

cakes

I remember my auntie making this cake at Christmas. She used to eat it with a glass of Madeira, and dunk it in the glass. Then she'd down the remains, crumbs and all, with a smile on her face – whether because of the wine or the cake, I don't know, but possibly as a result of both….

Madeira Cake

MAKES 1 X 18CM
(7IN) CAKE

175g (6oz) butter, plus extra for greasing

175g (6oz) caster sugar

3 large free-range eggs

250g (9oz) self-raising flour

about 3 tbsp milk

finely grated zest of 1 lemon

several thin pieces of candied citron or lemon peel, to decorate

Preheat the oven to 180°C/350°F/gas mark 4. Grease a 900g (2lb) bread or cake tin, line the base and sides with greaseproof paper and grease the paper.

Cream the butter and sugar together in a bowl until pale and fluffy. Beat in the eggs, one at a time, beating the mixture well between each one and adding a tbsp of the flour with the last egg to prevent the mixture from curdling.

Sift the flour and gently fold in with enough milk to give a mixture that falls reluctantly from the spoon. Fold in the lemon zest. Spoon the mixture into the prepared tin and lightly level the top. Bake on the middle shelf of the oven for 30 minutes.

Place the candied peel on top of the cake and bake for a further 30 minutes, or until a warm skewer inserted into the centre comes out clean. Leave the cake to cool in the tin for 10 minutes, then turn it out on to a wire rack and leave to cool completely.

This is obviously German, but it has always been very popular here. My version is the same as the classic, but with the addition of chocolate shards around the edge. I love it, but I only use tinned cherries. Who wouldn't love it? Chocolate sponge, double cream and cherries all piled up, with even more chocolate....

Black Forest Gâteau

SERVES 4

SPONGE
butter, for greasing

6 free-range eggs

150g (5 1/2 oz) caster sugar

125g (4 1/2 oz) self-raising flour

25g (1oz) cocoa powder

FILLING AND TOPPING
3 x 425g cans black cherries

2 tbsp cornflour

a good dash of Kirsch

750ml (1 pint 6fl oz) double cream, whipped

50g (1 3/4 oz) toasted flaked almonds

CHOCOLATE SHARDS
300g (10 1/2 oz) dark chocolate, broken into pieces

Preheat the oven to 180°C/350°F/gas mark 4. Grease and line a deep 30cm (12in) round cake tin.

For the sponge, break the eggs into a mixing bowl, add the sugar and whisk well until it reaches the ribbon stage, or is very light and fluffy. Carefully fold in the sifted flour and cocoa powder. Pour the mix into the prepared tin and bake for about 40–45 minutes, until cooked.

Turn out on to a wire rack and leave to cool.

For the filling, drain the cherries, reserving the juice. Put the juice into a pan and bring to the boil. Meanwhile, mix the cornflour with a little water to make a paste. When the cherry juice is boiling, mix the cornflour paste into it. Strain through a sieve over the cherries, also pouring through the Kirsch. Leave to one side to cool.

Cut the sponge into three layers horizontally using a sharp knife. Sandwich the three layers together using the whipped cream, half of the cherries and all of the almonds.

Melt the chocolate, spread on to a tray lined with clingfilm, and place in the fridge to set. When the chocolate is set, break it into large shards and stick them randomly around the edge of the cake.

Pile the remaining cherries on top of the cake and serve.

Carrot and Orange Cake

Carrot cake is good eaten with slightly whipped cream. In the States they make a heavier, darker version than this. The cake is at its best served simply.

SERVES 8

butter, for greasing

5 medium carrots, trimmed, scraped and sliced

juice of 2 oranges

125ml (4fl oz) corn oil

4 free-range eggs, separated

375g (13oz) caster sugar

350g (12oz) '00' pasta flour, or plain flour

15g (1/2 oz) baking powder

TO SERVE

200ml (7fl oz) double cream

2–3 tsp Cointreau

Preheat the oven to 180°C/350°F/gas mark 4 and butter a cake tin of 30cm (12in) in diameter.

Put the carrot in a pan, cover with water and add the orange juice. Bring to the boil and cook until tender. Drain and cool, then discard the liquid. Put the carrots in a blender with the corn oil and the egg yolks, and whizz to a purée. Transfer to a bowl.

Beat the egg whites until stiff, and set aside.

In another bowl, mix the sugar, flour and baking powder together, then fold into the carrot purée, until well combined. Now gently fold in the egg whites. Pour the mixture into the prepared tin and bake for 30–35 minutes.

When the cake is cooked, take it out of the oven and leave to cool on a wire rack.

Whip the double cream and stir in the Cointreau. Cut a slice of cake and serve with a dollop of the cream.

Carrot and Cinnamon Cake

Carrots were used in cakes as a cheap substitute for expensive imported dried fruit for hundreds of years. Serve with a dollop of crème fraîche or soured cream.

SERVES 8

300ml (10fl oz) sunflower oil, plus extra for greasing

225g (8oz) soft brown sugar

4 medium free-range eggs

175g (6oz) golden syrup

350g (12oz) self-raising flour

2 tbsp ground cinnamon

1 tsp bicarbonate of soda

275g (9 1/2 oz) grated carrot

Preheat the oven to 180°C/350°F/gas mark 4. Grease two 500g (1lb 2oz) loaf tins with sunflower oil.

Put the oil, sugar, eggs and golden syrup into a food processor and then add the flour, cinnamon, bicarbonate of soda and grated carrots.

Blend everything together, pour into the loaf tins and bake in the preheated oven for 40–50 minutes. Once cooked, leave to rest for 10–15 minutes before turning out of the tins.

Whoever is quickest gets a slice. Dive in!

Parkin

In Yorkshire we used to eat this on Bonfire Night, and it is one of those cakes, like ginger cake, that gets better after three to four days in a tin. It's dark and rich and, once cut into squares and placed in a sealed tin, becomes moister and eats even better.

SERVES 4

225g (8oz) self-raising flour

115g (4oz) caster sugar

2 tsp ground ginger

1 tsp bicarbonate of soda

55g (2oz) butter

115g (4oz) golden syrup

1 free-range egg

200ml (7fl oz) milk

Preheat the oven to 150°C/300°F/gas mark 2. Line a 20cm (8in) cake tin with greaseproof paper.

Sieve the flour, sugar, ginger and bicarbonate of soda into a bowl. In a small pan, gently heat the butter and syrup until melted. Beat the egg into the milk.

Gradually pour the butter and syrup into the flour mixture and stir well. Pour in the egg and milk mixture and combine until smooth.

Pour into the lined tin and bake for 1 hour.

Banana Cake

The great thing I find about this recipe is that the bananas help keep the cake nice and moist. A lot of banana cake recipes contain nuts such as almonds or walnuts, but I think it's nicer plain.

MAKES 1 CAKE

4 large ripe bananas

125g (4 1/2 oz) butter, softened, plus extra for greasing

250g (9oz) self-raising flour

200g (7oz) caster sugar

3 medium free-range eggs

3 tbsp golden syrup

Preheat the oven to 180°C/350°F/gas mark 4. Butter a large loaf tin.

Peel the bananas and put them into a food processor. Blend for 10 seconds to break them up.

Add all the other ingredients and blend again for 10 seconds. Scrape down the sides and blend again for a few seconds to mix everything in.

Spoon the mixture into the buttered loaf tin and spread evenly. Bake for 1 1/4 –1 1/2 hours, until well risen and firm to the touch. At this point, insert a small knife to test the cake; if it is pulled out clean and the tip is not wet, then the cake is ready.

Remove from the oven and leave to rest for 10 minutes before turning out of the tin and placing on a wire rack to cool a little. Serve the cake warm.

My gran used to swear by this sponge recipe and my auntie by the other one (*see* page 332), so you choose – they're both great.

Victoria Sponge

MAKES A 20CM
(8IN) SPONGE

200g (7oz) unsalted butter, softened, plus extra for greasing

200g (7oz) self-raising flour, sifted, plus extra for dusting

200g (7oz) caster sugar

1 tsp vanilla extract

4 free-range eggs

TO SERVE
double cream, whipped

raspberry jam

icing sugar, for dusting

Preheat the oven to 190°C/375°F/gas mark 5. Lightly grease and flour two 20cm (8in) sponge tins, at least 4cm (1½ in) deep. Line the bases with parchment paper.

Beat the butter and caster sugar together until well creamed. Add the vanilla extract. Gently mix the eggs together in a small bowl, then add, little by little, to the butter mixture. Once all the eggs have been combined, fold in the sifted flour and divide the mixture between the tins.

Bake for 20–25 minutes, until well risen and golden brown on top. Once cooked, turn out and leave to cool on a wire rack.

Spread one of the sponges with whipped double cream and raspberry jam. Top with the second sponge and sprinkle with a dusting of icing sugar.

Auntie's Sponge

Granny's sponge is the classic creamed sponge, while Auntie's is a whisked sponge. This one won't last as long as the other, but it's just as delicious.

MAKES A 20 CM
(8IN) SPONGE

50g (1 3/4 oz) butter, melted, plus extra for greasing

175g (6oz) plain flour, sifted, plus extra for dusting

6 medium free-range eggs

175g (6oz) caster sugar

TO SERVE
double cream, whipped

raspberry jam

icing sugar, for dusting

Preheat the oven to 200°C/400°F/gas mark 6. Grease and flour a deep 20cm (8in) sponge tin.

Place the eggs and sugar in a bowl and whisk to the ribbon stage. This will take a few minutes, so be patient.

Once the mixture has doubled in volume, fold in the flour. Carefully, but quickly, fold in the butter at the same time.

Pour into the tin and bake for 30 minutes. Test with a skewer in the centre – if it comes out clean, the sponge is ready.

Allow to cool for 10 minutes before turning out.

Finish by cutting in half horizontally and filling with whipped double cream and raspberry jam. Sprinkle with a dusting of icing sugar if you want to – I would!

Chocolate Biscuit Cake

This is any kid's favourite, big or little. Use this recipe as a starting point and experiment with other combinations of biscuits, dried fruits and nuts. Ginger biscuits or amaretti work well for a more grown-up version.

SERVES 8

125g (4 1/2 oz) dark chocolate, broken into pieces

1 tbsp golden syrup

125g (4 1/2 oz) butter

125g (4 1/2 oz) digestive biscuits, roughly crushed

100g (3 1/2 oz) ready-to-eat dried apricots, chopped

100g (3 1/2 oz) raisins

100g (3 1/2 oz) glacé cherries, halved

60g (2 1/4 oz) shelled hazelnuts, roughly chopped

Line a 450g (1lb) loaf tin with clingfilm, leaving enough to fold over the top when the tin is full.

Melt the chocolate, syrup and butter in a bowl in the microwave, giving it a stir to make sure all the ingredients are well blended.

Add the crushed biscuits, dried fruits and hazelnuts and stir well.

Tip the mixture into the loaf tin and shake to level it off. Fold over the clingfilm and put it in the fridge to set – this will take 1–2 hours.

This mixture will keep for up to two weeks in the fridge, if you can resist temptation for that long.

To serve, turn it out on to a plate, carefully peel off the clingfilm and slice. The cake is very rich, so try thin slices at first.

I don't care what all my cheffy mates think of me for putting this in a British book. I bet these little cakes won't even be able to set in the fridge before they're eaten.

Chocolate Cornflake Cakes

MAKES 12

50g (1³/4 oz) butter

100g dark chocolate, broken into pieces

5 tbsp golden syrup

80g (2 ³/4 oz) cornflakes

Place the butter and the chocolate pieces in a pan with the golden syrup and slowly melt over a low heat. When the mixture has melted and amalgamated, stir in the cornflakes.

Place paper cases on a tray and fill each one with a tbsp of the mixture. Put in the fridge to set.

Everybody loves Yule Log for Christmas, which must be something to do with the amount of chocolate that goes into it. For me, it's a bit sickly, but for all you chocolate-lovers, it has to go into the book!

Yule Log

SERVES 8

sunflower oil, for greasing

175g (6oz) good plain chocolate, broken into pieces

6 medium free-range eggs, separated

175g (6oz) caster sugar

FILLING

85g (3oz) good plain chocolate, broken into pieces

200ml (7fl oz) double cream, whipped

COATING

100g (3 1/2 oz) good plain chocolate, chopped

200ml (7fl oz) double cream

cocoa powder, for dusting

icing sugar, for dusting

Preheat the oven to 180°C/350°F/gas mark 4. Lightly grease a 30 x 20cm (12 x 8in) Swiss roll tin with sunflower oil and line with baking parchment.

Put the chocolate into a small heatproof bowl over a pan of hot water (the bowl must not touch the water) and heat gently, stirring occasionally, to melt. Leave to cool.

Whisk the egg yolks and sugar together in a large bowl until light and creamy. Place the bowl over a pan of hot water, add the cooled chocolate and stir to blend evenly.

In a separate bowl, whisk the egg whites until stiff but not dry. Carefully fold into the chocolate mixture.

Turn the chocolate mixture into the prepared tin, tilting the tin so that the mixture spreads evenly into the corners. Bake for 20 minutes, or until firm to the touch.

Remove from the oven. Place a clean, dry tea-towel on the cake, and on top of this layer another tea-towel that has been soaked in cold water and well wrung out.

For the filling, melt the chocolate as above. Cool.

Remove the tea-towels from the sponge and turn it out on to a piece of baking parchment. Peel the lining paper from the cake. Spread the melted chocolate over the cake, then spread the whipped cream on top. Roll up the cake from the long edge, using the paper to lift and help roll it forward.

For the coating, melt the chocolate as above. Allow it to cool slightly before adding the cream. The mixture should go smooth and glossy. Roughly spread this over the Swiss roll, then dust with cocoa powder and icing sugar. Serve.

There are many recipes for classic Christmas Cake. This is my auntie's old recipe, which worked for her, so it's good enough for me!

Christmas Cake

MAKES A 20CM
(8IN) CAKE

675g (1 1/2 lb) mixed dried fruit

115g (4oz) flaked blanched almonds

115g (4oz) mixed candied peel, chopped

115g (4oz) glacé cherries, well rinsed, then quartered

300g (10 1/2 oz) plain flour

1 tsp ground cinnamon

1 tsp freshly grated nutmeg

finely grated zest and juice of 1 lemon

225g (8oz) lightly salted butter

225g (8oz) soft brown sugar, light or dark

1 tsp vanilla extract

1 tbsp black treacle

4 medium free-range eggs

1/2 tsp bicarbonate of soda

1 tbsp milk

brandy

Preheat the oven to 140°C/275°F/gas mark 1, and line a 20cm (8in) cake tin with a layer of brown paper, then a layer of Bakewell paper.

Mix the dried fruit, almonds, peel and cherries in a huge bowl. Turn them well and add the flour, spices and lemon zest and juice.

Cream the butter and sugar thoroughly, then add the vanilla extract and treacle. Still beating, incorporate the eggs, then stir the mixture into the fruit and flour. Finally, dissolve the bicarbonate of soda in the milk and stir this into the fruit thoroughly as well. Add brandy to taste by the spoonful, until you have a soft dropping consistency.

Pour the mixture into the prepared tin and hollow out the top slightly. Bake for 3 1/2 hours, then test it with a larding needle or skewer (if this is just dry, the cake is ready). Remove the cake from the oven, when it is done, and leave it to cool in its tin.

When cool, remove from the tin and peel off the Bakewell paper and brown paper. Wrap in clingfilm, and then put into an airtight tin (or in foil). The usual thing is to keep the cake for at least a month before icing it, and to sprinkle it occasionally with more brandy.

To finish off the cake for Christmas, you will need Marzipan and Royal Icing (*see* page 341). Do not buy the marzipan ready-made – your own may not look as yellow as it does in the shop, but it will taste much better, I promise!

Marzipan

Why buy ready-made marzipan for a Christmas cake you've spent ages making when it can so easily be made at home?

COVERS A 20CM (8IN) CAKE

225g (8oz) icing sugar, plus extra for dusting

500g (1lb 2oz) ground almonds

1 large free-range egg (weighing about 75g / 2 3/4oz)

3–4 tsp lemon juice

GLAZE

1 tbsp apricot jam

Sift the sugar into a bowl and mix in the almonds. Beat the egg well, then add it and the lemon juice to the dry ingredients. Using a wooden spoon, beat to a firm paste, then knead on a work surface that has been sprinkled with icing sugar. (If you don't find most marzipan too sweet, add another 225g/8oz icing sugar and use 2 medium eggs instead of 1 large egg.)

Boil the jam and 1 tbsp water in a small pan, sieve it into a bowl and, while it is hot, brush it over the top and sides of the cake.

Roll out the marzipan to a circle a little larger than the cake. Using the rolling pin to lift up the marzipan, place it on top of the cake and smooth down over the sides.

Pat everything into place with your fingers, closing the cracks, and put the cake back on its rack.

Royal Icing

COVERS A 20CM (8IN) CAKE

4 small free-range egg whites

4 tsp lemon juice

1kg (2 1/4 lb) icing sugar, sifted

Whisk the egg whites until they are white and foamy but not stiff. Stir in the lemon juice, then the sugar, bit by bit, using a wooden spoon. When everything is combined, continue to beat the mixture until it is a dazzling white. Cover the basin and leave for an hour before using.

To ice the cake, have a bowl of hot water handy. Put half the icing on the cake, dip the palette knife into the hot water (it shouldn't be too wet), then use it to spread the icing. Cover the cake, then put on the remaining icing, either roughly to make a snowy effect or with the aid of a forcing bag and nozzles. Leave for at least two days to set before eating.

Dripping Cake

When I was a young lad, there always seemed to be pots of good country dripping in the kitchen. Beef and lamb fat were both added to the same pot ready to be spread on bread or toast to fill us up. My gran, Marjorie, was the ultimate country cook – the type nostalgic films now feature in comforting soft focus. Except mine was for real. This is her favourite family cake, which always seemed to be at hand whenever we wanted a hunk. It's what cookbooks would call a boiled fruit cake. Nowadays, not many of us have dripping pots, but you can still buy dripping. If it comes with a nourishing layer of meat jelly at the bottom, just scrape it off (save for adding to a stew) and use the clarified fat on top.

MAKES A 15CM
(6 IN) ROUND CAKE

**225g (8oz) mixed dried fruit
(with candied peel included)**

**95g (3 1/4 oz) clarified beef
dripping**

150g (5 1/2 oz) soft brown sugar

225ml (8fl oz) water

225g (8oz) wholemeal flour

1 tsp baking powder

1/2 tsp bicarbonate of soda

**a good pinch each of ground
cinnamon, nutmeg and allspice**

4 medium free-range eggs

Place the fruit, dripping, sugar and water in a saucepan and bring to the boil, stirring. Remove from the heat and leave to cool. (Gran would do this the night before.)

Heat the oven to 180°C/350°F/gas mark 4. Meanwhile, grease and line a deep round 15cm (6in) cake tin.

Sift the flour, baking powder, bicarbonate of soda and spices into a large bowl. Mix the fruit mixture into the dry ingredients with the eggs, beating well.

Tip the cake mixture into the prepared cake tin. Level the top and bake in the oven for about 1–1 1/4 hours until the top is golden brown and a clean metal skewer comes out clean when inserted into the centre of the cake.

Allow to cool in the tin for about 30 minutes, then turn out on to a wire rack and leave until cold. Peel off the lining paper and store in an airtight tin for up to three days. Slice and top, if you like, with jam and cream.

biscuits

These unusual shortbread biscuits are delicate and, once made, need to be handled with care, as otherwise they will drop to bits. To prevent this from happening, let them cool right down on the tray before lifting them off.

Jam Shortbreads

bakes

Scones

Scones (like 'stones') or scones (like 'swans')? Say it how you want, but the best way of eating them is with clotted cream and jam. Scottish by origin, they can be made with mashed potato, and they can be griddled or baked in the oven – there are so many variations.

SERVES 4

225g (8oz) self-raising flour, plus extra for dusting

30g (1¼ oz) caster sugar

a pinch of salt

30g (1¼ oz) butter, diced, plus extra for greasing

150ml (5fl oz) milk

GLAZE

1 free-range egg, lightly beaten with a little milk

TO SERVE

clotted cream

strawberry jam

Preheat the oven to 220°C/425°F/gas mark 7. Grease a baking sheet.

Put the flour, caster sugar and salt in a food processor and blitz briefly to mix. Add the butter and blend again until the mixture forms crumbs. Add the milk in a thin stream while mixing, stopping when the dough forms a ball. It should be moist, but not sticking to the sides.

Turn the mixture out on to a heavily floured surface, and form into a ball, then press gently into a 2cm (¾ in) thick round. Cut out the scones using a 5cm (2in) round cutter and put on to the greased baking sheet. Brush the scones with the beaten egg and milk.

Bake for 12–14 minutes. Remove and allow to cool slightly on a rack. Serve, while still warm, with clotted cream and strawberry jam.

Griddle Scones

These are so good eaten warm with some butter or with jam. But if you leave them to go cold they can be eaten like normal scones with jam and whipped cream.

MAKES 20

225g (8oz) plain flour

1½ tsp baking powder

15g (½ oz) caster sugar

a pinch of salt

1 free-range egg, beaten

about 150ml (5fl oz) full-fat milk

a knob of butter, for frying

Sieve the flour into a bowl with the baking powder, sugar and salt. Make a well in the middle, put in the egg, then the milk, and whisk to a thick batter, adding a little more milk if the mixture is too dry (you want the consistency of double cream). Leave to stand for 30 minutes at room temperature before using.

Preheat the frying pan, add a little butter, and test by cooking one scone first, then cook the rest in batches. A tbsp of batter will make one scone. As the bottom of the scones cook, after about 2 minutes, bubbles will come to the surface. Turn them on to the other side and cook for a further 2 minutes.

Keep the scones warm, wrapped in a cloth in a low oven, until all are done. Eat while still warm, with butter and jam.

You might think doughnuts are difficult, but they are made in much the same way as a simple bread – apart from the deep-frying, of course! They may take a while, but they're worth the wait, trust me.

Doughnuts

MAKES 5–10

250g (9oz) strong white flour, plus extra for dusting

a pinch of salt

40g (1 1/2 oz) caster sugar, plus extra for coating

25g (1oz) butter, softened

150ml (5fl oz) water

20g (3/4 oz) easy-blend yeast

some good jam (optional)

vegetable or sunflower oil, for deep-frying

Put all the ingredients except the jam, oil and coating sugar into a large bowl and mix together. Tip out on to a lightly floured surface and knead for 5 minutes. Put the dough back in the bowl, cover with a cloth, and leave for about 1 hour, until doubled in size.

Divide the dough into 85g (3oz) pieces and shape into balls. If you want, put 1 tsp jam inside each ball. Put on your floured surface, cover lightly with a cloth and leave to rise until doubled in size again.

Pour some oil into a large heavy-based pan and heat to 170ºC/340ºF, or a medium heat. Carefully lower each of the doughnuts into the oil and fry until brown, then roll them over and fry the other side. (If you have a problem with rolling the doughnuts over, then pierce them slightly with a knife to help you.) The frying should take no more than 5 minutes for both sides.

When they are browned, drain well on kitchen paper and tip them straight into a bowl full of caster sugar and coat well. Cool on a wire rack, then enjoy with a nice cup of tea.

Elizabeth Botham, a coffee and cake shop in Whitby, was where I first tasted Yorkshire brack. It's a bit like a fruit cake, but lighter, and has the taste and texture of sticky toffee pudding. The shop has either tea-infused or ginger-flavoured brack, and it's made fresh on the premises.

Yorkshire Brack

SERVES 6–8

675g (1¹/₂ lb) golden raisins

675g (1¹/₂ lb) dark raisins

450g (1lb) light brown sugar

250ml (9fl oz) cold strong breakfast tea

125ml (4fl oz) whisky or bourbon

butter, for greasing

550g (1¹/₄ lb) plain flour

4 tsp baking powder

a large pinch of salt

1 tsp freshly grated nutmeg

1 tsp ground allspice

3 free-range eggs, beaten

finely grated rind of 1 lemon

Soak the raisins and sugar in the tea and whisky or bourbon in a large bowl for 12 hours or overnight.

The next day, preheat the oven to 150–160°C/300–325°F/gas mark 2–3, and grease a 25cm (10in) round cake tin.

Sift together the flour, baking powder, salt, nutmeg and allspice, and add to the raisin mixture along with the beaten eggs and lemon rind. Combine well.

Put the batter into the greased tin, and bake for 60–80 minutes until firm to the touch.

When done, remove from the tin and let it cool on a wire rack. You can leave it simple and serve it with butter, or top it with a little icing.

These taste so good that you shouldn't just make them at Easter. They are great for brekkie with some Blueberry Sauce (*see* page 26) or fried caramel bananas, or toasted with strawberries and balsamic vinegar with a dollop of clotted cream. Better still, just serve with some good old homemade jam.

Hot Cross Buns

MAKES 18

BASIC BUN DOUGH

450g (1lb) strong plain flour

1 level tsp each of ground cinnamon, nutmeg and mixed spice

1/2 tsp ground mace

1/2 tsp salt

25g (1oz) fresh yeast

55g (2oz) caster sugar

150ml (5fl oz) milk

85g (3oz) unsalted butter, plus extra for greasing

1 free-range egg, lightly beaten

85g (3oz) raisins

55g (2oz) candied peel, chopped

ALMOND PASTE

225g (8oz) icing sugar, plus extra for dusting

450g (1lb) ground almonds

1 large free-range egg

3–4 tsp lemon juice

BUN WASH

a little beaten free-range egg

55g (2oz) caster sugar

5 tbsp water

Put the flour, spices and salt into a large warmed mixing bowl. Crumble the yeast into another bowl, add 1 heaped tsp of the sugar and 125g (4 1/2 oz) flour from the first bowl. Pour the milk into a measuring jug, and make up to 250ml (9fl oz) with boiling water straight from the kettle. Using a wooden spoon, mix this hot liquid into the yeast mixture. Go slowly so as to make as smooth a batter as possible. Leave it in a warm place to rise and froth up – this takes about 20 minutes.

Mix the rest of the sugar with the remaining flour, and rub in the butter. Form a well in the centre, and put in the egg and the frothy yeast mixture. Mix to a dough with a wooden spoon. Turn it out on to a floured surface and knead for 10 minutes, adding more flour as required, until the dough is coherent and tacky, but not sticky.

Wash and dry the mixing bowl, then grease with butter. Place the dough in it. Cover with a damp cloth, or put the whole thing inside an oiled polythene bag. Leave to rise to double its size. This can take anything from 1–3 hours, depending on the room temperature.

Punch down the dough, and knead in the fruit and peel. Roll the dough into a long sausage shape on a floured surface and cut it into 18 discs. Shape into round buns, then place them on baking sheets lined with parchment paper. Leave plenty of room to rise and spread.

To make the almond paste, sift the icing sugar and mix it with the almonds. Beat the egg thoroughly in a bowl, then add the lemon juice and the dry ingredients. Use a wooden spoon to beat everything to a firm paste. Knead it on a board or smooth surface, sprinkled with icing sugar. Roll out the almond paste and cut into thin strips.

To finish, brush the buns with the beaten egg and lay two strips of almond paste on each bun to form a cross. Leave the buns to prove for about 30 minutes. Preheat the oven to 230°C/450°F/gas mark 8. Bake the buns for 10–15 minutes. Meanwhile, boil the sugar and water together until syrupy. Brush over the hot buns when they emerge from the oven.

Crumpets

This is a real Yorkshire thing, although they have them in Lancashire as well. I call them crumpets, but in some areas they are called muffins. This recipe shouldn't be confused with the Scottish crumpet.

SERVES 4

500g (1lb 2oz) plain flour

15g (¹/₂ oz) salt

15g (¹/₂ oz) fresh yeast

650ml (1 pint 3fl oz) warm water

butter, for greasing and cooking

Sieve the flour and salt together into a bowl.

In a separate bowl, mix the yeast with 5–6 tbsp of the warm water. Whisk the rest of the water with the flour and salt then stir in the yeast mixture.

Cover and allow to rest in a warm place to rise. After 15–20 minutes, the batter is ready. If it is a bit too thick, loosen with a little warm water.

Warm a nonstick pan on the stove and lightly butter some metal crumpet rings or scone cutters. Melt some butter in the pan, too.

Place the rings in the pan and pour a little of the batter into each one, half filling them with the batter.

Cook on a gentle heat until holes appear in the top and the mixture starts to dry slightly around the edge. Turn over, remove the ring and cook lightly on the other side.

Real Christmas Bread

There are many variations of Christmas breads from country to country. This is my version, and it was invented purely because so often at Christmas we find we've quite a lot of mincemeat left over. It's very simple to make and uses few ingredients. I use fresh yeast, but if you can't find it, use dried (read the instructions on the packet).

MAKES 1 LOAF

500g (1lb 2oz) strong white flour, plus extra for dusting

100g (3 1/2 oz) mincemeat (bought or homemade, *see* page 260)

finely grated zest and juice of 2 oranges

finely grated zest and juice of 2 lemons

55g (2oz) unsalted butter

10g (1/4 oz) salt

25g (1oz) fresh yeast

280ml (9 1/2 fl oz) warm water

Place the flour, mincemeat, citrus zest and juice, butter, salt and yeast in a bowl and mix together. Gradually mix in the warm water to form a dough.

Place the dough on a lightly floured surface and knead for 4 minutes. Shape into a rough sausage shape, around 15cm (6in) across. Place on a baking sheet lined with baking parchment and leave aside to rise for 1 hour, covered with a tea-towel.

Preheat the oven to 220°C/425°F/gas mark 7.

Slash the top of the loaf with a knife and dust with flour. Bake for 25 minutes, until golden brown and hollow when tapped. Cool on a wire rack.

Grissini and Dips

This is a quick and simple party idea, hardly a recipe, and it's good for a mobile starter to a dinner party, too.

MAKES AS MANY AS YOU LIKE

thin breadsticks or grissini

selection of dips, perhaps including garlic mayonnaise, soft cheese and tapenade

toasted sesame or poppy seeds or fresh herbs, finely chopped

Dip the ends of the breadsticks or grissini in the garlic mayonnaise, soft cheese or tapenade. Then dip the dipped end of the stick into the toasted seeds or herbs.

Serve, dipped end up, in tall glasses or in a large jug, so people can dive in and help themselves.

Alternatively, you can just wrap the grissini in some Parma ham, which makes a great snack as well.

chutneys, jams & jellies

Plum Chutney

Give me chutneys, chutneys and more chutneys! I make this one from the plums from my trees in the garden. They are the dark flesh and skin type. If you can't get those, any plums will do, as this is a simple and quick way of making chutney.

MAKES 350G (12OZ)

500g (1lb 2oz) dark red plums

2 shallots, chopped

1 tbsp olive oil

100ml (3 1/2 fl oz) white wine vinegar

3 tbsp water

1 cinnamon stick

100g (3 1/2 oz) demerara sugar

Cut the plums in half down the crease, twist the halves in opposite directions and pull apart. Prise out the stones and discard. Roughly chop the flesh.

Place the shallots in a heavy-based saucepan with the oil and heat until sizzling. Sauté gently for 5 minutes until softened.

Add the plums, vinegar, water, cinnamon stick and sugar. Stir until the sugar is dissolved, then simmer for about 15 minutes, stirring occasionally, until softened and slightly thickened.

Meanwhile, heat the oven to 110–120°C/225–250°F/gas mark 1/4 –1/2 . Place a sterilized jam jar in the oven to warm (*see* below for sterilizing instructions). When the plum chutney is ready, spoon it into the jar. Seal with a lid and leave to cool completely before labelling. Store in a cool, dark place.

Gooseberry, Raisin and Green Peppercorn Chutney

This chutney is particularly good with grilled fish such as mackerel or tuna. It also goes well with most cheeses.

MAKES 900G (2LB)

600g (1lb 5oz) fresh gooseberries

2 medium onions, chopped

1 clove garlic, crushed

1/2 tsp mustard powder

juice of 1/2 lemon

300ml (10fl oz) cider vinegar or white wine vinegar

200g (7oz) raisins

a large pinch of salt

275g (9 1/2 oz) soft brown sugar

3 tbsp green peppercorns

To sterilize the jam jars, place them in a large pan and cover them with cold water. Bring to the boil and simmer for 10–15 minutes. Remove from the water and leave upside down to dry.

Put the gooseberries, onions, garlic, mustard and lemon juice in a preserving pan and pour in two-thirds of the vinegar. Bring to the boil, then reduce the heat and simmer for about 45 minutes, stirring occasionally, until thick.

Add the raisins, salt, sugar and the rest of the vinegar. Stir over a low heat until the sugar has dissolved, then simmer for up to 1 hour, stirring frequently, until thick and syrupy.

Stir in the peppercorns, then remove from the heat. Pour immediately into the hot, sterilized jars, and seal. Label and store in a cool, dark place.

Tomato and Apple Chutney I love this just with cheese on its own or even with some pan-fried cod or salmon.

MAKES 1.8KG (4LB)

300ml (10fl oz) malt vinegar

225g (8oz) brown sugar

100g (3 1/2 oz) sultanas

1 x 2.5cm (1in) piece fresh root ginger, peeled and finely chopped

2 red chillies, deseeded and chopped

1kg (2 1/4 lb) red tomatoes, roughly chopped

250g (9oz) apples, peeled, cored and chopped

200g (7oz) chunky shallots, roughly chopped

salt and pepper, to taste

Place the vinegar and sugar in a preserving pan and heat on the stove to reduce a little. Add the sultanas and cook until the vinegar and sugar start to caramelize. Add all the other ingredients, and bring to a simmer. Cover and cook gently for 20–30 minutes, stirring all the time.

Leave the chutney chunky, and not overcooked, which would make it more like a purée. Spoon into hot, sterilized jars, and label when cool (*see* page 368 for sterilizing instructions). Store in a cool, dark place.

Pear Chutney I did say I liked chutney!

MAKES 900G (2LB)

4 tbsp olive oil

1 tsp finely chopped fresh rosemary leaves

200g (7oz) sultanas

100g (3 1/2 oz) raisins

100g (3 1/2 oz) demerara sugar

400ml (14fl oz) cider vinegar

100g (3 1/2 oz) crystallized ginger, finely sliced

800g (1 3/4 lb) pears, cored and cut into wedges

1/2 tsp salt

1/2 tsp freshly grated nutmeg

2 tsp ground allspice

a good pinch of saffron

Heat a preserving pan and add the oil, rosemary, sultanas, raisins and sugar. Fry them until the fruit begins to caramelize.

Pour in the vinegar and boil on a high heat for 3 minutes. Add the rest of the ingredients, bring to the boil, then turn down to a simmer and cook until most of the liquid has evaporated. Because of the fruit, this chutney tends to stick to the bottom of the pan, so stir it well and keep an eye on it.

Spoon into hot, sterilized jars, filling them as full as you can, and seal while hot (*see* page 368 for sterilizing instructions). Label and store in the fridge when cool. It is important not to cook this too much as the pear wedges need to keep their nice shape.

Courgette and Black Peppercorn Chutney

I love this recipe, which I came across while in Yorkshire filming in a man's allotment. He was an amazing gardener who taught me the ins and outs of the carrot and the humble spud. His wife was an equally amazing cook, and she gave me a jar of this courgette chutney. I took it home, but didn't try it until some four months later. It was so good I tracked them down again, and she kindly gave me her recipe.

MAKES 900G (2LB)

2 small lemons

3 medium courgettes

2 onions, peeled and thinly sliced

100ml (3¹/₂ fl oz) dry white wine

3 tsp brown sugar

24 black peppercorns, coarsely crushed

2.5cm (1in) piece of fresh root ginger, peeled and finely chopped

a good pinch of salt

Peel the lemons, cutting away all the pith, then slice them thinly and discard the pips. Cut the courgettes in half lengthways, then across into 2.5cm (1in) pieces.

Combine all the ingredients in a preserving pan. Cover and cook over a moderate heat for 1 hour, stirring from time to time. There will be quite a bit of liquid at the end of the cooking time, but once the chutney has cooled, the consistency will be perfect.

Either bottle in hot, sterilized jars, or put in a bowl to serve (*see* page 368 for sterilizing instructions). Store in a cool, dark place.

Sweet and Sour Grape Pickle
Homemade pickles beat shop-bought ones any day. There is nothing better than reaching for a jar of your own pickle to add that extra kick to your meal!

MAKES 1 LITRE
(1³/4 PINTS)

750g (1lb 10oz) seedless white grapes

10 sprigs fresh tarragon

500ml (18fl oz) champagne vinegar or white wine vinegar

175ml (6fl oz) runny honey

1 tsp salt

Wash and dry the grapes. Put them in a large sterilized preserving jar with the sprigs of tarragon (*see* page 368 for sterilizing instructions).

Boil the vinegar and honey together for 2 minutes, then add the salt and pour the mixture over the grapes. Seal the jar immediately.

For the best results, store the pickle in a cool dark place for up to a month before opening.

Pickles and chutneys are not everyone's cup of tea, but they are a must in a book on British food. Together with jams and marmalades, they are staples for so many of us, but very few of us have a go at making them. This is an old recipe that I first used while at college. It takes a while to make, but it's worth it. My dad loves mustard pickle with pork pie. I like it with a ploughman's lunch or with some cold sliced meat, such as ham. But whatever you decide to serve it with, give it a go. Come back the pickle, I say.

Mustard Pickle

MAKES 1KG (2¼LB)

225g (8oz) table salt

500g (1lb 2oz) baby onions

250g (9oz) cherry tomatoes

500g (1lb 2oz) cauliflower florets

500g (1lb 2oz) cucumber, deseeded and cut into large dice

1 tbsp capers

1 tsp celery seeds

125g (4 1/2 oz) butter

25g (1oz) plain flour

500ml (18fl oz) malt vinegar

125g (4 1/2 oz) caster sugar

1 tbsp ground turmeric

2 1/2 tsp mustard powder

black pepper, to taste

Dissolve the salt in a large pan or bowl in about 4 litres (7 pints) of water and add the onions, tomatoes and cauliflower. Cover with clingfilm and keep in the fridge or in a cool place for 24 hours.

Drain, then add the diced cucumber, the capers and celery seeds and put in a pan. Cover with 2 litres (3 1/2 pints) of water and bring to the boil. Boil for 10 minutes.

Drain again and put the vegetables into a bowl.

In a separate pan, melt the butter, then add the flour and stir well over the heat to make a roux. Slowly add the vinegar, stirring all the time, and cook for a few minutes.

Add the sugar, turmeric and mustard powder, and season with black pepper before pouring over the vegetables. Put the vegetables into sterilized jars and seal (*see* page 368 for sterilizing instructions).

Leave for at least five days in a cool, dark place before eating, so that the vegetables can absorb all the flavour.

Every month as a child, I was woken by the smell of vinegar boiling on a hot stove below my bedroom. It was pickled onion day, and my father was pickling tonnes of onions. Left in a jar for just a week, they're fab. Love them or hate them, we used to eat them all the time with pork pie – a must. I had to stop eating them, though, when I started on the girl front, but hey – you can't have everything!

Hot or Cold Pickled Onions

SERVES 4

COLD

215g (7 1/2 oz) table salt

2.5 litres (4 1/2 pints) water

1kg (2 1/4 lb) shallots or small onions

600ml (1 pint) malt vinegar

HOT

1kg (2 1/4 lb) shallots or small onions

100g (3 1/2 oz) table salt

800ml (1 pint 7fl oz) malt vinegar

For cold – or uncooked – pickled onions, mix half the salt with half the water and add the shallots or small onions. Leave overnight.

Drain and peel the onions and make up the same brine with the remaining salt and water. Leave the onions in this mixture for about three days.

Drain the shallots again, and place them in pickling jars that have been sterilized (*see* page 368 for sterilizing instructions), then pour over the vinegar. Cover, seal and label, then leave for 3 months before eating.

For hot – or cooked – pickled onions, put the shallots or small onions in a saucepan of water and bring to the boil. Boil for 3–4 minutes. Drain and peel the onions and place on a tray. Dust all over with the salt and leave for a day.

Wash the onions well and simmer in a pan in the vinegar for 8 minutes before placing them in sterilized jars (*see* page 368), covered in vinegar. Cover, seal and label, then leave for three weeks in a cool, dark place before eating.

Cranberry jelly or sauce is now traditional with our Christmas turkey, although cranberries are indigenous to America. This jelly is also good with other cold meats, particularly ham. For more detailed intructions on jelly-making, see the next recipe.

Spiced Cranberry Jelly

MAKES 1 LITRE
(1 3/4 PINTS)

1kg (2 1/4 lb) Bramley apples

1kg (2 1/4 lb) fresh cranberries

1 tsp ground cinnamon

granulated sugar

Peel and chop the apples. Put the cranberries into a large pan as they are with the apples, cinnamon and enough water to just cover. Bring to the boil and simmer until the cranberries are soft.

Pass the mixture through a sieve or colander lined with a thin sterilized tea-towel, J-cloth or muslin (*see* next page) into a measuring jug. This may take some time: be patient – and never push it through. To every 600ml (1 pint) of liquid add 500g (1lb 2oz) granulated sugar.

Pour the mixture back into a clean pan and cook gently until it reaches 105°C/220°F on a sugar thermometer (or when a few drops on a cold saucer begin to set within a minute or two).

Pour into sterilized jam jars, cover while still hot and allow to cool and set (*see* page 368 for sterilizing instructions). Store in a cool, dark place.

Mint Jelly

My grandmother was never a lover of mint jelly: she couldn't understand why you put apples in it, and her mint sauce was simply some malt vinegar, a little sugar, some salt and chopped mint from the garden. But for me, mint jelly is a classic, great with any number of dishes. It needs to be made with apples to allow it to set, but it's simple to make.

MAKES 900KG (2LB)

1.8kg (4lb) cooking apples

55g (2oz) chopped fresh mint, including stalks, plus 2 tbsp finely chopped mint leaves

juice and finely grated zest of 1 lemon

1 tbsp white wine vinegar

approx. 675g (1¹/2 lb) caster sugar

Chop the apples coarsely, including the cores, and put them in a pan with the 55g (2oz) chopped mint, including stalks, the lemon zest and juice and the vinegar. Barely cover with about 1.2 litres (2 pints) cold water. Bring to the boil, turn down the heat and simmer gently for 45 minutes.

The proper piece of kit for the next stage is a jelly bag, but if you don't have one you could improvise. Line a colander with a double thickness of fine muslin and scald with boiling water to sterilize. Put this over a bowl, pour the contents of the pan into it and leave to drip through overnight. Don't try and hurry this process by pushing with a spoon or squeezing the bag, as this will force solids through and make the jelly cloudy.

The next day, measure the juice and put it into a pan with 450g (1lb) caster sugar per 600ml (1 pint) of apple juice. Bring to the boil slowly, then increase the heat and boil rapidly for about 8 minutes. Continue to boil for another 2 minutes, when the right amount of water will have evaporated and the frothing boil will have changed to a thicker rolling boil, with fat bubbles plopping noisily to the surface. At this stage the setting point should have been reached.

Remove from the heat, pour through a sieve into a warmed jug and then stir in the remaining finely chopped mint leaves. Test by putting a spoonful of the mix on a cold plate. The surface should set as it cools and will wrinkle when prodded. Pour immediately into warm sterilized jars (*see* page 368 for sterilizing instructions). Don't tilt them until set. Put on sterilized lids and keep in a cool cupboard. Once opened, keep in the fridge.

Chicory and Orange Jam

This is my all-time favourite relish, which I make in batches ready to liven up quick pan-fries. It goes really well with thick king scallops or plump free-range chicken breasts.

MAKES ENOUGH FOR
1 LARGE JAR

1 onion, chopped

1 fat clove garlic, chopped

25g (1oz) butter

1 tbsp olive oil

**5 heads fresh chicory,
thinly sliced**

**finely grated zest and juice
of 2 oranges**

2 sprigs fresh thyme

75g (2¹/₂ oz) caster sugar

250ml (9fl oz) dry white wine

Place the onion, garlic, butter and oil in a large heavy-based saucepan and heat until it starts to sizzle. Gently sauté for about 5 minutes, until softened.

Add the remaining ingredients and bring to the boil, stirring. Reduce the heat and simmer gently, uncovered, for 30–40 minutes until the chicory becomes transparent and wilted right down.

Once cooked, leave the jam to cool slightly before spooning into a warmed, sterilized jam jar (*see* page 368 for sterilizing instructions). Seal immediately and leave to cool completely. Use within a month.

Orange Marmalade

Thought to be English, orange marmalade was first made in Dundee in Scotland in about 1770. The Keiller Company there is one of the oldest producers of this fantastic product, but if you fancy giving it a go, here's an old recipe my gran and auntie once used. You must, however, use bitter, or Seville, oranges to give it that real 'just-like-granny-used-to-make' taste.

MAKES ABOUT
900G (2LB)

550g (1¼ lb) Seville oranges

juice of 1 lemon

1.4 litres (2½ pints) water

1.1kg (2lb 7oz) granulated sugar

Halve the oranges and, with a spoon, scoop out the insides, leaving the pith behind.

Place the orange juice, membrane and pips in a food processor and blend. Once the mixture is smooth, pass through a sieve into a large pan.

Using a tablespoon, scoop out as much of the pith from the orange peel as possible and then cut the peel into very thin strips. Add to the juice, then add the lemon juice and water. Bring to the boil and simmer for about 1–1½ hours, until the peel is tender and the mixture has reduced by half.

Add the sugar and mix over a low heat until it has dissolved. Boil for about 10 minutes, removing any froth from the surface with a large spoon.

After 10 minutes, spoon a little of the marmalade on to a cold plate – it should be like jelly. If it is still runny, cook for a further 5–10 minutes.

Leave to cool slightly before filling, sealing and labelling the sterilized jars (*see* page 368 for sterilizing instructions). Keep in a cool place until ready to use. Once opened, store in the refrigerator.

Onion Marmalade

This is bang in season around winter, and what could be better than a jar of onion marmalade given away as a gift? It goes brilliantly with melted cheese on toast, steak, roast fish and a huge variety of other things, either hot or cold.

MAKES 900KG (2LB)

1.8kg (4lb) brown onions, thinly sliced

100ml (3¹/₂ fl oz) olive oil, plus extra to cover the marmalade

1 tbsp chopped fresh thyme

175g (6oz) caster sugar

150ml (5fl oz) red wine

6 tbsp red wine vinegar

salt and pepper, to taste

Place the onions in a large, heavy-based saucepan with the olive oil and thyme, and cook over a moderate heat for 5 minutes. It is important not to let the onions brown at this stage or they will become bitter. Lower the heat, cover with a lid and cook for 20 minutes.

Remove the lid and add the sugar, wine, vinegar and some seasoning. Continue to cook, stirring from time to time, for about 20–30 minutes.

Once the jam is sticky, spoon it into sterilized jars (*see* page 368 for sterilizing instructions). Lightly cover the surface with olive oil and put on the lids. Keep in a cool place until ready to use. Once opened, store in the fridge.

Chunky Strawberry Jam

I find making jam one of the most rewarding things you can do, as you get to use the fruit at its best when it is in season and you reap the rewards throughout the rest of the year. That is, if you make enough — I never seem to as I keep deciding it makes a nice gift for someone!

MAKES ABOUT
675G (1 1/2LB)

600g (1lb 5oz) jam sugar

juice and finely grated zest of 1 lemon

1kg (2 1/4 lb) fresh strawberries, hulled and cut in half if large

Place the sugar and the juice and zest of the lemon in a large pan and heat slowly until the sugar has melted.

Add the strawberries and stir gently. Bring to the boil and cook for 3–4 minutes, or 10 minutes if you prefer a thicker style of jam.

Leave to cool slightly, skimming off any froth with a clean spoon. Spoon into sterilized jam jars, seal and label (see page 368 for sterilizing instructions). When cold, store in a cool, dark place.

Raspberry Jam

This is one of my favourite jams.

MAKES ABOUT
675G (1 1/2LB)

600g (1lb 5oz) jam sugar

juice and finely grated zest of 1 lemon

1kg (2 1/4 lb) fresh raspberries, picked over carefully

Make this jam exactly as the one above, merely substituting raspberries for the strawberries.

sweets
& treats

Chocolate Truffles

Dark-chocolate truffles, like these, are the quickest and simplest to make. Milk and white chocolate truffles need different chocolate, as dark sets more solidly – increase the amount by 115g (4oz). Mine are coated in cocoa powder. You can use icing sugar, coconut or grated chocolate, but if you do, roll the truffles in the coating while the chocolate is wet.

MAKES 20–30 TRUFFLES

300ml (10fl oz) double cream

300g (10 ½ oz) dark chocolate (70 per cent cocoa solids)

25ml (1fl oz) rum or brandy (optional)

COATING

200g (7oz) dark chocolate (70 per cent cocoa solids), broken into small pieces

55g (2oz) good cocoa powder

Place the cream in a pan and heat until hot, but do not boil.

Break the chocolate into small even pieces and place in a bowl. When the cream is hot, pour it slowly on to the chocolate and, using a whisk, mix well until all the cream is combined and the chocolate has melted.

Before you set this mix, add the rum or brandy, if using, then leave it to set for about 2 hours in the fridge.

Using a melon scoop dipped in hot water, spoon the mixture into balls. Place them on to a tray and put them back into the fridge.

Melt the chocolate for the coating in a bowl over a pan of hot water. Then stab each truffle with a fork, using it to dip the truffle in the chocolate and roll it in the cocoa. Place it on a plate and, once you have coated all the truffles, put them back in the fridge to set.

Festive Marrons Glacés

Marrons glacés are French crystallized chestnuts, but we Brits buy them enthusiastically at Christmas now too. If you don't want to just devour them out of the jar, here is something to do with them for a party dessert.

SERVES 4

300ml (10fl oz) double cream

a dash of whisky

a dash of Grand Marnier

25g (1oz) vanilla sugar (*see* page 393)

12 marrons glacés in syrup

25g (1oz) dark chocolate, grated

4 fresh mint sprigs

Whip the double cream until almost stiff. Add the whisky, Grand Marnier and a little of the vanilla sugar to taste.

Using 2 tablespoons dipped in hot water, spoon the cream on to the plates in rugby-ball shapes, three per plate. Place the marrons glacés on the side, three per plate, and drizzle over some of the syrup.

Drizzle the remaining sugar over the top along with the grated chocolate, garnish with a sprig of mint, and serve.

Why do people buy marshmallows when they are simple to make – just a sort of royal icing with gelatine in it? The sugar must be at the right temperature before you add it to the whipped egg whites. What a fantastic way of finishing a Hallowe'en or Bonfire Night party: having a pile of these with some sticks or skewers so that you can toast them on the bonfire.

Marshmallows

MAKES 675G (1 1/2 LB)

675g (1 1/2lb) granulated sugar

1 1/2 tbsp liquid glucose

14 gelatine leaves

3 medium free-range egg whites

vegetable oil

icing sugar, for dusting

cornflour, for dusting

1 1/2 tsp vanilla extract

Put the sugar, glucose and 200ml (7fl oz) water in a heavy-based saucepan. Add a sugar thermometer. Bring to the boil and cook until it reaches 127°C/260°F.

Meanwhile, soak the gelatine in 150ml (5fl oz) cold water and beat the egg whites until stiff. Lightly oil a shallow baking tray, about 30 x 20cm (12 x 8in). Dust it with sieved icing sugar and cornflour.

When the syrup is up to temperature, carefully slide in the softened gelatine sheets and their soaking water. The syrup will bubble up, so take care not to burn yourself. Pour the syrup into a metal jug.

Continue to beat the egg whites – preferably with an electric whisk – while pouring in the hot syrup from the jug. Do this very slowly, or the heat will cook the egg whites too much. The mixture will become shiny and start to thicken. Add the vanilla extract and continue whisking for about 5–10 minutes, until the mixture is thick enough to hold its shape on the whisk.

Spoon the mixture into the prepared baking tray, and smooth it with a wet palette knife if necessary. Leave for at least an hour to set.

Dust the work surface with more icing sugar and cornflour. Loosen the marshmallow around the sides of the tray with a palette knife, then turn it out on to the dusted surface. Cut into squares and roll in the sugar and cornflour. Leave to dry a little on a wire rack, then pack into an airtight box or jar.

Bloody Mary

The ultimate hangover cure! Make your own tomato juice or use tomato passata. The only other things you need are plenty of Tabasco sauce, a good wedge of lemon and, most importantly, loads of ice cubes. That way you get the Bloody Mary chilled right down, which is perfect for those mornings after the night before.

SERVES 1 (IF YOU LIKE IT STRONG!)

50ml (2fl oz) vodka

90ml (3fl oz) tomato juice (*see* above)

juice of 1/2 lemon

2–4 dashes Tabasco sauce

3 dashes Worcestershire sauce

freshly ground black pepper

ice cubes

1 lemon wedge

Place the vodka, tomato and lemon juices, Tabasco and Worcestershire sauces in a blender or a cocktail shaker and mix. Taste and season with black pepper and/or more of either sauce if needed.

Pour into a tall glass full of ice, and serve with the wedge of lemon on top of the glass.

Sweet Kir Royale

This is one of the best pre-dinner drinks around. It's this drink and Parma ham wrapped around thin, homemade bread sticks that I remember most about my hols a few years ago in Italy. A much cheaper option is to drink this while watching Corrie!

SERVES 6

6 tbsp Crème de Cassis

6 brown sugar cubes

1 bottle champagne or sparkling wine

Place a tbsp of Crème de Cassis in each of the champagne glasses along with a brown sugar cube.

Open the champagne carefully and pour it into the glasses at a 45 degree angle. Serve immediately.

Mulled Wine

Mulled wine is great served anywhere, especially when the nights are drawing in and you want something to really knock that sore throat on the head.

SERVES 8–10

3 bottles red wine

2 oranges, zest peeled with a peeler, then juiced

2 lemons, zest peeled with a peeler

2 vanilla pods, split

1 cinnamon stick

900g (2lb) caster sugar

3 cloves

4 juniper berries

1 bay leaf

Simply chuck everything into a saucepan with 1 litre (1¾ pints) water, bring it to the boil over a medium heat, and leave to infuse for 10 minutes.

Serve warm.

My auntie used to make toffee, which she served in a waxed bag, for Bonfire Night. This was really popular with all the kids! I think she learned the recipe from my great-great-grandmother, who had a corner shop selling toffee and fudge. My auntie would make a variety of toffees – some with raisins or sultanas, some plain, some with syrup and some, of course, with black treacle. To break it up, she used an old toffee hammer that she got from Terry's Chocolates when my father was manager of their restaurant in York (now sadly shut down). She always made it nice and soft, probably because she never refrigerated it. The toffee was kept in the biscuit tin with the commemorative plaque of Queen Elizabeth II from when she got married, a tin that I treasure to this day. My auntie sadly passed away several years ago, but the legacy of her toffee remains.

Treacle Toffee

MAKES 800G (1 3/4LB)

450g (1lb) demerara sugar

85g (3oz) unsalted butter, softened

1/2 tsp cream of tartar

100g (3 1/2 oz) black treacle

100g (3 1/2 oz) golden syrup

a handful of sultanas

Place the sugar in a heavy-bottomed saucepan with 150ml (5fl oz) water and heat until all the sugar has dissolved. Add the rest of the ingredients, apart from the sultanas, and put in a sugar thermometer.

Bring to the boil, brushing the sides of the pan down with a pastry brush dipped in water to stop crystals forming. Do not stir. When the sugar reaches 132°C/270°F, quickly and carefully fold in the sultanas. Pour the mixture into a 18cm (7in) tin lined with greaseproof paper and allow to cool. When set, break into pieces and store in a jar.

Toffee Apples

The first secret of good toffee apples is to get a nice apple. Make sure the apples are dry, or else the caramel won't stick. It's also important to add enough butter to your caramel.

MAKES 8

8 small, dry eating apples

toffee (as on page 390, but replacing the treacle with another 100g / 3 1/2 oz golden syrup, increasing the butter to 115g/4oz and omitting the sultanas)

Make the toffee as on page 390. When you reach the sultana stage (omitting the sultanas), stick a fork in each apple (forks are much better than sticks) and dip the apple into the caramel.

Immediately put the apple on a lightly oiled work surface or nonstick tray. Repeat with all the apples. Leave until cool and the toffee has set.

Vanilla Sugar

I can never understand, when walking around supermarkets, why people would want to buy prepared vanilla sugar, as it is so simple to make. You could easily sell it at a farmers' market for a quid – or, if you are more charitable, you could give it as a present. Otherwise use it in desserts, and it's great in coffee.

MAKES 500G (1LB 2OZ)

3 vanilla pods

500g (1lb 2oz) caster sugar

Chop the vanilla into pieces with a knife, and place in a blender with 100g (3 1/2 oz) of the sugar. Blend to break up the pieces.

Add the rest of the sugar and store in glass jars.

Coffee 'Mushrooms'

I invented this dish while working as a pastry chef at Chewton Glen. The guests there used to go on mushroom hunts, and bring back their booty, which was a great way of stocking the fridges and freezers with mushrooms – and the hotel guests had done all the work! This dessert seemed to suit the occasion!

SERVES 4

600ml (1 pint) good coffee ice cream, slightly softened

250g (9oz) dark chocolate (50–70 per cent cocoa solids)

good cocoa powder

icing sugar, sifted

TUILES

115g (4oz) unsalted butter, softened

140g (5oz) icing sugar

3 medium free-range egg whites

115g (4oz) plain flour

COFFEE SAUCE

1 tbsp instant coffee

2 tbsp caster sugar

125ml (4fl oz) double cream

Preheat the oven to 200°C/400°F/gas mark 6.

To start the 'stalks' of the mushrooms, take four large and four small dariole mounds and line them with clingfilm. Fill with the softened ice cream and re-freeze until set hard again.

Prepare templates for the tuiles using two margarine tub lids. Cut a large circular hole in one lid and a small circular hole in the other. Cream the butter and sugar together. Slowly add the egg whites to the mix, then fold in the flour. Place the templates on a baking tray, spread the tuile mix over the holes with a palette knife, then lift off the templates, leaving perfect circles. You need four of each size.

Bake for 2–3 minutes, until lightly coloured around the edges. Remove and place each disc of tuile over an eggcup or similar until cold. The soft tuiles will fold over into mushroom-cap shapes and become crisp.

To make the sauce, place the coffee and sugar in a teacup and add a little boiling water to dissolve to a very heavy syrup. Pour the cream into a bowl, then pour coffee on to it to colour and flavour it.

Grate the chocolate and scatter the gratings in a circle around the edges of the plates. Spoon the coffee sauce into the middle. Unmould the ice creams, removing the clingfilm, and stand these 'stalks' upright, one of each size on each plate, in the centre of the pool of sauce.

Turn the tuiles dome-side up, dust with the cocoa powder and icing sugar in a small sieve, and place the small mushroom 'caps' on the small mushroom 'stalks'; the large 'caps' on the large 'stalks'.

Serve the coffee mushrooms immediately.

Pork Scratchings

It's nice to offer your own scratchings with pre-dinner drinks, or you can even use them as a starter for a meal.

MAKES AS MANY
AS YOU LIKE!

pork rind (preferably from the loin)

fine salt

Cut any excess fat from underneath the pork rind.

Preheat the oven to 200°C/400°F/gas mark 6.

Instead of scoring the rind, cut into 5mm (1/4 in) strips, then sprinkle with salt. Bake for 30–40 minutes (or longer for thicker pieces), until the pieces become crunchy.

Hot Spiced Nuts

My sister once picked up some nuts in a pub, chewed on them for about half an hour, then spat them out, only to discover they were olive stones. (Sorry, sis!)

SERVES 4–6

55g (2oz) unsalted butter

175g (6oz) mixed nuts

1/2 tsp each of dried chilli flakes, medium curry powder, cayenne pepper and ground ginger

5 tbsp soft brown sugar

salt, to taste

2 tbsp chopped fresh parsley

Preheat the oven to 220°C/425°F/gas mark 7.

Melt the butter in a large sauté pan and sauté the nuts over a gentle heat for 3–4 minutes. Add the chilli flakes, curry powder, cayenne, ginger and sugar and cook for another 3–4 minutes.

Pour the nut mixture into an oven tray and dust with salt to taste. Stir, then roast for 5 minutes. Stir in the parsley and serve warm.

I like these with anchovies inside, but you can leave them out if you want. If you are going to add anchovies, buy those preserved in olive oil – these have less salt in them, and will taste much better inside the straw.

Cheese Straws

MAKES 24

1 x 375g packet ready-rolled puff pastry

55g (2oz) unsalted butter, melted

10 anchovies, drained and blended to a paste

2 tbsp sun-dried tomato paste

55g (2oz) Parmesan, freshly grated

2 tbsp chopped fresh flat-leaf parsley

salt, to taste

1 free-range egg yolk, beaten with 1 tbsp water

Preheat the oven to 220°C/425°F/gas mark 7. Place the pastry on a floured work surface, roll out slightly, then cut to create two squares. Using a large, sharp knife, trim the edges of the pastry so that the straws cook uniformly. Brush the pastry lightly with the melted butter.

Spread the first pastry half with the anchovies. Spread the other piece of pastry with the sun-dried tomato paste. Sprinkle both with Parmesan, parsley and some salt. Fold the bottom half of each piece over the top half, and gently press down. Roll out a bit to compress the filling. Brush the pastry with the beaten egg.

With a large, sharp knife, cut the pastry, lengthways, into 1cm (1/2 in) strips. Hold the ends between your fingers and carefully stretch and twist the strips in opposite directions.

Place the twisted strips on to lightly oiled baking sheets, spacing them evenly apart. Bake for 10–12 minutes, or until crisp and golden.

Remove the cheese straws from the oven and allow to cool on the baking sheet for 5 minutes to firm up. Using a palette knife, carefully transfer the cheese straws to a wire rack or serving plate.

index